DATE DUE

FEB 25 1978		MAY - 2 1978	
APR 26 1981		APR 22 1981	
DEC - 8 1989		NOV 29 1989	
			Printed in USA

A HALF CENTURY WITH
JUVENILE DELINQUENTS

PATTERSON SMITH REPRINT SERIES IN
CRIMINOLOGY, LAW ENFORCEMENT, AND SOCIAL PROBLEMS

A listing of publications in the SERIES *will be found at rear of volume*

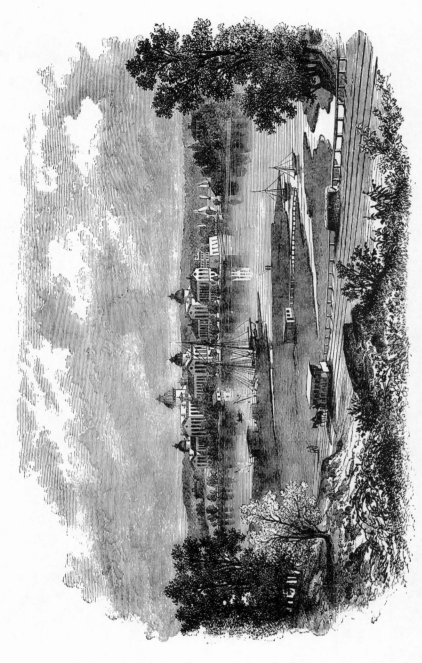

HOUSE OF REFUGE, RANDALL'S ISLAND, N. Y.

PUBLICATION No. 91: PATTERSON SMITH REPRINT SERIES IN
CRIMINOLOGY, LAW ENFORCEMENT, AND SOCIAL PROBLEMS

A HALF CENTURY WITH JUVENILE DELINQUENTS

*The New York House of Refuge
And Its Times*

BY

BRADFORD KINNEY PEIRCE

CHAPLAIN OF THE NEW YORK HOUSE OF REFUGE

With a New Introduction by
SANFORD J. FOX

Montclair, New Jersey
PATTERSON SMITH
1969

TO

THE MANAGERS

OF THE

SOCIETY FOR THE REFORMATION OF JUVENILE DELINQUENTS,

THIS RECORD OF THE

WISDOM, BENEVOLENCE, AND PIETY OF YOUR PREDECESSORS,

INTO WHOSE LABORS,

EMULATING THEIR SPIRIT AND EARNESTNESS,

YOU HAVE ENTERED,

IS

GRATEFULLY AND RESPECTFULLY DEDICATED.

INTRODUCTION TO THE REPRINT EDITION

The Reverend Bradford Kinney Peirce was part of the vast army of ante-bellum reformers who undertook to eradicate every evil that had ever afflicted American society. Emerson saw the movement sweeping into every corner of life. "Christianity, the laws, commerce, schools, the farm, the laboratory; and not a kingdom, town, statute, rite, calling, man, or woman, but is threatened by the new spirit." With change of this scope being solicited and demanded, an understanding of the motives and impact of the reformers goes a long way toward providing an insight into the evolution of the entire American experiment as it then stood. For this reason, Peirce's account of the effort to eradicate juvenile crime is a valuable source, and its reprinting at this time makes for a welcome contribution to American historiography.

There is, moreover, a specialized and important significance to this early child-welfare movement that derives from its close relationship to the establishment of juvenile courts in America three-quarters of a century later. Historians of that court have traced its ancestry to the opening of the House of Refuge in New York in 1825, claiming that, although the early part of the movement was concerned with providing institutions for juvenile offenders and the turn-of-the-century concern was with judicial procedures, it was all of a piece, evincing a steadily rising level of civilization. It is true that the parallels are there. But a close study of Peirce's history should produce a radical re-examination of what lay behind the founding of juvenile courts. It is clear, for example, that Peirce is essentially concerned with providing propaganda to justify and glorify the work of those involved with the creation and running of the House and not with writing its true history. Peirce tells of the praiseworthy work of Thomas Eddy, "the John Howard of America," as one of the charter members of the Society for the Reformation of Juvenile Offenders, but he tells us nothing of Eddy's earlier failure with the Newgate Prison in New York and how that experience might have shaped his views of dealing with juveniles. Only in passing does Peirce mention that the first year of the House's operations was marked with much rebellion on the part of the children, efforts to escape, and consequent severe punishment for this recalcitrant refusal by the children to acknowledge that unending benevolence was being bestowed on them. That there might have been some miscalculation in setting up the House, or worse, is never hinted at. The heroes of the drama can do no wrong. The same is true of those who wrote and spoke when the juvenile courts came into being, the most obvious piece of propaganda being their distorted presentation of the criminal justice system as a traditional enterprise of unmitigated cruelty toward children, whereas the fact of the matter is that it was, on the whole, benignly sensitive about treating children differently from adults.

The juvenile court reformers, like Peirce, also masked the anti-child-welfare aspects of their work. Nowhere, for example, does Peirce confront the problem created by the House being so religiously oriented, a problem which lay in the fact that its programs of worship and the many clerics in its administration were solidly Protestant, while large numbers of the children were Catholics. For the latter, and for their parents, this enforced involvement in heretical religion could hardly have been a reform. In this, the House of Refuge was, of course, merely participating in the virulent anti-Catholicism that played a major role in much of ante-bellum reform, but it is the sort of thing that barely emerges from Peirce's account. By juvenile court time, much had changed, although the impact of Populism on the court's roots, which accounts for so much of the change, is yet to be written. In this regard, it must be recalled that it was a down-state and rural legislature in Springfield that passed the Illinois juvenile court act in 1899, not the urban group of intellectuals in Chicago.

Probably the most striking Pickwickian reform that runs throughout Peirce's narrative is the matter of molding character and inculcating morality. A large part of this was concerned with training the children to be neat, diligent, punctual, thrifty, ambitious, etc. — all essentially an imposition of middle-class values on lower-class children. When coupled with the realization that movements of urbanization, industrialization, immigration, and Jacksonian

democracy must have appeared to the founders and supporters of the House to have created a propertyless mass
with no vested interest in maintaining the things the way
they "ought" to be, their effort to distill any seeds of radi-
calism out of the children in their charge appears as something quite distinct from child welfare.

Whether on balance Peirce and his fellow-workers
did advance the cause of children in trouble is a matter that
must await a competent historical inquiry. Certainly the
zeal and affection that went into the cause in the middle
third of the nineteenth century are at least as important to
such an inquiry as the laws and buildings that were its visible
accomplishments. And nowhere is this assiduous humani-
tarianism more fully or sympathetically described than in
this book.

—SANFORD J. FOX

Boston College Law School
January, 1969

PREFACE

JUST fifty years ago, in our city, the "Society for the Prevention of Pauperism," which finally was transformed into "The Society for the Reformation of Juvenile Delinquents," made its first report. Within this period the whole history of organized effort for the reformation of young criminals, and the rescue of young children from a life of crime, is included. With nearly all the movements in this direction, both in this country and Europe, the New York House of Refuge, in which the investigations of the Society have been practically embodied, has been directly or indirectly connected.

The best known and most honored names of the city have been associated with its establishment and progress, and it has enjoyed in their interest and efficient labors a warm and high place. But two of its original Managers are now living. The opportunity to collect personal and authentic statements in reference to its early history, outside of its documents, is nearly exhausted.

It was thought desirable by the present Managers of

the Society that these fading reminiscences should be revived as far as practicable, and that the history of the origin and progress of the institution should be gathered from authentic sources, and be embodied in some permanent form.

As the story of the Refuge runs parallel with that of every other institution of a similar character in the civilized world, and its system of discipline has been constantly examined by commissioners of other countries before establishing their own Houses, it seemed a legitimate outgrowth of its own history to recount the chief experiments in Europe and in the United States which have been originated since its own establishment.

No system for the cure of vagrancy and juvenile crime that has enjoyed an organized life in the last half century, presenting in itself any novel feature, has been intentionally omitted while recording the history of the New York Reformatory.

Almost every question in discussion among the friends of exposed children is involved in the sketch of the various fortunes of the Refuge; and, although the opinions of the writer, and of the Managers of the Society, may not be in accordance always with the judgments of others, still all candid inquirers will be gratified to examine the facts and premises upon which the convictions uttered in this volume rest.

From the valuable files of the Institution, from the rare collections in the rooms of the Historical Society, access to which has been generously proffered, from verbal statements of the few whose recollections run back with much freshness to the beginning of the century, from published lives of several of the principal actors, and from the quite extended literature, constantly increasing, upon the great questions of criminal and social reform, the materials for our volume have been drawn. The proper acknowledgments have been given in the body of the book.

The instances exhibiting the wholesome moral influence of the Institution, and recounting the successful lives of former inmates, could have been indefinitely multiplied, but the reader would have wearied under their constant repetition. We have selected a few average cases where all the circumstances have been well attested, as illustrating the different eras in the history of the Institution, and the various points discussed in the progress of the narrative. Many more striking records are found upon the Daily Journal and among the letters received and filed, but the full history of the cases has not been perhaps so well known. We have sought to select the records of those who had, in all human probability, passed through the years of peculiar temptation, and become settled in some positive position in life.

A more interesting or affecting series of volumes can hardly be conceived of than the thirty containing the histories, as they have been gathered from time to time, of every inmate of the House of Refuge, or the daily records embodying the incidents of nearly half a century, in so large and peculiar an institution as this.

While the volume has a local interest in the city of New York, and especially among the friends of the House of Refuge, we trust it may also be considered a contribution of some value in the discussion of that vital and interesting question, in every community, relating to the prevention and the cure of juvenile crime.

RIVERSIDE PARSONAGE, *Nov.* 13, 1868.

CONTENTS.

CHAPTER I.

LIGHT IN DARK PLACES.

CHAPTER II.

THE PHILANTHROPIST IN THE UNITED STATES.

CHAPTER III.

THE SOCIETY FOR THE REFORMATION OF JUVENILE DELINQUENTS.

CHAPTER IV.

THE FIRST HOUSE OF REFUGE.

CHAPTER V.

MR. HART'S ADMINISTRATION.

CHAPTER VI.

BELLEVUE.

CHAPTER VII.

RANDALL'S ISLAND.

CHAPTER VIII.

THE CONGREGATE SYSTEM IN REFORMATORIES.

CHAPTER IX.

THE CLOSE OF THE HALF CENTURY.

Mistake as to reformatory power; The weight of moral influence exerted by the institution; Death of Mr. Ketchum; Mr. I. C. Jones; Death of Col. Stevens; Edmund M. Young; Thomas B. Stillman, Walter Underhill; James W. Underhill; A permanent Chaplaincy; The duties of the office; Effect of liturgical service upon the inmates; Visits to indentured children; Visits to families in the city; Illustrations of their character and results; The civil war; Number of enlisted boys; Moral effect of army discipline favorable on the whole; the case of the dying soldier of Chickamauga; Incidents from the Daily Journal; The Society for the Protection of Destitute Roman Catholic Children; Managers have same powers as those of Juvenile Asylum, only limited to Catholic children; Established by donations and appropriations from the City Treasury; Boys and girls in separate institutions; Now established in West Farms; Description of edifice and system of discipline; The Christian Brothers; Brother Telliow; Boys younger than ours; Plans for the future; Present system of grades in the Refuge; Effect of it; How it opens before the new inmate and inspires him; The change of badge; Overseers of labor may not meddle with discipline; Illustrations of this; How all this affects the subjects of the House; Statistics to present time; Current expenses; Earnings of inmates; Effect of training on the whole; Call for a training-ship; Plan for rendering it economical and efficient; Advantages over the Massachusetts plan; Provision for mature young criminals; The direction of future reform; Charge of Recorder Hill; English press; The economy of all wise outlays in this direction, ... 284–317

LIST OF ILLUSTRATIONS.

A HALF CENTURY

WITH

JUVENILE DELINQUENTS.

CHAPTER I.

LIGHT IN DARK PLACES.

JOHN. HOWARD died at Cherson, on the Dnieper, while examining the Russian military hospitals to ascertain the cause and find a remedy for the plague which was sweeping away the soldiers by thousands—a willing martyr to his desire to relieve the sufferings of others—on the 20th of January, 1790. The inscription upon his statue in St. Paul's, London, among other impressive records, says, " He trod an open but unfrequented path to immortality, in the ardent but unintermitted exercise of Christian charity ; " and it closes with the devout hope, which has been abundantly realized, that this tribute to his fame, so richly deserved, " may excite an emulation of his truly glorious achievements."

He rested from his labors, but his works followed him. He had no lineal successors in the great mission of prison and hospital inspection, but his mantle fell upon many devout men and women upon both shores of the Atlantic.

Public attention had been thoroughly aroused to the physical and moral wants of imprisoned criminals, to the appalling increase of crime, and the importance of inquiring into its causes and of devising measures for its prevention. With the commencement of the next century Lord Brougham entered upon his brilliant public career, just terminated as this page is written,* and with his compeers wrought out the marvellous changes in the administration of criminal law, and instituted the numerous educational and social reforms which have given character and honor to the civilization of the nineteenth century in the British empire.

The denomination of Friends in England, embracing many persons of wealth and intelligence, seemed in a particular manner to charge itself with the duty of attending to the religious instruction of prisoners, and of continuing the work so worthily commenced by Howard.

When but fifteen years of age, Elizabeth Gurney, afterward well known as the devoted and saintly Elizabeth Fry, by repeated and earnest persuasion, induced her father to permit her to visit the House of Correction at Norwich. She was attracted by a "painful sympathy toward those who, by yielding themselves to the bondage of sin, had become the victims of human justice;"† a sympathy which had undoubtedly been awakened by the recitals to which she had listened at the "monthly meetings" of the Society.

In the commencement of the year 1813, four members of the Society of Friends (one of them being William Forster), with whom she was intimate, mentioned to her the cases of

---

* May 10, 1868.
† "Life of Elizabeth Fry," by Susanna Corder, p. 198.

several persons in Newgate prison, who were about to be executed. This occasioned her introduction to this noted prison
—at this time a shocking scene of brutality and crime—and the
commencement of a life-long interest in the moral improvement
of prisoners, especially those of her own sex.

The quadrangle in which the female prisoners were confined
was overlooked by the windows of the male prison. In four
rooms, covering about one hundred and ninety superficial yards,
three hundred women, with their numerous children, were
crowded—" tried and untried, misdemeanants and felons, without classification, without employment, and with no other superintendence than that given by a man and his son by night and
by day. In the same rooms, in rags and dirt, destitute of
sufficient clothing (for which there was no provision), sleeping
without bedding on the floor, the boards of which were in part
raised to supply a sort of pillow, they lived, cooked, and washed."*
With the proceeds of their begging from all visitors (for no restraint beyond what was required for their custody was placed
upon their communication with their friends outside), they purchased liquors from a regular bar in the prison.   Although
military sentinels were posted along the leads of the prison,
even the governor of it entered this portion with reluctance.
He advised Mrs. Fry and her companion, when they sought
admission, to leave their watches in his house lest they should
be snatched from their sides. This they declined to do. With
no attendant, Mrs. Fry and Anna Buxton (sister of Sir T. F.
Buxton, her brother-in-law) stood before this strange company.
" The sorrowful and neglected condition of these depraved
women and their miserable children, dwelling in such a vortex

* " Life of Elizabeth Fry," p. 199.

The Gospel in Prison.—John Randolph.

of corruption, deeply sank into her heart, although at this time nothing more was done than to supply the most destitute with clothes. She carried back to her home, and into the midst of other interests and avocations, a lively remembrance of all that she had witnessed in Newgate; which, within four years, induced that systematic effort for ameliorating the condition of these poor outcasts, so signally blessed of Him who said that 'joy shall be in heaven over one sinner that repenteth, more than over ninety-and-nine just persons who need no repentance.'"

She soon arranged a school in the prison, with one of the convicts for a teacher, and commenced a series of religious services, which not only produced remarkable results upon the immediate subjects of her labors, but greatly excited the public interest, and awakened faith in the possibility of redeeming, by the power of the Gospel, the most abandoned criminals from a life of sin. How characteristically John Randolph describes a scene which he witnessed in Newgate, while envoy plenipotentiary from this country to the court of St. James! " Two days ago," he says, "I saw the greatest curiosity in London—ay, and in England, too, sir—compared to which, Westminster Abbey, the Tower, Somerset House, the British Museum, nay, Parliament itself, sink into utter insignificance! I have seen, sir, Elizabeth Fry, in Newgate, and I have witnessed there miraculous effects of true Christianity upon the most depraved of human beings! And yet the wretched outcasts have been tamed and subdued by the Christian eloquence of Mrs. Fry! I have seen them weep repentant tears while she addressed them. I have heard their groans of despair, sir! Nothing but religion can effect this miracle; for what can be a greater miracle than the conversion of a degraded, sinful woman, taken from the very dregs of society? Oh, sir, it was a sight worthy the attention of angels ! "

The published accounts of this remarkable movement in behalf of those heretofore considered the outcasts of society, and abandoned to crime, awakened attention throughout Great Britain and America. Mrs. Fry was addressed by thoughtful minds in various lands, and solicited to make personal visitations and examinations of the principal prisons. In the Bridewell at Glasgow, Scotland, the keeper feared it would be a dangerous experiment to speak to the women. " They had never," he said, " listened to any reading except by compulsion, and were disposed to turn any thing of the kind into ridicule." The Scotch lady who accompanied Mrs. Fry, says : " A hundred women were assembled in a large room. She took off her bonnet, and sat down on a low seat fronting them. Then looking at them with a kind, conciliating eye, yet an eye that met every eye there, she said, ' I had better just tell you what we are come about.' She told them she had to deal with a great number of poor women, sadly wicked, and in what manner they were recovered from evil. Her language was scriptural, always referring to our Saviour's promises, and cheering with holy hope these dissolute beings. ' Would not you like to turn from that which is wrong? Would you not like for ladies to visit you, and speak comfort to you, and help you to become better? Surely you would tell them your griefs ; they who have done evil have many sorrows.' As soon as she spoke tears began to flow. One very beautiful girl near me had her eyes swimming with tears, and her lips moved, as if following Mrs. Fry. One old woman, who held her Bible, we saw clasping it with emotion, as she became more and more impressed.

The Prodigal.—London Philanthropic Society.

The hands were ready to rise at every pause, and these callous and obdurate offenders were, with one consent, bowed before her.   Then she took the Bible, and read the parables of the *lost sheep*, the *piece of silver*, and the *prodigal son*.   It is impossible for me to express the effect of her saintly voice while speaking such blessed words.   She often paused and looked at the poor women with a sweetness that won their confidence, applying with beauty and taste all the parts of the story to them, and in a manner I never before heard ; particularly the words ' his father saw him when he was yet afar off.'   A solemn pause succeeded the reading.   Then, resting the large Bible on the ground, we saw her on her knees before them.   Her prayer was devout and soothing, and her musical voice, in the peculiarly sweet tones of the Quakers, seemed like the voice of·a mother to her suffering child." *

At this time (in 1817) her two brothers-in-law—the excellent Samuel Hoare and Sir T. F. Buxton—her brother, well known in this country, Joseph John Gurney, and other of her personal friends, united in forming a society for the improvement of prison discipline and for the reformation of the juvenile depredators, who, at this time, " infested London in gangs." This resulted in the " London Philanthropic Society."   A large committee was appointed who met every fortnight, and sub-committees were constituted to attend to the various details. They were especially impressed with the importance of " taking from the streets boys who are under no parental control, exposed to every temptation, addicted to every vice, ignorant of all that is good, and trained by their associates to the perpetration of every crime."

* " Life of Elizabeth Fry," p. 301.

In a work written by Sir T. F. Buxton at this time, entitled
" An Inquiry whether Crime and Misery were produced or prevented by the Present System of Prison Discipline in England,"
he says : " When I first went to Newgate, my attention was
directed by my companion to a boy whose apparent innocence
and artlessness had attracted his notice.   The schoolmaster said
he was an example to all the rest ; so quiet, so reserved, and so
unwilling to have any intercourse with his dissolute companions.
At his trial he was acquitted upon evidence which did not leave
a shadow of suspicion upon him ; but I lately recognized him
again in Newgate, but with a very different character.   He
confessed to me, that, on his release, he had associated with the
acquaintances formed in prison.   Of his ruin I can feel but little
doubt, and as little of the cause of it.   He came to Newgate
innocent ; he left it corrupted."   In the same work is the testimony of a condemned murderer, of Douay, France : " I await,"
said he to one who kindly visited him, " the hour of execution,
and since you are the first person who has visited me, I will address you with confidence and conceal from you nothing.   I
am guilty of the dreadful crime for which I am to suffer, but
from infancy my parents neglected me.   I had neither a moral
example nor a religious education.   I was abandoned to the
violence of my passions.   I fell when young into bad company,
by whom I was corrupted ; but it was in prison that I completed my ruin.   Among the persons now in this apartment are
several boys, who, with pain I observe, are preparing themselves for the further commission of offences, when the term of
their confinement shall expire.   I entreat you to obtain their
removal into a separate ward, and snatch them from the conta-
gion of such associates.   Believe me, sir, and I speak from bit-

ter experience, you can confer on those boys no greater favor."
These extracts were introduced into the sixth report of the British " Society for the Improvement of Prison Discipline and for
the Reformation of Juvenile Offenders."

In one of their reports, they utter, with great wisdom, a
sentiment eminently true of exposed young persons, and applicable now and everywhere, that " it is the ordination of Divine
Wisdom that man cannot suffer from the neglect of man without mutual injury ; and that, by a species of moral retribution,
society is punished by its omission of its duties to the ignorant
and the guilty. The renewed depredations of the offender when
discharged from confinement, the crimes which he propagates by
his seduction and influence, spread pollution among all with
whom he associates, and the number of offenders thus becomes
indefinitely multiplied."

A long range of buildings was secured by the society, and
devoted to different mechanical trades, with dormitories for girls
and separate ones for boys—all enclosed by a wall. Within
this enclosure were also constructed a chapel, school-room, residence of officers, and warehouse for the reception and delivery
of manufactured articles. The boys were bound as apprentices
to the master-workmen for a certain number of years; they
worked throughout the day, and had a session of school four
evenings in the week. The girls were employed in making,
mending, and washing the boys' clothes and in different kinds
of needlework. At a suitable age the girls were placed out at
service, and the boys were sent to the colonies or to America.
In the annual report for 1823 the managers of the society say:
" The success of this institution satisfactorily proves that there
are few even among the most guilty who may not, by proper

discipline and treatment, be subdued and reclaimed, and justifies
the society in the conviction that no measure would be so efficacious in arresting the progress of juvenile delinquency as the
establishment of a well-regulated prison for the reformation of
criminal youth."

In 1849 the institution, which had accomplished a good work
among the exposed and criminal children of the city, was removed
to a farm at Red Hill, Surrey, in a rural district, three-quarters
of a mile from the Brighton Railway station.

In May, 1818, Prof. John Griscom, then in England, visited
the building and work-shops of the society. " Its great object,"
says Dr. Griscom in his autobiography, " is to afford an asylum
to the children of convicts, and those trained to vicious courses,
public plunder, infamy, and ruin. It is the peculiar distinction of
this society that they seek for children in the nurseries of vice and
iniquity, in order to draw them away from contamination, and to
bring them up to the useful purposes of life. Prisons, bridewells,
and courts of justice, afford materials upon which the society dis-
plays its bounty. They are seldom taken younger than eight
or nine or older than twelve. Within the buildings of the society
are more than sixty different wards. The apartments of the
girls are separated from those of the boys by a high wall, which
prevents all intercourse. . . . The principal trades pursued
are printing, copperplate printing, bookbinding, shoemaking,
tailoring, ropemaking, and twine-spinning. A portion of each
boy's earnings goes to his credit, and is given him at his discharge. . . . About one hundred and fifty boys are within the
walls, and more than fifty girls. The society has a house in
another part of the town, called the Reform, where the most
hardened offenders are first introduced, and where they are care-

fully instructed in the obligations of morality and religion and in school learning. When out of school, they are here employed in picking oakum. In passing through the workshops of this beneficent institution, where industry and skill were apparent, it was cheering to find that so many children were ' snatched as brands ' from criminality and ruin, and restored to the prospects of respectable and honorable life." *

The seed sowed by John Howard had begun also to produce the same harvests in portions of Germany and Prussia. John Falk was twenty-two years of age when Howard died—just the age to receive a powerful, practical impression from so noble an example. Of poor parentage, but with an insatiable love for books and learning, the heads of his native town of Dantzic, seeing the great promise of his youth, arranged to assist him through the university at Halle. They required only one thing at his hand : " If a poor child should ever knock at your door, think it is we, the dead, the old gray-headed burgomasters and councillors of Dantzic, and do not turn us away." † He never forgot the request nor his tacit promise—neither a poor nor a criminal child was turned from his door, even when he knew not from whence the next meal for those already dependent upon him would come.

In 1813, having lost, while residing in Weimar, four dearly-beloved and promising children within a few days of each other, " the bereaved parent resolved to become the father of those unfortunate children who had been deprived of a sound educa-tion and were in the path of crime and destruction. He founded the ' Society of Friends in Need,' for children of criminals and

---

* "Memoir of John Griscom, LL. D.," p. 166.
† " Praying and Working," by Stevenson, p. 28.

criminal children, and adopted, as a fit symbol for his establishment, the representation of some children converting on the anvil their chains into useful tools." *   The youths that came to him were many of them wicked and hopeless enough. One was a confirmed beggar at eleven, wretched and worn so that he had almost lost the marks of a human being ; another was so vicious, that he had been for some time chained like a wild beast ; still another had attempted to hack off his finger rather than work at the linen trade ; and one, a boy of sixteen, had murdered two little girls. ".Horrid, cannibal-like faces had they all," wrote Perthes of them in 1822, " with the image of the· desert unmistakably imprinted on their foreheads." †   The results of his discipline were encouraging on the whole, and he was able to write : " Could you see us, you would rejoice and bless God. The children of robbers and murderers sing psalms and pray ; boys are making locks out of the insulting iron which was destined for their hands and feet, and are building houses such as they formerly delighted to break open."   Hundreds of respectable tradesmen, clergymen, lawyers and doctors, schoolmasters, merchants, and artists dated the commencement of a life of usefulness and honor from the Reformatory at Weimar. Falk discovered, in his experiment, that among the chief means of criminal reformation, after moral and religious instruction, was honest and useful labor.   He became at length a wonderful believer in work.   He at first placed his boys out with different masters, but at last brought them together under his own eye, considering that in this way he could secure better

---

* Dr. Lieber, in note to " The Penitentiary System in the United States," by Beaumont and De Tocqueville, p. 108.

† " Praying and Working," p. 40.

discipline.   A few days before his death, he would hardly " let
the ring of the boys' hammers stop.   It rang in his ears like
music to the end." *

As early as 1816, Count Adelbert von der Reche Volmer-
stein commenced his truly Christian labors in Rhenish Prussia ;
gathering up " the poor, neglected, and abandoned children to
lead them to their heavenly Friend, and to shelter, feed, and
clothe them in His name." †   The bloody battles of the first
Napoleon had filled the country with orphaned children.   " A
young generation of swindlers, thieves, highway-robbers, and
malefactors of every kind, was springing up in consequence.
The back streets, the lanes and closes of the large towns were
crowded with them.   The public roads were unsafe, the prisons
were over-peopled.   What was to be done to stem the current
of this pernicious flood nobody could tell." ‡   A human exigency
is the Divine opportunity.   The soul of the count was stirred
within him by the sight of the misery and prospective ruin of
the youth of his country, and he was inspired of Heaven, as was
Howard before him for his pioneer work, to institute measures
for their redemption.

In 1819 his first formal Home, constructed for the reformation of youths, was opened with the most simple and touching
ceremonies : " It was evening—in noiseless quiet, the count
led the three children, which he had already adopted, up the
little hill which separated the asylum from his house.   (He
called this institution an ' Asylum for Neglected Orphans, and
Children of Vagabonds and Convicts.'   For a shorter title he

---

* " Praying and Working," p. 49.
† " The Charities of Europe," by De Liefde, vol. ii., p. 4.
‡ Ibid.

called it by the name of *Rettungs-Anstalt*, *i. e.*, Redemption Establishment.) He himself carried the lantern that illuminated their path; behind followed the teacher, with the bibles and hymn-books; after him came the housekeeper, carrying the bread and the ingredients for their first supper and breakfast; the children carried the fuel. 'Having entered the Orphan-house,' the count relates, ' we walked in solemn procession through all its apartments, singing hymns and praising God. We set apart each room to its purpose ; then we knelt down at the footstool of Him who had worked in us to will, and was working in us to do also, and besought that the labor should result to His glory.' "

The institution was soon crowded, and in 1822 an old abbey at Düsselthal, near Düsseldorf, about two miles distant from the original establishment, was purchased and prepared for inmates. Separate buildings for girls, and additional ones for boys, have been added from time to time ; and the institution, under the charge of Christian Frederick Georgi, who succeeded the count upon the failure of his health, and retained its direction until 1861, when he ceased " at once to work and live," has been one of the largest and most useful of the many reformatory establishments in Europe. Like nearly all the other European institutions, it has been supported by voluntary subscriptions, and its statistics seem small when compared with our American Houses of Refuge. Mr. Georgi's last report, made in 1861, showed that from the opening in 1819, a period of forty-one years, 2,200 young persons had been trained and sent out from its sheltering arms ; while, in the same period, more than 10,000 passed under the discipline of the New-York House of Refuge.

Berlin House of Refuge.

An institution somewhat similar to the Count's was established in 1819 for " beggar-boys," in the capital of Prussia, by Mr. Wadzeck; and in 1824 a number of gentlemen of Berlin formed a " Society for the Education of Children Morally Neglected," which resulted in the erection of a House of Refuge, under much the same discipline as American institutions bearing the same name.

None of these establishments received their inmates from the courts, nor held them upon legal warrants. The relation was voluntary on both sides. The children were generally under twelve, and were retained for a long period. But these experiments clearly illustrated the possibility of snatching from a criminal life and certain ruin children that had been already sadly perverted, and even guilty of serious offences. Public attention had also been turned to the most practical way of defending the community from a constant increase of its criminal class, by the rescue and reformation of its exposed youth.

CHAPTER II.

THE PHILANTHROPIST IN THE UNITED STATES.

To the denomination of Friends in the United States also are we indebted for the earliest efforts for the improvement of prisons, the mitigation of the criminal law, and the organization of the best measures for the prevention of crime. The visits and labors among them of English Friends quickened their zeal and suggested practical measures for the accomplishment of their object.

As early as 1786 a model penitentiary for the times was constructed through their influence in Philadelphia, a great modification of the sanguinary punishments of the day having been secured. Great improvements followed, resulting finally in the fully-developed Pennsylvania system of solitary confinement.

New York was the first State to follow the good example set by her sister State. In 1797 she adopted a new penal code and new penal system. The early experiments served to show the still unremoved evils of the existing system of prison discipline. The solitary system which had been chosen in Pennsylvania was thought to entail serious physical and mental results upon its subjects; finally, in 1823, in Auburn, where the first State Prison had been built, the State, after protracted discussions, inaugurated the silent, congregated plan of discipline,

which is now known throughout the civilized world as the
" Auburn system," and prevails more generally than any other.

As upon the other continent war filled the prisons and forced
into the streets for purposes of begging, and to secure an uncertain livelihood, the children of the poor and vicious, so the last
war between this country and England brought in its train its
usual concomitants of poverty and crime.   The large cities
would naturally feel the weight of this evil, and no one more
than New York.   The interesting discussions and practical experiments in Great Britain had attracted the attention of thoughtful philanthropists, whose sympathies had been awakened and
anxieties aroused by the great increase of the suffering and
dangerous classes in the country.

Among other intelligent and leading minds in the city of
New York, awake to every question affecting the education and
moral training of the community, and alive to every call of suffering, temptation, or poverty, was John Griscom, LL. D.,
Professor of Chemistry and Natural Philosophy.   He had removed, in 1808, to the city from Burlington, New Jersey, where
he had already established an enviable reputation as a teacher,
and especially as a lecturer in chemistry, then opening as a new
and very attractive field for scientific experiment.   As a teacher
and a lecturer in New York he more than sustained his previously acquired reputation, became one of her most honored citizens,
and by personal correspondence and visits held familiar relations
with the first scholars in the natural sciences in this country and
in Europe.   Professor Griscom was connected with the Society
of Friends, and intimately acquainted with the early advocates
of criminal reform connected with this society in England.
Moved by the condition of the poor and criminal class in the

city, in 1817 he invited several of his friends into the parlor of his house upon William Street, to consider some practical measure for the cure of pauperism and the diminution of crime.

His next-door neighbor, equally intelligent and interested with himself in such questions, was Thomas Eddy, also a Friend. He has been called with much propriety "the Howard of America." He was born in England, just about the time Howard was entering upon his life-work. His father emigrated to Philadelphia when he was a lad, and was an iron merchant in that city. Thomas came early to New York, with but ninety-six dollars in his pocket, but soon, through his industry and intelligence, secured remunerative employment. By 1794 he had acquired a considerable capital, and was engaged in many important financial undertakings. He was associated with De Witt Clinton in the great Erie Canal enterprise, and no inconsiderable cause of its final success was attributed to his indomitable perseverance and the peculiar confidence reposed in his judgment and integrity by the community.

With all his great, warm heart, he entered into the national and municipal movements for the amelioration of society. He was one of the pioneers in this country in the question of penitentiary reforms, one of the originators of banks of savings, one of the founders of the American Bible Society, and of the Institution for the training of the Deaf and Dumb. Of his efficient instrumentality in the establishment of the New York House of Refuge, Hon. Cadwallader D. Colden says, as published in the life of Mr. Eddy by Samuel Knapp: "I had a more intimate association with Mr. Eddy in this charity, from its origin to his death, than in any other of which we were members. Though there were many who participated with him in this humane-enterprise, yet I do not think it is going too far to say that its foundation and success were in a great measure owing to him ; at least it may be questioned whether, without his indefatigable exertions, this important measure for the prevention of crime would have been so soon adopted." At his death he left to the institution a handsome sum of money, the interest of which has been devoted to a library. Mayor Colden attributes to Mr. Eddy the peculiar discrimination of suggesting the *preventive* office of the Refuge. European institutions had been constructed for young criminals, but no one had secured the power from the State of withdrawing, from the custody of weak or criminal parents, children who were vagabonds in the streets and in peril of a criminal life, although no overt act had been commit-ted. The mayor well remarks : " Deprived of this power, the institution would lose much of its influence."

The thoughtful and practical mind of Mr. Eddy appreciated another want which has not yet been met, but is a pressing neces-sity in the administration of penitentiary discipline at the present hour. He wished to secure the establishment of an asylum for convicts who had finished their imprisonment, where employment could be afforded them at a proper recompense, until there should be some providential opening for them to begin life anew. The system of prison discipline now successfully inaugurated in Ire-land seems in a good degree to meet this important requisition, and to bridge over the heretofore fatal chasm between the hour of a convict's discharge, without character or means, and his entrance upon an honest remunerative employment.

The original suggestion of such an asylum may have been received by him from a communication made by Edward Liv-ingston, the father of legal and penitentiary reform in this country, to the Mechanics' Society, of New York, in 1803, when he was mayor of the city.   He proposed to the society, jointly with the city, to found an establishment in which to provide employment for strangers during the first month after their arrival in this country, for citizens who through sickness or casualty had lost their usual employment, for widows and orphans incapable of labor, and for *discharged or pardoned convicts from the State Prison*.   With his characteristic eloquence and humanity he remarks : " It must be evident that nothing will tend so much to defeat the principal object of reformation, and at the same time endanger the security of the city, as the situation in which those stand at the time of their discharge, who have undergone the sentence of the law.   The odium justly attached to the crime is continued to the culprit after he has suffered its penalty ; he is restored to society, but prejudice repels him from its bosom ; he has acquired the skill and has the inclination to provide honestly for his support.   Years of penitence and labor have wiped away his crime, and given him habits of industry and skill to direct them.   But no means are provided for their exertion.   He has no capital of his own, and that of others will not be intrusted to him ; he is not permitted to labor ; he dares not beg ; and he is forced for subsistence to plunge anew into the same crimes, to suffer the same punishment he has just undergone, or, perhaps, with more caution and address, to escape it.   Thus the penitentiary, instead of diminishing, may increase the number of offences." *   This paper simply anticipated the careful elaboration of such an addition to the penitentiary system, which appeared, in 1821, in the well-known and remarkable " Livingston Code," which he prepared for the State of Louisi-

---

* " Life of Edward Livingston," by George Havens Hunt, p. 94.

ana; a code, which, although not accepted, anticipated and became the model for all future modifications of criminal law and discipline, and made at the time of its publication a profound and practical impression upon the thoughtful men of Europe.   In his punitive and reformatory system, he provides—

A House of Detention ;

A Penitentiary ;

A House of Refuge and Industry ; and

A School of Reform.*

The latter was arranged upon a plan almost identical with that of the New-York House of Refuge, and may have guided the minds and hands of the noble men who constituted the system, which now for nearly a half century has justified the wisdom and benevolence of their work.

Mr. Eddy was in correspondence, at this time, with Mr. Livingston, with the cultivated William Roscoe the well-known English reformer, " and," says his biographer, " with some of the first men in Europe and the United States, upon the great objects of reform in prisons, hospitals, penal codes, schools, and almost every other topic which the best minds of the civilized world are now discussing."   With his foreign correspondents he was in the habit of exchanging public documents upon all these subjects, and had accumulated in his library reports and addresses, exhibiting the progress of European reform in almost every direction.   " His object and unshaken purpose seemed to be," says Mayor Colden, " to diffuse, by every possible means and reasonable effort on his part, a liberal, enlightened, humane, active, and Christian public spirit.   He possessed, far beyond the race of ordinary men, the philanthropy of Howard ; and,

---

* "Life of Edward Livingston," by George Havens Hunt, p. 268.

under the influence of so illustrious an example, he appeared to be willing to devote himself ' to survey the mansions of sorrow and pain,' and to mitigate human misery, in whatever form it might meet the eye or awaken sympathy."

Another gentleman present at this informal meeting was John Pintard, a public-spirited merchant of the city, who was afterward very efficient in the organization of savings banks, and was the founder of the New-York Historical Society.

Mr. Pintard preserved to the close of his life his interest in the reformatory institution which finally grew out of this preliminary meeting. The writer has before him a manuscript letter, written January 4, 1826, after the House of Refuge had been a year in operation, addressed to his friend Isaac Collins, expressing his " great satisfaction on reading the first report," and making two valuable suggestions in reference to indentured children. The first was, that they should not be discharged until they could read, write, and cipher, " as far as the rule of three ; " and the second, that they should have an entirely new suit of clothes throughout, so that, " when taking leave of the house and of those they leave behind, they may go abroad with a ' freedom suit,' and walk erect like regenerated beings, with a new character in society. The impression would operate alike favorably on the liberated and upon those looking forward to the happy day of their release." He adds : " A Bible, I presume, is always given on these occasions." The letter closes with the characteristic and affecting sentence : " Accept these hints from one who, almost past the days of active exertion, keeps a steady eye on the progress of benevolent and useful institutions, among which the House of Refuge ranks next to our free schools."

As the result of this informal meeting, a number of influential gentlemen were invited to meet at the New-York Hospital on the 16th of December, 1817. General Mathew Clarkson, a general officer in the American army in the Revolution, afterward vice-president of the American Bible Society, was chairman of this meeting, and Divie Bethune, a benevolent merchant, noted for his interest in Sabbath-schools, and for the distribution, at his own expense, of Bibles and tracts, was secretary. A committee was appointed " to prepare a constitution and a statement of the prevailing causes of pauperism, with suggestions relative to the most suitable and efficient remedies." * The meeting also constituted itself into a " Society for the Prevention of Pauperism."

The first regular meeting of the society was called upon the 6th of February, of the ensuing year, and a full and elaborate report was made upon the causes and remedies of pauperism. The paper attracted much attention in England, and was translated at the instance of a similar society in Geneva.

The interest of the officers of the society was at once awakened by the condition of the criminal institutions connected with the city; and in the second report, bearing the date of December 29, 1819, attention is called to the fact that in the Bellevue Prison there was no separation made between mature and juvenile offenders. " Here is one great school of vice and desperation," they say ; " with confirmed and unrepentant criminals we place these novices in guilt,—these unfortunate children, from

---

* This committee was composed of the following gentlemen : John Griscom, chairman ; Brockholst Livingston, " an accomplished scholar, a brilliant advocate, and a successful judge," Garrett N. Bleecker, Thomas Eddy, James Eastburn, Rev. Cave Jones, Zachariah Lewis, and Divie Bethune.

Hon. CADWALLADER D. COLDEN.   p. 39.

ten to eighteen years of age, who, from neglect of parents, from idleness, or misfortune, have been doomed to the penitentiary by condemnation of law." With great force and propriety they start the pregnant inquiry, " And is this the place for *reform ?* " As a remedy, the report recommends the erection of a building, at a moderate expense, within the precincts of the penitentiary, for the younger convicts.

Hon. Cadwallader D. Colden was at this time mayor of the city. He was an eminent lawyer, and as noted for his public spirit as for his noble character and large attainments. He freely yielded his valuable services and influence to every form of public benevolence that sought his aid. With characteristic modesty and nobility of mind he yielded to others the generous praise of being most efficient in the establishment of the House of Refuge, but his colleagues in the management of that institution, upon his death in 1834, bear unqualified testimony as to the inestimable value of his public services at Albany and Washington, as a magistrate in the city, as a manager and as the president of the Board for eight years, in behalf of that institution.

When in January, 1830, his removal from the city rendered it necessary for him to resign his office as president of the Board, he remarks in his letter to the managers : " There is nothing in which I have been concerned to which I look back with more satisfaction than I do to the share I have had in the establishment of an institution, which, in itself, and as an example, should it not be destroyed by jealousy and prejudice, will, I am convinced, have a benign influence on the condition of mankind."

His widow, in acknowledging the deserved tribute of respect paid to him by the managers, says : " This was indeed his most favorite institution among the many over which he presided, with that zeal and anxious care which his benevolence of character always prompted."

The mayor at this time was the presiding judge of the Municipal Court. He was particularly interested in that portion of the report referring to the depraving influence of the prison over the youths committed to its custody. Many young persons of both sexes were brought before his court, and he had found, that if they were sent to the penitentiary, for even a short period, they were no sooner liberated than they returned to a life of crime. He responded to the report of the society in an admirable letter, protesting against the herding of young and old convicts together, especially females, and offering heartily to correspond with them in efforts for the removal of this evil.

The report of the society for 1821 was written by Mayor Colden, and in it he inquires : " Shall it in future times be said of New York, that she has educated a portion of her native youth with a gang of felons in the penitentiary ; and this, too, because these youths have in their infancy been abandoned by the hand that should have protected them? Under the present state of things, the penitentiary cannot but be a fruitful source of pauperism, a nursery of new vices and crimes, a college for the perfection of adepts in guilt. The condition of the Bridewell is no better."

At how favorable a period were these energetic movements for the relief of the poor, and for the reformation of vicious and criminal children, originated ! It was just upon the eve of the flood of immigration which has since then poured into our country, chiefly through New-York City, as a great gateway. The population of the city was still homogeneous in a good degree ; its government was in the hands of its ablest men, and enjoyed the

confidence of its citizens ; and its men of substance and in telli-
gence were marked by their public spirit and interest in the
general welfare of the community. The population of the city
at this time was 123,000—one-eighth of its present census.

Mayor Colden recommended for consideration thirteen top-
ics, as bearing upon the question of Pauperism, the last of
which was Juvenile Delinquency. In 1822 the society issued
an exceedingly interesting and valuable paper upon " the Penitentiary System in the United States." The committee appointed to consider the subject consisted of the honored names
of C. D. Colden, Thomas Eddy, Peter A. Jay, Rev. James Mil-
ner, D. D., Rev. Cave Jones, Isaac Collins, Richard R. Ward,
and Charles G. Haines. Mr. Colden was to have drawn up the
report, but being at this time elected to Congress, the pressure of
public and professional duty rendered it impossible for him to
perform this service. It was therefore committed to Adjutant-
General Haines, an able and influential lawyer of New York,
chiefly interested in political and public questions. It was a
very elaborate and extended work, exciting general attention in
this country and in Europe. The report argues with great force
the necessity of providing new and separate prisons for juvenile
offenders, and insists upon the possibility of securing, as a general
rule, the reformation of the young criminal. " These prisons,"
the report goes on to say, " should be rather schools for instruction than places for punishment like our present State prisons,
where the young and old are confined indiscriminately. The
youth confined there should be placed under a course of discipline severe and unchanging, but alike calculated to subdue and
conciliate. The wretchedness and misery of the offender should
not be the object of the punishment inflicted ; the end should be

his reformation and future usefulness. Two objects should be attended to : first, regular and constant employment in branches *of industry that would enable the convict to attain the future means of livelihood ; and secondly, instruction in the elementary branches of education, and the careful inculcation of religious and moral principles. The latter would be vitally important." In reference to the incidental expense of such institutions, the report urges the obvious inquiry : " Which, then, is the cheapest, to take five hundred juvenile offenders, and render the great part of them honest and useful men, by a new course of punishment, attended with no extraordinary expense, or to thrust them into our present penitentiaries, with a moral certainty of their coming out with new vices and with fresh desperation—with the moral certainty of their either being in prison as a public burden their whole lives, or of their living, when out, by depredation and knavery ? "

The special committee appointed to write the next annual report determined to consider almost solely the question of juvenile delinquency. The head of this committee, and the author of the paper read, was James W. Gerard, Esq., still living to mark the ever-widening circle of influence resulting from the establishment of an institution, the first specific proposition for which was the act of his own hand.

The necessity for some institution to meet the wants of the children constantly brought to the bar of the mayor's court was seriously felt by every one connected with the administration of justice in the city. Hugh Maxwell, Esq., was then district attorney ; he distinctly recollects (remaining with us still, as he does, in a hale and honored old age) both the difficulties and the dangers attending the trials of youths accused of crimes. Juries, on account of their tender age, were unwilling to convict and send them to prison. They would therefore be discharged, with a feeling of impunity, to be returned to the court again in a few days for more serious offences. If conviction were secured, the children were sure to be corrupted and ruined by the influences of the Bridewell. Says Mr. Maxwell, in answer to the inquiries of the committee, of which Dr. Griscom was chairman, appointed after the report of Mr. Gerard was read : "That many of these youths might be saved from continued transgression no one can doubt, who will examine the statement which I have made from the records of the police office for 1822. This abstract contains the names of more than four hundred and fifty persons, male and female, none over the age of twenty-five, many much younger, and some so young as to be presumed incapable of crime. Many others not mentioned have been discharged, from an unwillingness to imprison, in hope of reformation, or under peculiar circumstances. It would be indeed difficult to determine who would and who would not be influenced by such an institution to leave the paths of vice ; unworthy objects might be received, imposition practised, yet surely, out of three or four hundred miserable beings, some would be found worthy of protection, and desirous of amendment." He further remarks : " Many notorious thieves infesting the city were at first idle, vagrant boys, imprisoned for a short period to keep them from mischief. A second and third imprisonment is inflicted, the prison becomes familiar and agreeable, and at the expiration of their sentence they come out accomplished in iniquity. At each term of the court the average number of lads arraigned for petty theft is five or six, and I regret to state that lately high crimes have been perpetrated in several instances by boys not over sixteen, who at first were idle street-vagrants, and by degrees thieves, burglars, and robbers."

The gentlemen associated with Mr. Gerard, in the committee appointed to consider the question of Juvenile Delinquency, were J. W. Stearns, M. D., and Hiram Ketchum, Esq. The report, which was written by Mr. Gerard, and which embodied the idea afterward realized in the House of Refuge, its paper yellow and its ink pale with age, is still preserved by its honored author, as an interesting and memorable relic, and as a production upon which his surviving family will look as a significant memorial of the early dedication of his valuable services to the best interests of the young people of his generation.

Ever Yours
James W Gerard

Jany. 4" 1863.

CHAPTER III.

THE SOCIETY FOR THE REFORMATION OF JUVENILE DELINQUENTS.

JAMES W. GERARD, Esq., was at this time a young lawyer, and had been practising in the city for a few years. His profession and his inclination led him to take an intelligent interest in the current questions of the day relating to pauperism and crime. He became a manager of the Society for the Prevention of Pauperism, and relates a striking incident occurring about this time, which drew his mind in a special manner toward young offenders.

The first criminal case that he was called to defend was that of a fine-looking, well-dressed lad, of fourteen years of age. He was the son of respectable parents ; he had been arrested and brought to trial for the theft of a canary bird. The case was heard in the mayor's court before Mr. Colden, and was prosecuted by Mr. Maxwell, the district attorney ; the three, judge, attorney, and counsel, were not long after associated together in an institution for the reformation of just such young criminals. Mr. Gerard attempted to secure the discharge of his client upon the ground that a canary bird, being *feræ naturæ,* was not a subject of larceny ; but in this plea he was overruled by the court. To save the boy from what seemed to his counsel would be his certain ruin, he pressed upon the jury the fact, that as there was no separate prison for boys, he would be thrown into the company of old and hardened villains, whose conversation and influence would utterly corrupt him, and extinguish every spark of honesty within him.   The jury, eager to find any loophole to permit them to escape deliberately condemning a boy to certain moral ruin, yielding to the persuasion of the advocate rather than to the law in the case, refused to find him guilty, and the boy was discharged.   The sequel was a sad one, and deeply impressed upon the mind of the young lawyer the importance of securing, in such a case, some positive and powerful reformatory agency to counteract the effect of temptation and evil habits. The boy, emboldened by this easy acquittal which followed his first offence, very soon fell into the commission of more serious crimes.   Under the tuition of those he met during his limited term in the penitentiary, he became a confirmed criminal, and some years since died in prison, while serving out a sentence for larceny.   Singularly enough, while he was in prison a fortune of eighty thousand dollars was left to him.

The early incidents in this case led Mr. Gerard to the conviction that something should be done to rescue the youth of both sexes, who were in peril of a criminal life, from their inevitable corruption if left to themselves or committed to the penitentiary. An incident which Mr. Gerard related, at the opening of the new house on Randall's Island, forms a very happy counterpart to the one which so powerfully impressed his mind with the peril of exposed children, and justifies the wisdom of the plan which he had the honor to place before the community, for the first time, in a tangible form.   Within a month, he remarked at that time, he had met one, now a man, and an active man of business, who had been checked in a career of temptation and wrong-doing by his reception into the House of Refuge and by the discipline which he there received. When the person referred to addressed him he had forgotten his name, but his face was very familiar to him. He was now a thriving man of business in the city; he had not forgotten the short addresses which Mr. Gerard, then a manager, in the early days of the House of Refuge, had made to the boys. "One such case," Mr. Gerard remarked, "compensated for all the labor he had bestowed, in aiding to form this most valuable institution;" and he added with great force, "doubtless if that person sees the report of this day's proceedings, he will pour out in the gratitude of his heart a silent blessing upon those who snatched him from ruin."

In preparing his report, Mr. Gerard visited the Bridewell, Penitentiary, and State Prison, and conversed with police justices and criminal lawyers, that he might have full and correct information upon the subject. For suggestions in reference to the course pursued by the London Philanthropic Society in the work of juvenile reform, and for documentary statements, he went to Isaac Collins—a name inseparably connected with the most important reformatory institutions of New York and Philadelphia. He was the son, and a successor, with his brothers, to the business of the well-known printer and book publisher of the same name, whose octavo family Bible, published at the close of the last century, having been subjected to eleven proof-readings, was considered so free from errors, that it became at once the standard for critical appeal whenever the English translation alone was concerned.* The sons followed the religious persuasion of their father, that of a Friend, as well as his form of business. Mr. Collins's circumstances enabled him

---

* "New American Encyclopædia."

early, as his tastes and sense of duty drew him, to devote his personal attention to the most important benevolent and moral movements of the day. He was in correspondence with English Friends, and familiar with the reformatory measures which had been taken in Great Britain. From the first, until he removed to Philadelphia, he was one of the most active and efficient managers of the House of Refuge. In a convention of the friends of juvenile reform, held in this city, in May, 1857, over which Mr. Collins presided, Mr. Gerard, in an introductory address, remarked : " From you, Mr. Chairman, with whom I freely consulted, I received most useful hints and information. You were, at that time, not only one of the leading managers of the Society for the Prevention of Pauperism, but were actively engaged in numerous philanthropic plans for the improvement of the pauper population of our city, and you lent me, I remember, a report of a kindred establishment in London, from which I made extracts of individual cases, appended to my address." In his own opening remarks, upon this occasion, Mr. Collins expressed the satisfaction he felt in remembering the services he had been able to offer, in the establishment and early years of this " great Christian institution." He felt a sadness, he said, as he recalled the names of the noble band of philanthropists with whom he had been associated in the undertaking, and who had been since " gathered to their eternal rest "—names of which the State might justly be proud—" the Clintons, the Coldens, the Allens, the Jays, the Cornells, and many others. * . . . My heart swells with gratitude," he continued, " to find that this institution, which, in its inception,

---

* " Proceedings of a Convention of Managers and Superintendents of Reformatories," New York, 1857.

may be compared to a grain of mustard-seed, has grown to a great tree, which now spreads its branches through many of our States."

On Friday, February 7, 1823, a meeting of the Society for the Prevention of Pauperism was called "in the large assembly-room of the City Hotel, Broadway." It was extremely cold, but so much interest had already been awakened in reference to the objects of the society, that a good audience was present, many ladies being of the number. The chair was taken by the Rev. Cave Jones, and Mr. Gerard read the annual report, which was almost wholly devoted to the consideration of the subject of juvenile delinquency. "Those who are in the habit," he says, "of attending our criminal courts as jurors, or otherwise, must be convinced of the very great increase of juvenile delinquency within these few years past, and of the necessity of immediate measures to arrest so great an evil. What increases the cause for apprehension is, that punishment produces no reformation, and the young convict is no sooner released from prison than he is again arraigned for other crimes, until time confirms him to be a hardened offender, whom youthful indiscretion, or the force of example, at first caused to deviate from rectitude. Had he been taken by some friendly hand, on his discharge from prison for his first offence, and taught to know his faults and how to mend them, instead of passing his days in crime, and perhaps ending them on a gallows, he might have become an honest and a useful man."

The inability of the public schools to correct this evil, the sad condition of the unclassified penitentiaries, already containing a large number of youths of both sexes, are dwelt upon at length. The report then insists that "there should be a separate

building for the imprisonment of young offenders both *before* and *after* trial. If we may so speak, we should endeavor to hide it from themselves that they are prisoners.

" The consciousness of crime and punishment, and consequent disgrace, at once break down the spirit of youth, and their independence of character. If it were possible, they should hear no clanking of chains ; feel no restraint of bolts and bars : they should be made to think rather that they are in a place of instruction and WORK, preparing for their future support and usefulness, than in a prison suffering punishment as an atonement for their offences."

The report alludes to certain experiments, successfully tried in the Eastern States and in Philadelphia, to classify juvenile offenders by themselves, and finally develops the most vital idea of the whole paper. " Connected," says Mr. Gerard, " with juvenile delinquency, there is a subject which the Board beg leave to lay before the public and our civil authorities, which, if acted upon, they are confident would greatly reform and prevent the increase of young offenders : it is the project of a House of Refuge for young delinquents when discharged from prison." (Mr. Gerard, it will be seen, had not considered the still more important office which the Refuge was to render to the young in anticipating a criminal life, and offering them a shelter and training before they had entered the walls of a prison. His suggestions, which follow, are still applicable and full of significance.) " Our penitentiaries are now thronged with young men and women over sixteen, but under twenty-five ; " (and his remarks, after nearly half a century, are strikingly pertinent to their case at the present time. To meet this exigency should be one of the first movements of philanthropic men in our land :) " Let

us for a moment dwell upon the condition and feelings of a youth when he is let loose from prison upon the termination of his punishment. How hopeless and helpless is his case; without money, without friends, without the means of gaining his bread, even with the sweat of his face, and above all without character! No hand is extended to guide him on his way; no tongue speaks to him the voice of comfort; no smile of welcome lights up the face of friendship. All who know him shun him. He bears the mark of Cain upon him; all hands bid him depart, all doors are closed against him. He feels as if the world were a desert, and he alone in it; as if the prison he left contained all his friends and all his ties, and as if its gate, when it closed upon him, shut him out from a home. Thus viewing the world, and thus viewed by the world, can he repent and reform? No opportunity is given him to do so. He is driven to seek the haunts of lawless men, for such alone will receive him; he is compelled to theft and robbery, because he cannot starve. He is sought after and tempted by old offenders who are always on the watch for young proselytes to join them in their depredations upon society; and he is again convicted and punished, and again let loose upon the world, riper in years and iniquity. This is no picture of the fancy, no story of exaggeration; it is the history of hundreds of our youth who are annually discharged from our prisons, and again and again committed to them.* Ask our

* While these pages are being written, a fine-looking young man calls at the door. He was discharged the day before from the penitentiary. He had heard the writer preach to the prisoners. His home is in England. He was a finished book-keeper, and had been a clerk in a book-store; but, upon the failure of the firm that employed him, he found a position on board the Hamburg line of steamers. While under the influence of liquor, in a sailor boarding-house in our city, he committed the offence (far from being a serious

officers of justice and judges, and they will tell you that the
statement is true.   They will tell you that the faces of young
offenders grow familiar to them from the frequency of their conviction, and that they do not know what to do with them, as imprisonment works no repentance.   We have official information
that between one and two hundred young persons, from the age
of seven to fourteen years, are annually brought before the police
on charges involving various degrees of crime ; and it is the
opinion of our magistrates that all between those ages can, by
proper means, be reformed and made useful members of society.
. . . To support a House of Refuge would require funds to
procure a suitable building where the children could receive
moral and religious instruction, and be taught some of the more
simple mechanic arts.   The greater part of the young convicts
are the children of poor and abandoned parents, and commence
their career by street-begging and petty pilfering.   Those who
preferred it, and these doubtless would be many, when their
minds were properly wrought upon, their character changed, and
the seeds of virtuous principles had taken root, might be bound

one) which sent him to prison.   When he called, he had not eaten since his
discharge, and, for want of other shelter, slept in a station-house.   He
offered himself as store-keeper on board a steamer, and his examination was
entirely satisfactory, until, frankly and truthfully answering the questions
asked him, he told the person inquiring, that he had just come from the
penitentiary.   This closed the engagement at once.   Now what shall this
man do ?   Does the community propose to starve him in addition to incar-
cerating him ?   Two accomplished pickpockets were discharged at the same
time ; being Englishmen also, they offered to take him into company, and to
guarantee him a good living.   They had confederates and comfortable quarters awaiting them.   How unwise and uneconomical to force a man under
such circumstances upon so serious a temptation !   One of these young men
was thirty-five years of age.   He had practised his *profession* for eighteen
years ; seven of these years he had spent in prison.   What a heavy tax upon
individuals and upon the whole community he had laid in this time !

out in the country to farmers, or sent to sea as apprentices to masters of vessels. The offender now feels that he has regained his character, he hopes the world has forgiven him and perhaps forgotten his offence, and he feels himself to be once more a part of society. If but one out of ten could by such an establishment be saved from ruin, it would repay all the efforts of its founding and of maintaining it. It should be supported by subscribers and contributors, and placed under the direction of benevolent and competent men, many of whom our city can boast, who would gladly undertake it. The Legislature, convinced of its utility and economy to the public treasury in saving them the support of many convicts, would doubtless patronize it by ample contributions."

All these moderate expectations have been abundantly realized in the history of the House. The report was well received, and was ably supported in eloquent addresses by Hiram Ketchum, Thomas Fessenden, and Theodore Sedgwick, Esqs. The latter gentleman related in his speech a touching incident of a child who had that day been detected in stealing, who was but four years of age. The editorial columns of Colonel Stone's paper (who was greatly interested afterward in the Refuge, and was for fourteen years a manager), the *Commercial Advertiser*, for the three succeeding days, were devoted to the report and sketches of the addresses delivered upon the occasion. The report itself was afterward published in a pamphlet form, and widely circulated.

Thus far the Society had simply modified the offensive name of the place of confinement for young offenders, from a prison, with all its offensive and disgraceful associations, to a House of Refuge; it was still to be a refuge to those that had been in prison, or a separate place of confinement for young criminals. Individuals, indeed, had suggested the preventive work to be performed, as in the instance of Mr. Eddy.   The next and final stage was to entirely divest the Refuge of its penitentiary associations, and to permit magistrates to send into its sheltering and nurturing folds the vagrant and perilled children of the streets—thus, in a degree, anticipating the corrupting influences of early evil associations.

On the 12th of June, 1823, at a meeting of the managers of the Society, upon the motion of Isaac Collins, a committee was appointed to prepare a detailed plan for a House of Refuge. Prof. Griscom presided at this meeting, and was added to the committee and made its chairman.   The following gentlemen were associated with him : Isaac Collins, Cornelius Dubois, James W. Gerard, Hiram Ketchum, and Eleazer Lord.

The admirable report, that embodied the whole idea of the House of Refuge, and formed the foundation upon which the institution has rested for its first half century, was written by the chairman, who remained, from its establishment until he removed from the city, one of its most active and respected managers. When, at the age of seventy-seven years, after a life of great usefulness, in the enjoyment of an enviable reputation, and in the peace of the Gospel of Christ, respected and beloved, he " fell asleep," the managers of the Society for the Reformation of Juvenile Delinquents thus recorded their appreciation of his services in the founding of their institution, in their twenty-eighth annual report : " His name," they say, " may deservedly take rank among the foremost of those enlightened philanthropists to whom society is indebted for the plan of the House of Refuge. The discipline and working of reformatory institutions had long occupied

his attention, and he had obtained, by extensive inquiries and observation, especially during his travels in Europe, much valuable
information upon the subject. The experience he had thus
acquired caused him to be selected as chairman of that committee of the old Society for the Prevention of Pauperism, whose
admirable report developed the plan of the House of Refuge,
and led to its establishment. Dr. Griscom was the author of
several of the earliest annual reports of the society, was one
of its first vice-presidents, and continued his active services in
that position till his removal from the city in 1832."

In his report he took the ground that " the children of neg-
lectful, intemperate, vicious parents, and those who are trained
to sin, should be *saved from prison* even though they may have
been guilty of actual crime." He says : " Every person that
frequents the out-streets of this city, must be forcibly struck
with the ragged and uncleanly appearance, the vile language, and
the idle and miserable habits of great numbers of children, most
of whom are of an age suitable for schools, or for some useful
employment. The parents of these children are, in all probability, too poor or too degenerate to provide them with clothing fit
for them to be seen in a school, and know not where to place
them in order that they may find employment, or be better cared
for. Accustomed, in many instances, to witness at home nothing in the way of example but what is degrading ; early taught
to observe intemperance, and to hear obscene and profane language without disgust ; obliged to beg, and even encouraged to
acts of dishonesty, to satisfy the wants induced by the indolence
of their parents,—what can be expected but that such children
will, in due time, become responsible to the law for crimes which
have thus in a manner been forced upon them? Can it be con-

sistent with real justice that delinquents of this character should
be consigned to the infamy and severity of punishment, which
must inevitably tend to perfect the work of degradation, to sink
them still deeper in corruption, to deprive them of their remaining sensibility to the shame of exposure, and establish them in
all the hardihood of daring and desperate villany?   Is it possible that a Christian community can lend its sanction to such a
process without any effort to rescue and to save?   If the agents
of our municipal government stand toward the community in
the moral light of guardians of virtue ; if they may be justly
regarded as the political fathers of the unprotected, does not
every feeling of justice urge upon them the principle of considering these juvenile culprits as falling under their special guardianship, and claiming from them the right which every child may
demand of its parent, of being well instructed in the nature of
its duties before it is punished for the breach of their observ-
ance?   Ought not every citizen, who has a just sense of the
reciprocal obligations of parents and children, to lend his aid to
the administrators of the law, in rescuing these pitiable victims
of neglect and wretchedness from the melancholy fate which
almost inevitably results from an apprenticeship in our common
prisons?"

The report introduces extended statistics of the criminal
juvenile population of the city, gathered from the records of the
district attorney, Hugh Maxwell, Esq., and from the keepers of
the Bridewell and Bellevue Prison.   "From the exposition thus
given," the report goes on to state, "of the subjects referred to
their consideration, the committee cannot but indulge the belief
that the inference which will be drawn by every citizen of New
York, from the facts now laid before him, will be in perfect

accordance with their own—that it is highly expedient that a
HOUSE OF REFUGE FOR JUVENILE DELINQUENTS should, as soon
as practicable, be established in the immediate vicinity of this
city."

Of the character of the House the report remarks : " The
design of the proposed institution is to furnish, in the first place,
an asylum, in which boys under a certain age who become
subject to the notice of our police, either as vagrants, or house-
less, or charged with petty crimes, may be received, judiciously
classed according to their degrees of depravity or innocence, put
to work at such employments as will tend to encourage industry
and ingenuity, taught reading, writing, and arithmetic, and most
carefully instructed in the nature of their moral and religious
obligations, while, at the same time, they are subjected to a
course of treatment, that will afford a prompt and energetic
corrective of their vicious propensities, and hold out every
inducement to reformation and good conduct . . . Such an institution would in time exhibit scarcely any other than the character of a decent school and manufactory. It need not be invested
with the insignia of a prison ; it should be surrounded only with
a high fence, like many factories in the neighborhood of cities,
and carefully closed in front.

Secondly, the committee have no doubt that, were such an
institution once well established and put under good regulations,
the magistrates would very often deem it expedient to place
offenders in the hands of its managers, rather than to sentence
them to the City Penitentiary. The gradations of crime are
almost infinite ; and so minute are the shades of guilt, so remote
or so intimate the connection between legal criminality and
previous character, that it would often be judged reasonable

to use all the discretion which the law would possibly admit in deciding upon the offence and the destination of juvenile delinquents ; and every principle of justice and mercy would point, in numerous cases of conviction for crime, to such a refuge and reformatory, rather than to the Bridewell or City Prison.

" A third class, which it might be very proper to transplant to such an establishment, and to distribute through its better divisions, are boys, some of whom are of tender age, whose parents, either from vice or indolence, are careless of their minds and morals, and leave them exposed in rags and filth to miserable and scanty fare, destitute of education, and liable to become the prey of criminal associates."

For a fourth class, Dr. Griscom introduces those young persons, often alluded to before, for whom, as yet, the community has made no provision, and who have never been transferred to the House of Refuge ; " youthful convicts, who, on their discharge from prison, at the expiration of their sentence, finding themselves without character, without subsistence, and ignorant of the means by which it is to be sought, have no alternative but to beg or steal."

The last class which he mentions is that of " delinquent females, who are either too young to have acquired habits of fixed depravity, or those whose lives have in general been virtuous, but who, having yielded to the seductive influences of corrupt associates, have suddenly to endure the bitterness of lost reputation, and are cast forlorn and destitute upon a cold and unfeeling public, full of compunctions for their errors, and anxious to be restored to the paths of innocence and usefulness. That there are many females of tender age just in those predicaments in this city, none can doubt who surveys the list of last year's culprits, furnished by the district attorney." Guarding with great wisdom against receiving those too mature in age and crime, he remarks : within such limits, " it is our decided opinion—an opinion founded not only upon the reasonableness of the proposition, but upon the result of similar institutions in Europe—that destitute females might form one department of the establishment, and with advantage to the institution. Occupying apartments entirely distinct from those of the other sex, and separated from them by impassable barriers, the females might contribute, by their labor, to promote the interests of the establishment, and at the same time derive from it their full and appropriate share of benefit."

Upon the expediency of thus uniting the two sexes in the same institution we shall speak hereafter, and give the matured judgment of those that have watched the experiment of half a century, and observed and read what has been done and said by others.

Prof. Griscom enters into full details in reference to the importance of classification, based upon character and designated by some badge, open to the free competition of all the inmates ; thus inspiring self-respect and a wholesome ambition. He treats, also, with remarkable judgment, the various questions relating to food, hours of labor and recreation, and the more difficult one of moral and corporal punishment. He proposes the plan which was realized in the establishment of the Refuge, of associating with the managers a supervisory committee of ladies, by whose " discretion, tenderness, and fidelity," the interests of the department for girls should be judiciously considered.

" The introduction of labor," he remarks, with prophetic

wisdom, " would constitute an important feature in the concern, not only as a means of diminishing its expense and promoting its moral influence, but in order to supply its subjects with that instruction and with those habits, which would enable them, on leaving the House, to procure a decent and honest livelihood."

We reluctantly abridge the valuable practical suggestions of this extended report, as they are as instructive at the present hour as when first read, forty-four years ago. The paper concludes with such stirring appeals as these : " Your committee can but cherish the lively expectation that, when the public mind comes to be impressed with the nature and importance of these various considerations, there will be but one opinion of the necessity and expediency of providing a place in this city which shall serve as a real penitentiary to the younger class of offenders, and as a refuge for the forlorn and destitute, who are on the confines of gross criminality. . . . If the actual situation of these several classes of criminal and destitute beings in this city does not open a door for Christian benevolence, as inviting in its promises of good as any of the various kinds of charity, either at home or abroad, which claim the attention of our citizens, your committee think they might in vain seek to explore the miseries of their fellow-creatures, with the hope of exciting the feelings of commiseration, and the energies of active and unwearied humanity. Can it be right that we should extend our views to the wants of those who are thousands of miles from us, and close our eyes upon the condition of the worse than heathen that wander in our streets? Shall our hands be opened with distinguished liberality to the means of civilizing and reforming whole nations in the remotest quarters of the globe, and closed to the obvious necessities of the outcasts of our own society? Your committee mean no reflection whatever on the schemes so actively prosecuted of doing good in distant parts of the earth; but surely if this we ought to do, the other we ought not to leave undone."

This report was first read and sanctioned by a large private gathering held at the New-York Hospital; and on the 19th of December, 1823, a very large meeting was convened in the assembly-room of the City Hotel, Mayor Colden presiding on the occasion. Before this audience, including the most substantial men of New York, the report was again read, and its recommendations were earnestly supported in addresses delivered by Peter A. Jay, Esq., Rev. Dr. Wainwright, Mr. Joseph P. Simpson, Hiram Ketchum, Esq., Prof. McVicker, James W. Gerard, Esq., Hugh Maxwell, Esq., and Mr. Divie Bethune.

The district attorney, Mr. Maxwell, in his speech, replete with moving incidents and statistics, drawn from his personal experience in the criminal courts of the city, estimated that at least two hundred young persons might be annually snatched from a life of crime by such an institution—a very moderate limit, in view of the actual history of the House of Refuge since its establishment. It has sent out into society an average of three hundred every year during its existence, and the lowest estimate of the number of these that have done well has been seventy-five per cent.

The *Commercial Advertiser* of the 24th of December, of this year, has a very full and interesting account of this meeting. Without reporting each speaker, it embodies the chief thoughts and suggestions of all. "The object of the House of Refuge," it says, after vividly portraying the previous ruin which inevitably befell the young criminal if imprisoned for his offence, " is to afford to young offenders an asylum where they will be received with open arms and friendly hearts.   At the knock of the poor, friendless, homeless, penitent young convict, its portal will be raised, and he will be received by benevolent men, whose duty and whose pleasure it will be to instruct and reform him.   His rags will be taken off ; the principles of virtue and religion will be instilled, and he will be made, as far as possible, to forget that he has ever been the subject for a prison.

" The House of Refuge will resemble a large school-house and manufactory.   The boys will be taught the elements of a practical education ; they will be put to labor at simple mechanic arts, which will afford them afterward the means of support. When their minds are expanded by education, and good principles are elicited and confirmed, they will then leave the Refuge with such a certificate of character that mechanics, and farmers, and captains of vessels, will receive them into their employ, and they will become useful members of society."

The interesting paper, read by Prof. Griscom, met with universal acceptance from the audience ; and their feelings were so aroused by the addresses of the eloquent speakers, that the meeting unanimously resolved that such an institution as had been described should be at once established, and that a society should be formed for the Reformation of Juvenile Delinquents. Eight hundred dollars toward the realization of the plan were subscribed before the meeting adjourned, and the city was districted to be canvassed for further donations.   Eighteen thousand dollars were in this way readily secured for the commencement of the enterprise.

The old Society for the Prevention of Pauperism having

accomplished its appointed task, was "translated, that it should not see death," into the new Institution for the Reformation of Juvenile Delinquents, and entered at once upon the practical realization of the theories that had long been discussed. Dr. John H. Griscom very happily remarks, in reference to this change: "Like a pebble dropped into the bosom of a lake, itself disappeared from sight, but the ripple which it created will continue to expand until it shall have reached the utmost verge of time, and embraced within its widening and humanizing circle unnumbered thousands who will confess its happy influence over their present and future destinies."

To give an organic form to the movement, twenty-five managers were nominated and appointed, who should retain their position until the Society, constituted of its subscribers and life-members, should be regularly organized under an act of incorporation which was to be obtained from the State Legislature.* Of this committee, Hugh Maxwell and J. W. Gerard are the only survivors. Judge Duer, presiding justice of the Superior Court of New York City, held in great esteem for his eminent judicial abilities as well as for the dignity and impartiality with which he discharged the duties of his office, died in 1858. His sound judgment, his large legal experience, and his benevolent sympathies, rendered him a valuable counsellor in preparing the organic law of such an institution as the House of Refuge.

---

* The following persons were elected at this meeting as managers: C. D. Colden, J. Griscom, J. M. Wainwright, Alderman Wyckoff, Judge J. T. Irving, an honored and able judge of the Common Pleas, and brother of Washington Irving, C. Dubois, John E. Hyde, Dr. Ives, J. W. Gerard, Isaac Collins, J. Curtis, Dr. J. Stearns, R. Olmstead, J. Grinnell, R. F. Mott, Stephen Allen, Judge John Duer, A. Burtis, John Targee, Thomas Eddy, Samuel Cowdrey, and Hugh Maxwell.

Upon all these committees we notice the name of Cornelius Dubois. No one did more to aid in raising and managing the funds which were requisite, and for which the necessity at times became pressing, than this highly-respected and sturdy merchant. He took a lively and intelligent interest in all the measures relating to the establishment of the House of Refuge. In the language of his brother managers, recorded in the twenty-second annual report, " He saw the great evils attending the disposition of our juvenile criminals, and with other philanthropists obtained the act incorporating this institution. In its infancy, when it was looked upon as an experiment, and depended mainly for its support on private charity, he was untiring in his exertions to extend its means of usefulness, and place it beyond the embarrassment of pecuniary want. For eighteen years he filled the office of treasurer, and discharged its duties with accuracy and untiring industry until within a few months of his decease."

No name during his able ministry in this city was more familiar to, or respected among, its citizens than that of Jonathan Mayhew Wainwright, who, when he died, had been for about two years provisional bishop of the Protestant Episcopal Church in the diocese of New York. His graceful and impressive eloquence, the influence of his high social position, and his active sympathies, were generously proffered to the Society in its birth. He was one of its incorporated managers, and remained for some time upon its Board.

April 7, 1826, Robert F. Mott, a well-known and wealthy citizen, a highly-respected member of the Society of Friends, an intelligent and earnest laborer in every work of charity and reform, especially interested in the public schools, wrote to the

president of the Society for the Reformation of Juvenile Delinquents : " I find myself obliged by continual ill-health and a
prospect of leaving the city for some time, to tender my resignation as a member of your Board.   As I have never served
any institution with greater pleasure, so I have never left one
with greater regret."   Upon his death, in 1826, his colleagues,
with much feeling, bear their testimony to his great worth and
probity of character.   " To those who knew him well," they
say, " little need be said in favor of his worth.   He was the
friend of the friendless, and the advocate of the poor.   Unob-
trusive in his manners, yet steady in his purpose, nothing could
swerve him from the path of duty, or divert him from the main
object of his life, which was the good and welfare of his fellow-
creatures.   He has early finished his course of rectitude, and
has left for the approval and imitation of others a bright example of active and disinterested worth."

The temporary board of managers made an earnest appeal
to the public, which appeared in the issue of the *Commercial
Advertiser*, February 26, 1824, stating clearly the object proposed in the movement for the salvation of young offenders.
They append their names to this call upon the charity of the community, with their places of residence, to which contributions
could be sent.   It is an interesting local fact, showing the growth
of the city, that at the time only one of their number lived as
far up as Grand Street ; this was Dr. Griscom, who had just
removed from William Street to the corner of Elm and Grand.

" We are aware," they say, " of the responsibility we assume.   We anticipate the difficulties of an untried path.   We
are sensible of the time and attention it will require at our
hands, and of the discretion that will be requisite in every stage

of its operation.   But all we want, as an encouragement to perseverance, is the promptitude and efficiency of your coöperation.
Even at a time when so much feeling has been excited and
liberality manifested on behalf of the grievances and sufferings
of a far-distant nation (the Greeks), we hesitate not to prefer
our claims upon the charities of the bountiful and the sympathies of the benevolent, in favor of the wretched of our immediate borders. . . . We are fully persuaded of the practicability of the scheme we have undertaken, and of its truly
beneficial tendency."

On the 29th of March, 1824, an act of incorporation was
secured from the Legislature, then assembled in Albany.   This
act, and all the subsequent legislation in behalf of the institution, will be found in the Appendix to this volume.   With all
the changes and additions that have taken place since that day,
the closing sentence of the second section has remained un-
altered : " *And it is hereby further enacted,* That no manager of
the said Society shall receive any compensation for his services."
A half century of constant and efficient labors, sometimes very
exacting and perplexing, have thus been yielded by the best
citizens of the city and State, without any further recompense
than that which comes from above, and the realization of that
truth of our Lord that it is " more blessed to give than to receive."

In making the twelfth annual report, the writer remarks :
" They " (the managers) " have no pecuniary interest in the institution—no end to gratify but humanity.   Their time and talents
are voluntarily and cheerfully devoted to this cause, and if they
have any regret it is that all their fellow-citizens who are qualified
do not inquire into the merits of the institution, and do what they

can to increase its usefulness. They are still of the opinion, heretofore frequently expressed, that this voluntary management, prompted solely by feelings of philanthropy, is the best mode of governing the institution, and that its utility would be seriously impaired if any different course were to be pursued. So well satisfied are they on this point, that they earnestly desire to see the multiplication of similar establishments not only in this country but in Europe. If *all* the juvenile delinquents here and elsewhere could be introduced into Houses of Refuge, and enjoy the advantages of a moral and religious education, there would soon be much fewer candidates for the prison and the gallows ! "

A very good summary of the most important powers of the managers, as bestowed in their several acts of incorporation, is embodied in the fifth annual report which they made to the Legislature. " The Legislature," says this report, " has very much enlarged the objects of our institution and intrusted to its managers powers that have not heretofore been delegated. These are essential to its beneficent action, and mark the great difference between it and other similar institutions that previously existed, however similar they may be in name. If a child be found destitute ; if abandoned by its parents, or suffered to lead a vicious or vagrant life ; or if convicted of any crime, it may be sent to the House of Refuge. There is in no case any other sentence than that it shall ' there be dealt with according to law.' That is, it may, if not released by some legal process, be there detained, if the managers should think it unfit to be sooner discharged, until it arrives at age. Parents or guardians, from the time it is legally sentenced to the Refuge, lose all control of its person. When it is believed that a child is reformed, the managers have power, with its consent, to bind it as an apprentice, till the age of eighteen years " (now twenty-one), " if a female ; and if a boy, till the age of twenty-one.   It is these important features that mark the difference between our institution and all others that previously existed ; and it is in this sense that we may say with truth that the New-York House of Refuge was the first of its kind ever established."

It cannot be supposed that the State would have intrusted such powers into the hands of any but her most reliable citizens ; and every one must see how sacredly such powers must be guarded and governed by justice and righteousness in the board of management.

These powers have been often questioned before the courts, on both technical and constitutional grounds, but the decisions of the highest tribunals have not only sustained the fundamental law of the House, but, in several instances, in elaborate opinions, have set forth the great underlying principles justifying the bestowment upon persons, acting in *loco parentis*, of these extraordinary powers for the sole behoof and well-being of the child. Several of these decisions, rendered in our own State, in Pennsylvania, and in Maryland, will be found in full in the Appendix to this volume.

The character and standing in society of the gentlemen who from the first have held the management of the Refuge have been a satisfactory assurance to the community that these powers would be conscientiously exerted ; and there has never been an occasion when this conviction has been disturbed.

Through errors in the commitments of the courts, the Board has seen many a promising child, on a writ of *habeas corpus*, discharged to certain ruin, through either the weakness or wickedness of a parent or guardian ; but they have never failed, whenever a child has been discovered to have a decent home and respectable parents, and has shown good evidence of amendment, to return it to the custody of its own friends.

Our judges have often undoubtedly suffered as keenly, but have probably felt themselves unable to dismiss a writ as summarily, as did the recorder of the city in a case tried before him in 1829. A child, ten years of age, was committed to the House. The father kept a house of bad repute. The mother, who was shockingly intemperate, employed the child, day after day, in begging victuals and old clothes. The infamous persons that frequented her father's house would often take this little girl with them, entering houses on the pretence of begging, and using the child to cover their thievish practices. " When she entered the House," says the superintendent, " she was as black and dirty as a chimney-sweep ; her muslin was the color of the earth, it being all the garment of the kind she had." When she was thoroughly cleaned and clad in a neat, plain dress, she attracted all observers by her interesting appearance. Her parents, enraged at the loss of their gains through her begging and thieving, brought her on a writ of *habeas corpus* before the recorder. " The judge examined the case with much attention, interrogated the child, discovered that she preferred the Refuge to her father's house, seemed pleased with her clean and sweet appearance, and then looked with disgust at the dirty heap of clothes in which she had come to the Refuge ; suddenly addressing the lawyer, ' Sir,' said he, ' if I should give you this child, my conscience would not let me sleep to-night ! ' "

CHAPTER IV.

THE FIRST HOUSE OF REFUGE.

PERHAPS the earliest suggestion, as to the place that afterward became the site of the first House of the Society, was made by Rev. John Stanford, D. D., a highly-respected and able Baptist clergyman of the city. He had a private academy, and was also the pastor of a church. In 1811, having previously preached in the almshouse, he was appointed by the city government to be its chaplain, and eventually the field of his labors "embraced the prisons, hospitals, and charitable asylums of the city." *

He was a venerable man at this time, over seventy years of age. In an extended report, very interesting and thoughtful, rendered to the city government, December 22, 1823, and published in the *Commercial Advertiser* of the 17th of January, 1824, the old divine calls the attention of the authorities of the city to the fact that, on January 21, 1812, he had presented to them, in a report, an outline of a plan for the establishment of an asylum for vagrant youth, " with its promising advantages to prevent pauperism and the commission of crime." He remarks, that since his duties had led him into the peni-

---

* " American Encyclopædia."

tentiary, " a tenfold weight of conviction had pressed upon him, of the importance of a separate place for the reception of vagrant children." His plan, as drawn out in his report, is an almost perfect anticipation of the organization of the Juvenile Asylum. He suggested also, at this time, in connection with the House of Reform upon the land, what might be called a naval department. He was a half century in advance of his times ; but when a reform school-ship rides the waves of New-York harbor, the wisdom, piety, and patriotism of old Doctor John Stanford will be fully justified. His plan was very simple and practicable. He proposed to have navigation taught in the asylum upon the land, and, by masts and rigging, to give a general idea of a sailor's duty. A small vessel, which could be used from time to time, under a proper sailing-master, would give the boys that exhibited a predilection for the sea such an opportunity to become sufficiently acquainted with the ordinary requisitions upon a sailor as to render them capable of offering valuable services on board any vessel in the mercantile marine or United States service. " I recommend," he says, " that the greatest attention be paid to raise boys for sea service, the advantages of which will be found to be of the highest value. . . . In proportion as your trade and commerce increase, you require seamen of your own without being indebted to foreigners, and the institution will lend, in this respect, its friendly aid to establish your independence on the water. The youth you have rescued, on whom you have bestowed your kindness, will naturally form an attachment to the interests of the country, and nobly contend for its rights and its honors."

In his report, he proposes to the city council that the United States Arsenal at the fork of the Bloomingdale and Old Post roads should be obtained and set apart for the discipline and training of neglected and exposed children.

In conclusion, he adds: " Through my advanced age, I scarce allow myself the luxury of indulging a thought that I shall be permitted to live to see such an asylum in operation. I could not withhold my pen from presenting you this paper upon the subject ; and if at present it may not be found useful, it may be deposited among your papers, and prove of some advantage when my hand can write no more."

His last suggestion, however, met with an unexpectedly favorable result, and he was permitted to take a conspicuous part in the inauguration of a refuge for abandoned children, which his experience in the penitentiaries had shown to be such a pressing necessity, on the site of his own nomination.

The managers made an application to the city council for a grant of land for the proposed institution, and the committee to whom the request was referred recommended " that the piece of ground lying at the junction of the Bloomingdale and Old Post roads, on which the United States Arsenal was situated, which was granted on the 17th of November, 1807, by the corporation to the General Government, upon the express condition and understanding that the same should be used for the purpose of an arsenal and deposit of military stores, and whenever it should cease to be used for such purposes it was to revert to the corporation, should be conveyed to the board of managers of the Society for the Reformation of Juvenile Delinquents, whenever they obtained from the General Government a conveyance of the interest they had in the ground." In addition to this they proposed to convey to the society the triangular plot in front, formed by the junction of the roads. They cordially add : " That they feel a pleasure in expressing their approbation of the laudable objects which the society has in view.   Perhaps," they remark, " no institution is more desirable in our city than one which affords a place of refuge for neglected and depraved children, just entering upon the paths of vice, where they may be reclaimed from their bad habits, their minds instructed in the rudiments of learning, and their time devoted to some useful employment.   The committee believe that such an institution, properly regulated and conducted, would not only tend to improve the condition of society by lessening the commission of crime, and the number of convicts sent to our prisons, but would have a tendency to diminish the expenses of the city incurred on that account."

It was understood that the General Government was proposing to change the site of its arsenal, as its distance from navigable water rendered it inconvenient, and the gradual approach of population dangerous.

The memorial of the society to the Government at Washington, seeking for the release of these grounds and buildings, met with great favor.   Mr. Calhoun, then Secretary of War, the Vice-President, and Colonel Bomford, at the head of the Bureau of Ordnance, cordially received and favorably considered the application.   Colonel Bomford said : " The humane objects contemplated by the society you represent merit and must receive universal approbation.   The officers of the Government are disposed to aid the objects of the Society by any measure which can be adopted, consistently with a due regard to the public interest."   Lieutenant Monroe, stationed near the city, was ordered to give a personal consideration to the matter, and to report at once.   The result was, that the government stores

were removed to Castle William, and the large barracks, a
house suitable for the superintendent and his family, outbuild-
ings and walls, were surrendered to the Society for the sum
of six thousand dollars, four thousand of which was afterward remitted to the Society, upon a petition drawn up by Dr.
Griscom, and presented in the name of the managers to Congress.

This site, containing about four acres of land, then so favorable for the object to which it was to be devoted, was about a
mile from the habitable portion of the city, and two miles from
the City Hall. It was surrounded by cultivated farms, groves,
open and rough fields blooming in their season with wild flowers,
and wearing all the aspects of the country to the little city
Arabs gathered there from the narrow streets of the town. It
is now in the heart of the city, forming the charming park,
known as Madison Square, lying between Twenty-third and
Twenty-sixth Streets and the Fifth and Madison Avenues. It
was then considered so far out of town, that a lady of the city
recollects, when young, being invited to visit the institution ;
the day was devoted to the object, and she was so fatigued by
the jaunt that she was sick for a week, as the consequence.

Here, on the first day of January, 1825, in the old soldiers'
barracks, occupied during the War of 1812–1815, purified,
refitted, and prepared for a limited number of inmates, the New-
York House of Refuge was opened with appropriate and impressive services.

Money and influence could secure an available site, and
arrange and furnish comfortable rooms, but the whole success
of this most difficult and delicate experiment would turn, in a
large measure, upon securing, in the superintendent, qualities

that gold cannot always purchase. The first one, especially, had quite an untrodden path to explore.

Among the officers of the Society for the Prevention of Pauperism was Mr. Joseph Curtis, who had served for several years as its secretary. His excellent wife was a member of the Society of Friends. He was a diligent, intelligent business man, but was ruined, with many others, in his business by the war. In 1820 he became the superintendent of the business of James P. Allaire, and through the general probity of his character, and the confidence he had won from the business community, he obtained for this great mechanic that bank credit which was alone necessary to secure for his brilliant capabilities an adequate field of development.

Mr. Curtis had been personally active in all the public charities of the day, he was endowed with a peculiarly generous and unselfish disposition, and was especially interested in the young and every thing that related to their happiness or improvement. He had been particularly prominent in securing the State act of manumission, by which New York became in the widest sense a free State, which was passed in 1817 ; having pressed the matter upon the community, in connection with Peter A. Jay, Cadwallader Colden, Isaac M. Ely, and others, and also upon the Legislature, for a period of eight years.

He was accustomed to refer to the 17th day of February, 1817, " when he froze his face in mounting the bleak hill to the capitol, at Albany, as one of the proudest of his life. ' I feel I have not quite lived in vain,' he was accustomed to say, ' when I consider the passage of the Manumission Act ; the memory of it will smooth my dying pillow.' " * A pair of very

---

* " Life of Joseph Curtis," p. 59.

handsome silver pitchers, happily inscribed and engraved, were given him by the Society, as a testimony of their appreciation of his labors in its behalf.   Dr. Bellows, in the funeral sermon which he preached, upon the decease of Mr. Curtis, well remarks, that "fifty years ago the ignorant, the weak and abandoned, the slave, the prisoner, the blind, had not drawn to themselves the attention even of the Christian; and when we are estimating the claims on our gratitude of the founders of our public schools, the projectors of asylums and houses of refuge, the starters of emancipation, we are not to forget that the lamp of their charity sprang up in utter darkness, and was trimmed without the notice of men, and fed by none of the sympathy and admiration of society at large."

An affecting illustration of the genuine kindness of his heart was the beautiful tenderness with which, for twenty-six years, he personally undertook the care of an imbecile brother.   This care he never delegated to a servant.   "His dress was scrupulously attended to, and his person cared for as a tender mother cares for her child.   The poor invalid was liable to sulkiness— to fits of passion.   His gentle brother and his eldest daughter, and they alone, could manage and subdue him.   As he grew older he lost the use of his limbs, and for two years prior to his death was confined to a chair on wheels."   The dying words of the poor imbecile were, "Brother Joseph."   And the response from the unfailing affection of his brother was, "My dear, your mother waits for you."   "He was a harmless man," said Mr. Curtis gently to one of his children, as he looked upon his brother's face in the coffin, "he has filled his mission, and now, daughter, my work is finished."   And so indeed it proved, for in just three months he followed him.

His Power to awaken Affection.—His Last Gift to Refuge.

This was the spirit of the man whom the providence of God at the moment seemed to indicate as the fit person to introduce the novel experiment of attempting the reform of young delinquents. He retained the position but little more than a year. His was simply the office to open the way and afford a worthy lesson to younger successors. While inimitable in his power to win the affections of the young, and overflowing with paternal goodness toward the sad, misguided youths sent to his institution, others might excel him in managing the multifarious details of such an establishment, and even in the administration of discipline.

One might be surprised, in reading the records of the first year of the Refuge, at the number and severity of the punishments and the repeated efforts of escape and acts of rebellion, such as never occur now, with the census at one thousand inmates, when so mild and loving a man was at its head, if he had not learned the wonderful effect of regular employment, gentle but unvarying discipline, and the constant inspiration of a positive expectation of discharge to be earned by good behavior, faithfulness, diligence, and studiousness.

Mr. Curtis, when he left the Refuge, never removed his interest from it. He became one of the most ardent and efficient friends of the public-school system in the city. For years he visited the institution upon Sabbath afternoons, to address the children. One of his last requests to his family was that his portrait might be sent to the Refuge, that the children might continue to look upon the face of him who never spoke of them without a moistening eye. To this day that face, hanging upon the wall of the superintendent's office, glances down its benign benediction upon every new-comer as he enters the institution, and upon the discharged child as he receives his farewell counsels, and goes out again into a life of temptation.

On this first day of January, 1825, the Board of Managers, with several members of the Corporation, and with quite a concourse of citizens, met at the House to open with simple services an establishment, the full results of which for good no human mind could estimate. Six unhappy, wretched girls and three boys, clothed in rags, and with squalid countenances, had been already brought in by the police, and were present to give a practical illustration of the nature of the task before them. An address, appropriate to the occasion, was made by Hugh Maxwell, Esq., one of the managers. " And not an individual," says the writer of the first report, " it may safely be affirmed, was present, whose warmest feelings did not vibrate in unison with the philanthropic views which led to the foundation of this House of Refuge."

In May of the present year, 1868, Mr. Maxwell was present at the Sabbath service of the Refuge, and addressed the children. About a thousand, with their officers, were present in the large and beautiful chapel of the institution. With emotions which he found it very difficult to suppress, he contrasted the gathering in January, 1825, the nine unhappy-looking children, with the great animated and interested audience before him—the low, inferior building, rendered barely comfortable for seventy children, and the palace-like structure in which they were now worshipping. More than twelve thousand children have been the successors of this first handful of delinquent girls and boys. But more than this result was inaugurated at this New-Year's dedication of a house of reform. During this period, in our own country, more than twenty such institutions have been established, and there have been gathered within their walls from forty to fifty thousand perilled or criminal youths.

p. 78.

THE FIRST HOUSE OF REFUGE.

By the 21st of October of the year of opening, Mr. Maxwell, whose office as district attorney enabled him to speak with authority upon this point, was able to say: " I am happy to state that the House of Refuge has had a most benign influence in diminishing the number of juvenile delinquents. The most depraved boys have been withdrawn from the haunts of vice, and the examples which they gave in a great degree destroyed. Before the establishment of the House, a lad of fourteen or fifteen years of age might have been arrested and tried four or five times for petty thefts, and it was hardly ever that a jury would convict. They would rather that the culprit, acknowledged to be guilty, should be discharged altogether, than be confined in the prisons of our State and county. This rendered the lad more bold in guilt, and I have known instances of lads, now in the House, being indicted half a dozen times, and as often discharged to renew the crimes, and with the conviction that they might steal with impunity. I might enlarge on the benefits of this noble charity were it necessary. Of this I am certain, that no institution has ever been formed in this country by benevolent men, more useful or beneficent."

During the years that have elapsed since the opening of the House, Mr. Maxwell has been permitted often to have interesting illustrations of the effect of the training of the institution upon individuals brought to his notice. Persons well situated in life, bearing excellent characters, when meeting him in public conveyances, remind him of their recollection of his securing their committal to the House of Refuge, and of his addresses to the inmates, as a manager. For a period of ten years, he passed nearly every Sabbath afternoon at the House. Once, not long since, crossing in the ferry-boat from Nyack to Tarrytown, a gentleman, who had driven on board with a fine team of horses and an elegant carriage, and whom he learned afterward to be a man of property and reputation, having a beautiful family growing up around him, came to him and offered his hand, remarking, " You do not remember me ? " Mr. Maxwell had to assure him that he could not recall his name or his face. The gentleman then reminded him of a scene in the court-room, and all the circumstances came back freshly to his remembrance. A lad was brought up for trial, and Mr. Maxwell was so struck with his appearance that he moved the court to save him the disgrace of the penitentiary, and to commit him to the House of Refuge. The recorder was much interested in his behalf, and addressed him with kindly counsels. Many particulars of the youth's history had passed from Mr. Maxwell's recollection, which are preserved on the records of the House. The boy was between seventeen and eighteen ; he had been a clerk, and held in much esteem, in the office of Aaron Burr, but had chosen evil associates of both sexes. He was made an officer in the Refuge after a few months, having by his handsome address won the confidence of Mr. Curtis, and was permitted to visit the city. He again fell into temptation while enjoying this indulgence, and was finally returned as an inmate to the House. His life was not entirely regular for the first few years after his discharge, but the last account, many years before he met Mr. Maxwell, was favorable. He gratefully acknowledged the benefit he had received from the discipline of the Refuge.

In reading the first report and the daily record of the first year, one familiar with the present condition of the House of Refuge cannot fail to be impressed with the peculiar moral aid which constant, regular, and somewhat exacting (so far as the attention is concerned) employment gives in the work of reforming these vicious and almost always mentally and physically indolent children. Their occupation at first was miscellaneous, working in the garden, aiding the repairs and construction of buildings, shoe-making and tailoring, and the general housework. The superintendent of the first year speaks of "a restlessness and an effort to escape, rendering a constant guard necessary." The most conspicuous items in the first volume of the daily journal are those that relate to attempted or successful escapes.

Something more than the warm, paternal affection which was lavished upon them, and which did not fail in numerous instances to call out the strongest filial returns, and even the delightful scientific addresses and conversations which beguiled the time of their meals and other hours, was found requisite to bring these children of lazy and vicious habits into a love of wholesome work, and to a manly self-restraint.

No person connected with reformatory institutions made so strong an impression upon the members of the two conventions of the officers and friends of these establishments, held in 1857 –'59, as the gentleman at that time superintendent of the Reform School in Chicago. He was apparently the father of a large family, and had rendered walls and bars unnecessary by the strong moral and social cords which he had succeeded in throwing around his boys. He could trust them everywhere, and was constantly sending them to the city, and permitting them uncommon indulgences. All this was delightful to hear, and had every appearance of being the simple expression of the actual facts. The gentleman himself was conscious of no flaw in his system of discipline. But his successor, after a short period, found the institution in a shockingly demoralized condition.   This well-meant indulgence had proved the ruin of many of the inmates. The boy-officers, in whom he had trusted, had abused their opportunities to their serious injury, and the inmates who had been permitted to visit the city had been guilty of crimes, while availing themselves of his confidence.

These are human children, but their affections and passions have been fearfully perverted, and they require something different from the ordinary training of an indulgent home to enable them to overcome the evil habits of years.   Indeed, many of them have fallen into sin, not through the lack of kindness at home, but through the manifold temptations of the streets and the peculiar weakness of their moral natures. It was only a few years after the opening of the House, that the superintendent sent a gentleman to the managers with the following introductory letter : " The bearer, Mr. J—— W——, Jr., has been known to me for about three years, from the circumstance of his occasionally sending donations to the House of Refuge of boxes of chocolate, etc., he being a manu- facturer of the same.   He is unfortunate in one of his sons, and fears that inevitable destruction will be the boy's doom, if not placed in the House of Refuge.   Mr. W—— called on Alder- man Burtis for an order to send him there, but, on account of his being sixteen years of age, he declined giving his consent thereunto, but wished him to make application to the Board this evening.   Mr. W—— says that his son is small of his age. His frequent tokens of benevolence call upon your fatherly kind- ness to aid in stopping the boy's progress in vice."

There has not been a period in the history of the institution when this class of boys has not been represented in considerable numbers among its inmates. The sons of some of the shining lights of the New-York bar and of several of the clergy have, from time to time, passed through its halls, and in every instance, we believe, with profit.

In 1858, C. W. P., seventeen years of age, was sent to the House. He had a comfortable home and good friends. The absence of his father (who was a sea-captain) from home, and the indulgence of his mother, left him without parental control. Not fancying school, he was permitted to seek employment. He fell among bad associates, frequented places of vicious amusement, lost his position, and became quite dissipated. For a theft of a considerable sum of money, which he finally confessed, he was arrested. The court, struck with his intelligence, and reluctant to send him to the certain ruin of the penitentiary, obtained permission to commit him to the Refuge, although above the legal age.

For some months he was restless, and exposed himself to severe discipline. After a time, however, he yielded, and began to develop manly and hopeful qualities. At the close of the year he was permitted to ship on board a whaling-vessel. He afterward entered the merchant service. He has been for a long time master of a vessel. His voyage, before the last, to China, was made as master of the fine steamer A——o. Pleasantly married, and living near the city, he never fails to report himself when in port, or to express his grateful remembrance of the rigid but just and wholesome discipline of the House.

Regular labor, in connection with regular hours, daily, for tuition in school, wonderfully calms this restlessness, so peculiarly the characteristic and second nature of these children of the street. The large sum which it now annually secures toward the support of the institution (nearly fifty per cent. of the whole present outlay) is the smallest benefit accruing to the in-

mates of the House from their labor.   Every child, from
the oldest to the youngest, has a daily task wisely adapted
to its age and ability.   A trade in most instances is thus
secured, upon which the youth may rely for his own support and for that of those dependent upon him.   Hundreds of
young persons are now in the city, following the trades which
they learned at the Refuge.   But the crowning advantages
arising from this system of labor are, the habits of attention
and industry which are not merely inculcated in the shops, but
are actually developed and cultivated.   These children come to
the institution almost universally heedless and indolent.   They
have never been put to serious labor, and seem almost to have
lost the capacity of entering upon any work requiring intelligence and skill.   This condition of mind has rendered their
attendance upon school almost profitless, even if they have been
sent.   The boy enters the shop.   The simplest form of labor he
is about to undertake, requires careful attention.   There is no
escaping the necessity of yielding his whole mind to the work.
It is a slow and painful process at first, but it is almost universally successful.   A new capacity is developed, as novel and
pleasantly exciting to the boy as to his friends.   He can work,
and labor brings its grateful sense of self-respect, and awakens
a wholesome ambition for the future.   The beneficial effect of
this is immediately felt in the schools.   The boy takes hold of
his books with the same attention that he has just given to his
work, and his success in the latter assures him of the same in
the former if he is duly diligent.   And the benefit of this is seen
in his moral and religious life.   He comes to the chapel and to
daily devotions with this same newly-formed habit of giving his
mind wholly to the business before him.   This, in some degree,

may account for the extraordinary attention yielded by our inmates to all the religious services of the House.   The workshop
has become literally a " means of grace," and an efficient hand-
maid of the schools.   A cultivated gentleman of Massachusetts,
who is particularly interested in the public-school system of that
State, remarked, when passing through the shops, that some such
simple form of labor would be a beneficial complement of common-school instruction.   The celebrated Swiss school, which
has enjoyed such a wide reputation in Europe, and secured
many pupils from the United States (the Hofwyl School of Industry), was conducted upon this plan, combining labor with
scholastic education.

Indolence is the mother of ignorance and impiety.   It is the
aimlessness and helplessness of these vagrant children that make
them so certainly the victims of temptation.   Every inmate
leaving a reformatory should be able to say, " *I learned to work
there.*"   On some accounts the shop offers a more wholesome
discipline to these youths than the farm.   The latter wearies
the body without awakening the mind or imperatively demanding the attention.   These " children of the desert " require a
stronger counter-irritant than the work of the field to summon
into action the slumbering energies of thought and will.   From
the shop, if their natural inclinations draw them to the country,
they may be safely removed to the farm, with habits of care and
industry formed that could not be nurtured by agricultural pursuits.

In the second report, we have assurance how early this truth
had made its impression upon the minds of the Board : " The
boys, when in health, are kept strictly employed during the
hours appointed for labor, at chair-making, tailoring, brass-nail

manufacturing, and silver-plating.   The object being not only to keep them employed, but to teach them some trade by which they may obtain a livelihood when set at large."—The chief office, however, of this work was distinctly set forth in the first collection of " rules and regulations."—" The introduction of labor," it states, as its opening paragraph, " into the House of Refuge, will be regarded principally with reference to the moral benefits to be derived from it.   If the employment should be unproductive of much pecuniary profit, still the gain to the city and State will eventually prove considerable, from the reformation and consequently the reduced number of offenders."

The profit to be derived from labor has never been permitted to lengthen for an hour the time of the child's restraint in the House.   Whenever the character and education of an inmate justified the discharge, no circumstance connected with the value of the labor, or experience or reliability of the youth, in the shop or House, has been allowed a moment's consideration.   The contractor at one time offered a large advance if the experienced boys were retained in the House for a few months longer.   The late Charles M. Leupp, a respected and wealthy merchant, whose large business experience, excellent judgment, and rare humanity, were devoted to the interests of the institution for many years before his lamented death, when he heard the proposition announced in the Board, rose in his seat, and with much feeling protested that never, without his condemnation, should an inmate be retained, even for the most limited period, for any purpose of pecuniary profit.   Labor must be, he held, entirely subordinated to the great work of reformation, and when that was effected, the inmate was wronged were he retained longer in their custody.   This sentiment was unani-

Effect upon a Boy of Good Family.

mously sustained by the Board.   Eight hours in the early years were devoted to labor, which is an hour more than at present, four to study in the school, and the remainder of the twenty-four to rest and recreation.

The period of labor, it ought to be stated, is much shortened by the diligence of the inmate.   Moderate stints are given to inspire and reward activity, and long before the tardy children reach the appointed limit of daily labor, the yards are ringing with the joyful voices of those who have completed their tasks, and are thus enabled to extend the hours of recreation.

A letter received from a young man by the author, while writing this history, bears a significant testimony to the effect of this discipline of sharp labor upon a boy of good parentage, but of perverted habits.   He was between seventeen and eighteen when committed for stealing.   He had been united with a church in the city of Brooklyn, but had been drawn aside into evil company, and had a strong inclination to theft.   His pleasant address, and his interesting family relations, awakened much sympathy in his behalf.   Instead of being placed in the shop, he was employed in the light work of taking care of the halls. Opportunities offered to test his character, and this strange habit of appropriation was found to be still his master.   He was sent to one of the hardest positions in the shop, and remained there for months, and this is his testimony, after more than a year's absence in well-doing from the House, written in a hand nearly as perfect as copper-plate engraving: " If you should look over the roll-book, you will see my name opposite the House—number —, and I am quite sure you will remember me.   What I want to say is, what the Refuge has done for me.   It was the turning-point in my life.   I shall never forget the lesson I learned there.

When I was there, I thought it was hard when Mr. Jones placed me in the shop, but now I thank him for doing it. Before that I was asleep, but that brought me to my senses. When I was in the shop burnishing, I made up my mind that, when I was discharged, I would live a Christian life, and I have followed it up. The Refuge dealt with me as the man did when he had a bird that could sing but wouldn't sing—*he made him sing*. I allowed the devil to build a wall all around me, but he could not put a top over it; so that I could get *up*. This I have begun to do, and, with God's help, I mean to continue."

The institution began early to bear fruit. Many evidences was the first superintendent permitted to see, in after-days, that his labors had not been in vain. It was his custom to gather the children together each evening around a long table, he sitting at the head, and to invite them to ask him questions upon such subjects as might occur to their minds, the various processes of manufacture, and curious questions in science. These questions, with great pains-taking and interest, he would answer. " I remember," says a friend, writing to his daughter, " that once a boy, aged about twelve years, inquired, ' What attracts the magnet to the north pole?' I see your father's face *now*, as after a pause, he replied, ' The future life of a boy asking *that* question is marked and determined.'" Either, as suggested, the natural taste of the boy, or the interesting lecture upon his own question, or the inspiring commendation of Mr. Curtis, one or all, resulted in a life upon the sea. The lad became a highly-respected shipmaster, and acquired a fortune. He lost his life some twenty years afterward on a voyage from a Southern port to New South Wales.*

* " Memoir of Joseph Curtis."

His daughter after his death received a letter from a gentleman, who, when he came to the. House, was entirely without education, and had since enjoyed no opportunity of adding to that which he received at the institution. He spent his early life after his discharge in trading-voyages to foreign ports, but at the time he wrote his letter was filling a place of trust, offered him by one of the first and most honored citizens of New York. He was enabled to bestow upon his seven children an education, the want of which he had felt. He expressed no reluctance to have his letter used, but remarked : " My children know, and thank God, that it was Mr. Curtis who made me the man I am. . . . My first sight," he says, " of Mr. Curtis was in 1825. I was in prison and under the law for crime. I was an orphan, well acquainted with all the crimes that man, woman or boy, can commit. I hated all that was good in man or woman till I saw Mr. Curtis, and for some months I hated him, till his kind love won my love. His first conversation with me was all kindness, to show me I would not be punished for the crimes I had committed, but for any thing I should commit while under his charge ; that if I told the truth, and did as well as I knew how, he would make a man of me. At first I could not believe. I had heard too many persons promise the same ; but he was the only man who, under all circumstances, never forgot his promise to any boy or girl, to my knowledge, and I had a good chance to know. His first point to gain was to convince each boy and girl that he did not wish to punish them, but to gain them by love ; for when he had to punish, he would talk long and kindly to the boy or girl, till the tears would flow from his own eyes, and then from the person that was to be punished, till those that were looking on felt more sorrow for his feelings than for the boy.   He would say, ' My son, it is hard, I feel it hard, but the body must suffer to make the mind obey.'   His plan was for the boys to try each other by jury, and he was the judge.   Each boy made his complaint and called witnesses, and then it went to the jury, and if found guilty, the number of stripes was named by the foreman, and Mr. Curtis put it on ; not in anger, but in mildness, telling them all the time how it grieved him.   The boy, after punishment, had no hard thoughts of him, but felt truly sorry and ashamed to offend him.   The first *capital offence* (as the phrase was with the boys), which I committed, was an attempt to run away by getting over the wall.   Another boy and myself hid under Mr. Miller's dwelling-house at dusk, and when the roll was called, we were missed. We were soon found, and, oh ! the sensation, the dread of meeting that kind face, with so kind a smile, was worst of all.   ' My son,' he said, ' have you got tired of doing well?   I am very sorry that you could not believe me that this was a good home, and the best you could have at present.   Now I must punish you, and it hurts me more than it does you.'   One case that happened to myself, bears very strong upon my mind even to this day.   After trying to escape, and being caught, how powerful was the punishment of his taking me to walk with him alone, and putting his arm around my neck and his hand in my bosom, and speaking such kind words that it ought to win any one !   I mention a case to show his reliance on a good God, which occurred in 1826 or '27.   There was a rumor of the world coming to an end ; and on one particular night there was to be a ring around the moon, and, sure enough, there was, and many began to fear.   About eight o'clock that summer evening, he said, ' My sons, you see that ring as they have foretold.   It de-

A Case of Severe Discipline.

notes nothing to fear for those that do as well as they know how.' He talked kindly and long till our fears departed." Many other illustrations of the paternal manner of his old superintendent, this grateful young man, redeemed from a life of crime, records in his letter.

He was sometimes very severe in the administration of corporal punishment, but his characteristic love of the boy always appeared like a bow in the cloud, spanning the storm.

" Two boys, known as hard cases, were sent to the Refuge from the Sessions. Soon after their commitment, one of them attempted to escape, was detected and punished. His companion reproached him for submission, and with an oath threatened resistance to the death under kindred circumstances. Mr. Curtis happened to overhear the young rebel, and his course was at once taken. It may not be improper to premise that the instrument of chastisement used by him, though incapable of bruising, was capable, when applied to sensitive cuticles, of producing a stinging and smarting sensation, exceedingly painful. When the boy was brought before him, Mr. Curtis said : ' W——, you have attempted to overthrow my authority by inciting your fellow-inmates to insubordination, and have imposed upon me the painful necessity of punishing you. Remove your jacket.' ' I won't.' This refusal was immediately followed by a smart application of the whip to one cheek " (a very dangerous experiment, in view of the liability permanently to injure the eye, and one that would not be permitted under the present discipline of the House), " with a repetition of the order to remove his jacket. ' I won't, by —— ! ' The whip fell with added force upon the opposite cheek. The contest lasted for several minutes, the boy preserving his dogged obstinacy, and Mr. Curtis his quiet

determination to subdue him. At length the jacket was taken
off and petulantly thrown upon the floor.   ' Take up your garment and hang it orderly over the back of your chair.'   This
command was also obeyed, but with a reluctance that was not
submissiveness. ' Now remove your shirt.' Here the boy burst
into tears ; but he stripped himself of his under-garment, and
stood nude, humiliated, and subdued.   The poor young wretch
expected to be flayed alive ; but no such purpose rested in the
gentle heart of his conqueror ; his object was accomplished, and
he only said, ' W——, you have compelled me to punish you
against my will ; you have compelled me to enforce an obedience
which should have been willingly yielded ; now resume your
garments, take your seat in your class, and avoid again subjecting me to the pain you have this day occasioned me.'   The boy
did so ; his conduct from that day forth was irreproachable, and
he is now one of the wealthiest oil-merchants in one of our
Eastern whaling ports." *

An auxiliary Board of Ladies was constituted to have the
superintendence of the female department of the House, and
this Board has been perpetuated until the present.   Ladies of
high reputation and well-known benevolence have cheerfully
met the labors and responsibilities incident to this important
work, and have not only yielded their valuable suggestions, as
to the reformation of their own sex, to the managers, but have
proffered their warm sympathies and counsels to the officers of
the female department, and often addressed and prayed with
the girls.   "In their weekly visits," says the first report, " a
part of their time is employed in hearing the girls recite portions of Scripture, and other pieces which they have committed

---

* "Memoir of Curtis," p. 81.

to memory. The advantages to be gained by the continued superintendence of the Ladies' Committee, as the institution becomes enlarged and the employment and exercises of the girls are multiplied, cannot be anticipated without feelings of particular satisfaction. In addition to their oversight of the domestic regulations and of the employment of the girls, their conversations with these unfortunate children, their admonitions, their encouragement, their patient efforts to gain upon their sensibilities, to enlighten their judgments, and to implant, however slowly and discouragingly, the pure principles of integrity and religious obligation, all strengthened by their clear and pertinent explanations of Scripture truths,—cannot fail to come powerfully in aid of the instructions of the matron in effecting the moral improvement of her charge."

This expectation has been realized. These long-continued and invaluable services, rendered for Christ's sake, have met with their reward on earth in the testimonies of many redeemed women, and in heaven, in the blessed words of the Master: " Inasmuch as ye have done it unto one of the least of these, ye have done it unto me."

The spirit manifested by these ladies during the long history of their services is faithfully embodied in the example of the first one of their number that fell at her post. Mrs. Sophia Wyckoff, the wife of Alderman Wyckoff, a devoted friend and most efficient manager of the institution, was equally interested as a member of the Ladies' Committee. Her generous gifts and profitable visits to the House continued to the last of her life. The ladies in their report rendered by their secretary, Sarah C. Hawxhurst, with affecting simplicity, remark: " She was indeed one of those who fed the hungry, clothed the naked, and

visited the sick and imprisoned; and we humbly hope that she
has her inheritance with those who are blessed of God our
Father. Her last moments were consoled with the belief that
she should be permitted, through the merits of her Redeemer,
to join the heavenly company in praising and adoring the King
of kings and Lord of lords."

Mrs. Sarah C. Hawxhurst, sister of Isaac Collins, and fully
sympathizing with him in his interest in the well-being of the
young and the rescue of the unfortunate and criminal, was the
secretary of the Ladies' Committee from the first until her removal from the city in 1847. In May of that year the superintendent records this well-deserved testimony in his daily journal:
" Although far advanced in years, she has been one of the most
active and efficient of the Ladies' Committee since the organization of the institution; she will be greatly missed by her associates; and her fervent prayers and pious exhortations in the discharge of her duties among our girls will long be remembered by
many of them, and we trust for their good."

The sixth annual report very happily remarks: " It is
woman who invests charity with her most beautiful drapery,
while her deeds of beneficence increase her own loveliness.
Could there be an excess of charity, woman would be prodigal,
' but in charity there is no excess; neither can man or angel
come in danger by it.' "

In view of the good influence of an institution under such
supervision, we may properly join now with a committee of the
State Senate, in 1830, in saying: " It is extraordinary that,
while we see at every corner of our streets so many youthful
females abandoned to vicious courses—while so many of them
are prosecuted as vagrants and criminals—so few should be found

in an asylum where, under the guardianship of the most amiable of their own sex, they would receive religious, moral, and
useful instruction, and, when they left the walls that confined
them, would be put into a right path."

The proportion of girls who seemed when they left the House
to take a decidedly virtuous course has not been so large as
that of the boys.   Vice gives a woman's nature a more terrible
wrench than a man's.   It is harder for her to draw a veil over
the past; it seems constantly to come back to her to rebuke her
and to overwhelm her with disgrace.   Her opportunities to rise
are not comparable with the boy's, who finds a hundred doors
opening before him, while she finds nearly every honorable door
closed.   Most ladies are less patient with the frailties of their
sex than men, and less hopeful of their redemption. . Against a
great weight of doubt and many obstacles an erring girl has to
struggle up to a respectable character.

But even the first report commences the series of very
encouraging incidents, which form the touching and appropriate close of every succeeding annual record.   They read with
natural variations like the following: " D. W., aged fifteen, was
with the last two girls" (whose records preceded this) " on the
commission of their robberies, and sent to this place by the
police on her being detected.   After remaining a sufficient time
to convince the superintendent that she felt a desire to reform,
agreeably to her own wishes, she was bound to a gentleman in
the western part of the State.   In a letter, under date of the
30th of August last, he states, ' that her conduct has been good;
she has given less cause of complaint than he should have reason to expect from a girl of her age taken from one of our well-
regulated families in this part of the country.   The lessons

taught her while under your care appear to have made a proper, and, I think, a lasting impression on her mind. She evinces a disposition to learn what is good, and such work as is proper for her she performs with ingenuity and neatness.'

" J. G., aged between sixteen and seventeen. She has lived in several places, but in none to any advantage to her principles or habits. Her last place in Bancker Street, Albany, led her to form evil associates ; she was taken up by the watch, being in bad company, and was committed to the House. With her conduct since in the House the superintendent has had better reason to be satisfied than with that of any other of our female subjects, notwithstanding the vicious life she led the last year before she came into this establishment. She has many good traits. After being in the House a few weeks, she became willing to yield to restraints, and to attend to the advice given to her. She has a good disposition and pleasant manners. She was indentured the beginning of last month."

The preservation of our records, and the careful gathering, from time to time, of incidents in reference to the after-lives of our inmates, enables us to follow the two girls for a period of ten years after their discharge. The first, having honorably fulfilled her indentures, was respectably married, and removed to the West. The latter remained, faithfully discharging her duties in the family where she was bound, but afterward was again drawn aside from the path of virtue, and was living with a person whose name she did not honestly bear. It would be by no means safe to say that all the efforts for the salvation of the latter were lost. Who knows but the sinful woman, recalling the merciful invitations of the Saviour, of whom she had learned in the House, "when she thought thereon, wept bitterly," and again found pardon at the hand of Him who " came to seek and to save that which was lost"?

In the twenty-eighth annual report, Robert Kelly, Esq., then president of the Board, a peculiarly thoughtful and careful observer, and a man of superior intelligence, remarks upon the success of reformatory agencies among female subjects : " There have existed in the community, and in the minds of judges and magistrates, doubts as to the success of this department of reform, which our experience by no means justifies. It is a part of the prevailing impression on the subject of female reformation ; an impression which exercises an unhappy influence upon them, and paralyzes the sympathies of the benevolent on their behalf. For their benefit, and the advantage of society, it is, therefore, highly desirable that the facts should be extensively known in regard to the success which has attended the operations of the female department of the House of Refuge, as exhibited in a trial of twenty-eight years. We are free to say, that with young girls, not hardened by a long-continued public life of shame, the chances of reformation are quite as good as with boys of the same age. Those more advanced in years and evil are unfit subjects for our establishment, and likely to exercise a corrupting influence ; but we can point to girls who were brought from the lowest haunts of infamy, where they had been living one or two years, that are now well married and perfectly respectable. We have never experienced any difficulty in obtaining good places for our girls ; indeed, the demand has always exceeded the supply."

Immediately upon the opening of the institution, the construction of a separate building for the girls was undertaken. This was completed and furnished, and was then opened in the presence of the managers, the mayor and Common Council, members of the Legislature, and a large number of citizens, on the morning of the 25th of December, 1825 ; a more appropriate Christmas service can hardly be conceived. Singularly befitting is the Gospel of the Nativity to the opening of a Refuge for young outcasts, of whom it may be said, as of their Saviour, " There was no room for them in the inn." A very appropriate and original discourse was delivered by Rev. John Stanford, A. M., upon the text—" Take this child away and nurse it for me, and I will give thee thy wages " * (Exodus ii. 9). " The service," says a note, appended to the sermon, which was published for general circulation by the Board of Managers, " was concluded by the children, *alone*, singing an hymn. The recollection that those sixty-three unfortunates had just been rescued from vice and the paths of the destroyer, and were now employed in singing the praises of the Lord, together with the melody of their voices, produced a most impressive effect upon the whole assembly."

By the time these improvements were completed, the managers found that the fund which had been so generously contributed had been exhausted, and some claims upon them were not yet met. The Legislature had made at its last session an annual appropriation of $2,000 ; but in view of the increased numbers that could now be received, the current expenses would call for a considerable addition to this appropriation. The managers, therefore, inquire, " Ought such an institution as this to rest for its support on the voluntary contributions of the charitable of a city, whatever may be the extent of the benevolence which it is calculated to excite ? Is it of that local and

---

* We have given this unique discourse in the Appendix.

incidental character which places it in the class of those objects
which are fitted merely to awaken the impulse of spontaneous
charity? Can there be a more legitimate and worthy object of
legislative provision than the education of the destitute? And
of all classes of the destitute, have not they the most emphatic
claim to the charity of public instruction, who have the misfortune to be drawn into the vortex of crime by the force of
inevitable suffering, by the urgency of guilty parents, or by the
excitement of guilty associates? . . . We are encouraged,
therefore—nay, emboldened and animated—in the belief, that
upon the face of our unvarnished statement, there will not be
found an individual member either of our city or State Legislature, who will say that an institution erected for such objects,
and commenced under such auspices, ought to be left to struggle
with the embarrassment of an uncertain support, but rather that
it ought to enjoy that ample countenance, which the wealth and
prosperity of our State enable it so freely to extend to institutions exclusively beneficent."

De Witt Clinton was Governor of the State ; the managers
of the House of Refuge were his intimate friends ; he had become personally interested in their benevolent movements, and
familiar with the discipline of the new institution. In his
message he says : " The best penitentiary institution which has
ever been devised by the wit and established by the beneficence
of man is, in all probability, the House of Refuge in the city
of New York, for the Reformation of Juvenile Delinquents.
. . . During the short period of its existence its salutary
power has been felt and acknowledged in the haunts of sin,
and in the diminution of our criminal proceedings. I cannot
recommend its further encouragement in language too em-

phatic, and I do believe if this asylum were extended so as to comprehend juvenile delinquents from all parts of the State, that the same preserving, reclaiming, and reforming effects would be correspondently experienced."

The Governor ever remained a strong friend of the House of Refuge. Mr. Maxwell, in his happy speech at the opening of the present House, in referring to the early friends of the institution, spoke warmly of Governor Clinton. " When his friend, Mr. Collins," said the eloquent speaker, " once told him that he feared the Legislature were about pass an act to defeat the objects of the founders of the House of Refuge, ' Then,' said he, ' I shall put in my veto.' "

Cadwallader D. Colden, then in the Senate, made a report upon this portion of the message. It was thought that provision for the accommodation of two hundred would meet all the requisitions of the State. An additional act was passed by this Legislature, empowering the managers to receive children convicted of criminal offences in any city or county of the State, and also providing that the Commissioners of Health, answering in many respects to the present Commissioners of Emigration, should pay over to the managers of the House of Refuge any surplus over what was required to defray the expenses of the Marine Hospital, from the moneys which had been collected from passengers across the seas and from sailors. The occasion for this direction of the funds thus collected was the fact that the flood of immigration, just beginning to break upon the Atlantic shore, was one of the leading causes of the increase of juvenile vagrancy and crime.

To meet the demands of the whole State, extensive additions were made to the buildings, and considerable pecuniary obligations were incurred. Difficulties in construing the act arose between the managers of the two societies, and the Board of the House of Refuge was forced to appeal again to the Legislature. Its memorials always met a ready hearing and secured a favorable response. After several changes, during succeeding years, in the manner of dividing the expense of the support of the institution between the city and the State, the present arrangement was devised. The comptroller pays annually eight thousand dollars; the licenses of theatres, shows, circuses, etc., the prolific sources of juvenile delinquency, affording about an equal amount, are accorded to the managers of the Refuge. The institution receives its quota from the public-school fund, determined by the average of its inmates, amounting to about the same sum as the previous one. The State allows forty dollars per capita, and has from time to time, by special grants, met the requisitions of the Society for the increased accommodations required by the growing number of inmates under its care. The labor of the inmates has usually covered the balance, amounting last year to nearly fifty per cent. of the whole current expense.

For five or six years, until the House was placed in permanent and well-defined relations to the State, contributions were taken up at the annual meetings and collected from yearly subscribers.

The internal, educational, and spiritual interests of the institution were most thoroughly considered and watched over by the body of earnest and intelligent men elected annually, by the subscribers forming the society, to superintend the House. Being managed by an incorporated society, the institution has never experienced the inconvenience and injury arising from political changes, but permanence in its administration, economy, strict accountability and harmony, have marked its history from the opening to nearly the close of its first half century.

From the first until the present hour, the managers have given their personal attention to the government of the institution. They have availed themselves of all the talent and experience of their officers, but have, of their own judgment, finally assumed the responsibility of the various features of its economy and discipline before they have been carried into operation by the executive officers.   By this course the superintendent and his assistants have been defended from personal misapprehensions and suspicions, and the institution from ill-considered experiments and changes.   At first the Acting or Executive Committee took cognizance of all the interests of the institution, in the *interim* of the monthly meetings of the Board.   As the number of inmates increased, this committee was subdivided into School, Indenturing, and Executive Committees, still one in their relation to the Board.   But upon the organization of the new Refuge on Randall's Island, three distinct permanent committees were constituted—the Executive, the School, and the Indenturing Committee.   The first two meet every week.   Before the Executive Committee every interest of the institution passes.   Every supply that is required first receives their order, and the purchaser is designated by them.   Every bill must be audited by this committee before it is submitted to the Board or can be paid by the treasurer of the society.   All the suggestions of the superintendent are laid before this committee, and must receive their sanction, or be submitted by them to the Board at their meeting, before they can be crystallized into the rules of the House.   The School Committee make weekly visitations to the schools, and hold their supervision and discipline in their hands.   The Indenturing Committee meet now once a fortnight, and before them the friends of the children are permitted to appear to seek their discharge.   At first they met certainly once a week, and generally much oftener.   "They consider it their duty to examine minutely and rigidly into the certificates and other evidence of the character, situation, and circumstances of every applicant for apprentices ; to ascertain, in like manner, the disposition, turn of mind, and general fitness of the individual children from whom the selection is to be made ; and in addition to all this, to maintain, as far as practicable, a general acquaintance with the situation of the children after they are indentured, and especially with reference to their treatment by their employers.   No adequate idea can be conveyed of the amount of time consumed, of active exertions made, and patient investigation submitted to, in the performance of these important duties."

When, at the close of 1834, the lamented death of Heman Averill, Esq., occurred—"a man," say his brother-managers, " of unblemished character, of the strictest integrity, piety, and benevolence, who, without ostentation or parade, sought to do good to all who needed it, and looked for his reward in a better world, where he has gone to enjoy the recompense of a well-spent life"—this testimony was borne to his unsparing labors upon this important committee : " His services as chairman of the Indenturing Committee were of the first importance to this institution, the duties of which require much foresight and knowledge of mankind ; and it is owing in a measure to the great interest he felt for the welfare of the youths sent out of the Refuge, and the unwearied pains he took to ascertain the character, disposition, and temper of the applicants for apprentices, that the boys generally have been so happily situated in the families where they are placed." Upon his death an indentured lad wrote back, expressing his sorrow, and remarking that " he had lost a good friend."

Through all this long period until the present time, this laborious service has been patiently borne, or rather cheerfully proffered ; and now that the institution has reached the census of a thousand, it can readily be imagined how heavy a tax upon the time and sensibilities of this committee must be the work of properly and conscientiously discharging between nine and ten hundred youths from their custody annually, so that they may feel themselves that, all things considered, the best thing possible had been done for them. No small amount of anxiety and care has been called forth in behalf of those that have been indentured to secure their rights and to defend them from abuses.

The result of this close supervision has been, that no funds of the institution have ever been perverted to personal uses, no suspicions have prevailed in the community that the moneys provided by the State and city have been unwisely expended, and the officers have always been defended in their acts of discipline, by the responsibility of men well known and respected by their fellow-citizens. Every act, both of officers and committees, has been a matter of record. The daily journals of the institution have been kept from the beginning, and are all preserved. Each committee has its book of minutes, and all are submitted to and read before the whole Board at their monthly meetings. The story of every child that has crossed the threshold of the Refuge, and of the after-life, so far as it could be gathered, has been carefully kept. It is not an uncommon occurrence for a person to visit the institution, to learn the particulars of his own early life, as they were collected from various sources upon his admission to the House.

The proper disposition of the children, after their training in the institution, became a matter of solicitude at once in the Board. The boys were all committed through their minority, and the girls until their eighteenth year. By an amendment to the law, the girls are now committed for the same period as the boys. It was never proposed to retain their inmates longer than to become satisfied of their reformation. To return many of them to the city, was to insure their relapse into their old habits. The adjoining country, with its wholesome farms, mechanic-shops, and house-service, offered wide and constant opportunities for placing the children in respectable positions upon articles of indenture. From time to time special efforts have been made to find positions for the older boys in the mercantile and United States marine service; many were shipped, in Nantucket and New Bedford, upon whaling-voyages; and for the younger boys, whose parents were dead, or in no condition to provide for them, homes were found in the Western States.

The special work of the Children's Aid Society was anticipated by the Society for the Reformation of Juvenile Delinquents as early as 1828. Mr. Hart writes in the daily journal, May 10th: "We saw the eight boys for Ohio start in good spirits, and Mr. King appeared to be pleased with his charge. It excited considerable warm good-feeling, to see so many little fellows bound for such a good and suitable place from the House of Refuge, among the passengers on board the steamboat."

The records of the Refuge abound with such instances as the following: F. C. was sent from Brooklyn when eleven years of age. His father was dead; his mother had married again.

His home became an uncomfortable place to the boy, and he took to the streets.   He became a little pest in the neighborhood, and was frequently under arrest for theft.   In 1858 he was sent with a company of children to the West, and placed in a good family in Illinois.   When he came to the institution, he could neither read nor write, but before his discharge, in about two years, he had advanced finely in the school.   In his new home he found good friends.   In an interesting letter, written a year after his discharge, he announced his union with the church, and the happy change in his affections which he had experienced. The war called him into the army, where he served honorably until his discharge.   He then reported himself at the Refuge— a fine-looking young man, with his moral principles evidently well preserved during the peculiar temptations of army-life.   He afterward became a teacher in a Western House of Refuge, writing most intelligent and judicious letters upon matters relating to the discipline of such institutions.   His last letter to the superintendent is from Council Bluffs, where he was a student in a law-office, preparing himself for practice in that profession.

Three children, two brothers and a sister, were sent to the institution as vagrants.   The father was dead, and the mother was a miserable, intemperate woman, in whom the love of liquor had destroyed all natural affection.   The elder brother and sister were placed in families not far from the city.   They are now grown up, and greatly respected.   The sister is well married, and has a little family of her own.   The younger brother, Emerson, was sent to the West.   From his excellent home there last year this letter was received:

"Your note of inquiry was duly received.   In answer to it, allow me to say, Emerson is still with me; is honest, industrious,

Leaving the Place not an Evidence of the Ruin of the Child.

improved in education, and is healthy. He attends church and Sabbath-school regularly. I see nothing to hinder him from being useful in the future. Besides the above, I would inform you, that in a short time, if he lives, he will enter the elementary department of the Capitol University, at Columbus, Ohio, with a view of taking a regular course, preparatory to entering the Theological Seminary. Should God spare his life, some of you, perhaps, may hear him calling poor sinners to the Saviour."

The fact that many leave their places before their indentures expire, is by no means so discouraging a matter as might at first be supposed. From our success in obtaining information of a large number that have thus anticipated their legal discharge, we are convinced that they have not left good principles behind, nor forgotten the instructions of the Refuge. Sometimes they have been impelled by ill-treatment, but often by the natural restlessness of youth. The chaplain of the institution, some time since, was looking over a volume, bearing the imprint of the House, while riding in the city cars. A stout, well-dressed man, apparently about forty years of age, with a remarkably intelligent face, and a pleasant address, was sitting by his side. Glancing upon the title-page, and seeing the imprint, he asked, " Are you connected with the Refuge?" Upon an affirmative reply, he remarked that about thirty years before he was an inmate of the institution, while it was situated on Madison Square. He was a small boy at the time, had fallen into bad company, and would have been ruined had not the Refuge opened its doors for his rescue. He gave his number in the House at once, although it was among the early hundreds, and his story on the records fully confirmed what he said of himself. He had been accounted a pretty hard little fellow.

He was indentured to a family in Norwalk, Connecticut; but, after a few years, ran away and went to sea.   When he returned, however, he visited his old home in Connecticut, where he was loved by the family as a son.   Since then he had often visited them, and when the chaplain met him, had just returned to the city from a call upon them.   He had risen from the lowest to the highest position in the ship, and had been both ship-master and ship-owner in the China trade.   He preserved a very grateful recollection of the old Refuge on Bloomingdale Road.

The religious culture of the children, from the opening of the House, was looked upon as the vital element of reformation. Men and women of marked religious character were selected to fill its offices of discipline and instruction.   The daily services, morning and evening, and at meals, were those of a Christian family, and on the Sabbath, Sunday-school instruction, and addresses from different clergymen and laymen, and from devoted members of the Board, who were rarely absent, varied and rendered impressive the exercises of the day.   Afterward a regular chaplain was appointed, who became responsible for the public preaching, but had no duties to perform during the week. Of the excellent men filling this office we shall speak hereafter. When the inmates had come to number almost as many as a small village, and more than the majority of congregations, it was thought desirable to have the chaplaincy a permanent office in the House, and to have its occupant devote his whole time, to the appropriate work of his calling, among the inmates and officers.   The legitimate expansion of his work would be a visitation of the homes of the children from the city, to learn the prospects of the child if he should be again discharged to the custody of his parents, and also of the homes of the indentured children in the country, to discover how far they were enjoying their rights at the hands of those who were profiting by their services.

It has been the object of the Board to render the Sabbath both a delight and a means of grace to the children. At first the day was crowded with exercises, and was a burden too heavy to be borne. It had two sessions of Sabbath-school and two public services. It was not a day of rest in any measure, and bodily weariness destroyed the effect of its religious lessons. Now there is one public service in the morning, every portion of which, but the sermon and the extemporaneous prayer, is arranged liturgically, so that it is the worship of the children, and not merely a round of religious exercises conducted in their presence. In the afternoon they have their Sabbath-school. The remainder of the day is devoted to their religious books and papers, and to quiet recreation. It is, perhaps, affirming only the simple truth to say, there is not a youth in the institution who does not look forward with pleasure to the Sabbath services. Clergymen and Christian laymen of all denominations are cordially invited to the pulpit of the House, but the exercises are always conducted with the same regularity, and deference to a proper religious taste, and reverence for the house of God that is thought indispensable in churches for adults, where these children are soon to worship. While every effort is used to render the instructions simple, attractive, and impressive, especial care is taken not to turn the services of the chapel into a succession of miscellaneous, amusing, or wearisome addresses.

There has been no period of any length in the long history of the institution when there have not been affecting illustrations seen of the power of the Gospel to soften and sanctify the hearts of depraved youths.   Every report bears touching testimony in confirmation of this.   In the fourth report, the managers remark : " In almost every case, we do not say in all cases, the discipline of the institution works a reformation.   The moral faculties are awakened, the thoughts of the young offender are turned, often with regret, upon his past life, and he is led to resolve on a better course.   In many instances, the child not only thinks of his future condition in this world, but his mind is filled with a concern for his eternal as well as his temporal welfare ; a conviction is produced that our happiness in this life, as well as in that which is to come, depends on a due application of our moral and physical faculties.   The transition of a being from a life of want, ignorance, idleness, corruption, and hopelessness, to the enjoyments in the Refuge of comfort, to the relief which is afforded to the mind by constant and useful employment, to the knowledge of good and evil, to the hope of obtaining an honest living, and to the consolations of religion, must be to him as a new birth."

A little Irish orphan-girl who had been quite unhappy and irritable at first, under the discipline of the House, became very anxious to overcome her temper, and to be a disciple of Jesus. Her prayers were very earnest and touching.   Every one noticed the change in her temper and life.   She has been indentured for some months, and thus writes, under the date of Sunday morning : " I am in my little room, reading my Bible and thinking of you. You do not know how I should enjoy to hear one of your sermons once more.   I think of you and the rest of my loving friends on Randall's Island.   Every Sabbath I hear the bells of the churches, and it puts me in mind of my dear old chapel.   I never shall forget the beautiful and interesting story that Dr. Wise re-

lated to us of Jack's *bads* being blotted out " (Charlotte Elizabeth's touching story of her deaf and dumb *protégé*). " I think
that beautiful little story brought me to repentance, and I still
have hopes of my soul's being saved through Christ.   I have the
Bible that Mr. Jones " (the superintendent) " gave me when I
left for my pleasant home, and I hail it as a treasure and a
jewel to my soul.   I have a very pleasant home in the country,
and go to church every Sabbath."

The inmates themselves have yielded affecting testimonies as
to their estimation of the moral influence of the Refuge.   " We
have known children," says the writer of the twelfth annual report, " who, after they have left the institution, have deviated
again from the paths of rectitude, but who still retained such a
sense of the moral care extended to them, that they have actually
persuaded children younger than themselves, who were on the
road to ruin, to enter the House, and seek its paternal care.
One young girl, who was thus persuaded by a former (but then
tempted) inmate to seek the protection of the Refuge, was undoubtedly saved from destruction, and she is now the wife of a
farmer in a neighboring State.   We may also mention the case
of a boy whose two brothers were received into the House some
time after his reception.   He went to sea on a suitable opportunity offering, and remained absent for a considerable time.
On his return to New York, he learned that one of his brothers,
who had been indentured during his absence, had left his place
improperly.   He immediately went in pursuit of him, and, after
much difficulty, discovered where he was, and had him returned
to the House of Refuge.   Being on the eve of a second voyage,
he felt anxious to secure for his erring brother the continued
kindness of his old teachers before his departure."   Such in-

stances as these have been of repeated occurrence in the history of the House.

To aid in preserving the tone of piety among the officers of the institution, whose constant intercourse with the inmates has so much to do in moulding their characters, for years a weekly lecture has been sustained, and for a portion of the time social religious exercises and a Bible-class. These services have been particularly interesting and profitable.

At the opening of the institution, a library of nearly five hundred volumes was formed by the donations of the managers and others, and by purchase. " The boys who can read," says the Library Committee in the second report, " avail themselves of the privilege of obtaining books. It is not unusual to observe them reading at table when their meals are finished, as well as during their leisure hours, and particularly on the Sabbath."

By the application of bequests to this object, libraries, amounting in the aggregate to over two thousand volumes, are now enjoyed by the different divisions of the schools in the institution, and a valuable library of over one thousand standard works has been donated and purchased for the benefit of the officers of the institution.

The schools, from the first, collecting the children, properly classified, from four to five hours every day, in their school-rooms, have met the highest commendations from the public-school superintendents.

To their second report, the managers append the report of the sub-committee, to which was assigned the duty of providing books and school apparatus; in which, after referring to the rooms chosen for the schools, they say : " The necessary arrange-ments for this important part of our system having been com-

pleted, the boys' school was opened and conducted on the mon-
itorial plan of education.   The committee have frequently
visited the school, and Dr. Griscom has repeatedly delivered
familiar lectures on natural history and natural philosophy,
which have instructed and interested the children, and have been
listened to with eager attention. . . . We are persuaded that
if such lectures were more frequent, and accompanied with simple experiments, very beneficial results would be discovered."
The beautiful school-rooms, provided for the female department
in the present House, with their four teachers, afford a pleasing
contrast to the limited provisions made for girls at the opening.
A school-room was appropriated for their use, where they might
receive instruction from the teacher of the male department,
" *when he is not engaged with the boys.*"   The report closes with
a recommendation that has been most faithfully met, that the
" committee should visit the Refuge during the school-session, at
least once in each week."

The schools have kept up in every respect with the great improvements in the public-school system during the last half century ; and now, as to convenience of arrangement, classification,
and modes of instruction, compare favorably with the popular
schools of the city.

The number of male teachers has been gradually decreased ;
so that now but two besides the Principal are in charge of over
eight hundred boys.   It often occurs that a lady is left alone
with four hundred boys before her.   No difficulty on this account
has ever occurred.   The assistant teachers are carefully-trained
and well-educated Christian ladies.   There has never been an
unfavorable result attending the introduction of ladies into the
department of instruction, but, on the contrary, the oldest and

coarsest of our boys have exhibited a deference and a self-respect in their presence that has benefited themselves as much as it has gratified their teachers.   They have more than met for the time the craving of the boy's heart for a mother and sister, by their ready sympathies and gentle words.   There are no names that remain longer, or are embalmed with pleasanter memories, than those of their lady-teachers, after the lads are discharged from the Refuge.   It is not an uncommon, and always a touching, sight to see the teacher following her pupil to the hospital, when he is suffering from disease, and expressing in her looks and thoughtful attentions a consideration that is a medicine to a sick body as well as to a sorrowing heart.   The advance in rudimental education has always been fully abreast of the attainments of children, of the same age and time, under instruction, in the public schools.   Several fine teachers date their earliest ambition to become instructors, to the interest awakened in their minds while members of the school in the Refuge.

In the twenty-second annual report, the managers remark that they have found it necessary to employ additional teachers, and have engaged two young gentlemen, one of whom, Mr. David Brown, "was once an inmate of the Refuge, and is a happy instance of the good influence of this charity.   Here he laid the foundation of his education, and as his mind developed under the influence of moral and religious instruction, he learned to discriminate, and to choose that course which led to respectability and happiness.   By that light he has been guided, and has been enabled to become a successful and efficient teacher in that very school, where he learned the first lessons in morality and virtue."

O. F. B. was an Irish boy, employed in a printing-office before he was committed to the House, but he had been out of employment for some time, frequenting the streets with bad companions. He was arrested, with others, for an act of petty larceny. He could not read when he came, but became interested in his studies in the school, and made excellent improvement in the House, where he remained about two years. He was indentured to a farmer in our State—an intelligent Christian man, who gave O. every opportunity that could have been expected in the position he occupied. The young man became deeply interested in religious things, and united with the church. His love of study had followed him, and he sought continually to improve himself. He was finally employed to teach the village school, and gave good satisfaction. During the war he served in the army for nine months, but the condition of his health forced his discharge. He visited the Refuge a few years since, and passed the Sabbath there. In the school he delivered a very interesting and modest address to the boys, referring to his own connection with the institution, and impressing upon them the truth that under God's blessing their future was in their own hands; that all that was done for them would be in vain, if they did not exert themselves. The impression of the speech was decided and wholesome, as may readily be believed. He is now at the head of a large public school in one of the chief interior cities of New York, well married, and enjoying the respect of the community.

M. P. was as pitiable a little girl in many respects as ever came into the sheltering arms of the Refuge. She was an orphan, had early been left motherless, and had fallen under the worst influences. After some advancement in school, and marked improvement in character, she was indentured as a house-servant in New Jersey. Falling under religious influences that nurtured her in the life upon which she had entered in the House, she united with the Baptist Church. When her time of service expired, she felt a strong desire to improve herself, and bravely undertook the task of hiring herself at house-service, practising the closest economy, and, when she could secure a small sum, she·would avail herself of a term in an academy. Her money expended, she would return cheerfully to her work again. A Baptist clergyman called the attention of the chaplain of the institution to her case. He visited her, and found a peculiarly modest young woman, earnestly struggling for an education, in order that she might better serve her Master in any field of labor where He might call her. The managers, upon learning the circumstances, immediately made arrangements for her to prosecute her studies more favorably, but still in connection with her own labor, not being willing to weaken the noble self-dependence which she had thus far manifested. At the present time she is one of the most successful and respected teachers in a public institution, holding and deserving the regard both of the heads of the establishment and of her pupils.

CHAPTER V.

MR. HART'S ADMINISTRATION.

For personal and family reasons Mr. Curtis resigned his position as superintendent, which took effect July 1, 1826. The managers were particularly fortunate in the selection of his successor. Mr. N. C. Hart was at this time a very successful teacher in the male high-school of the city. His personal presence was becoming to his position—of medium size, very stout, with a face beaming with good-nature, and with a pleasant voice. He thoroughly understood boy-nature. His school discipline, says Mr. Seaton, one of the superintendents of the public schools, was peculiar and admirable. At the least sign of disorder, he would seem about to strike his bell a powerful blow, but he never touched it. The lightning with him was made to do its work without the thunder. He was a faithful and greatly-beloved member of the Methodist Church, and was noted for the simplicity, sweetness, and depth of his piety.

Beaumont and De Tocqueville, in their report upon "The Penitentiary System in the United States," speak in these strong terms of Mr. Hart: "If a model of a superintendent of a House of Refuge were required, a better one, perhaps, it would be impossible to find than that which is presented by Mr. Wells" (of Boston) "and Mr. Hart. A constant zeal, an indefatigable vigilance, are their lesser qualities; to minds of great capacity they join an equanimity of character, the firmness of which does not exclude mildness. They believe in the religious principles which they teach, and have confidence in their own efforts. Endowed with deep sensibility, they obtain still more from the children by touching their hearts than by addressing their understanding. Finally, they consider each young delinquent as their child; it is not a profession which they perform, it is a duty they are happy to fulfil."

Mr. Hart had the hearty fellowship and support of his predecessor, who served upon the Board of Managers the next year.

He was inaugurated, Sunday, July 2, 1826. The managers of the Society and a large number of visitors were present on the occasion. Rev. Mr. Stanford preached an appropriate sermon, and Hon. C. D. Colden, president of the Board, delivered an address to Mr. Hart. " We know," says Mr. Colden, in his charge, " that you have left an establishment where your services have been preëminently useful, and we are persuaded that you have been induced to change your situation with a view, not of personal advantage only, but by considerations of public benefit." He pays a fitting tribute to the retiring superintendent: "Hitherto the institution has answered the most sanguine expectations of its friends, and its success must be in some measure imputed to the exertions, industry, and good conduct of your predecessor. He has no less share than any other member of the institution in its organization. While we receive you with every feeling of cordiality, and with perfect confidence that, under your administration, the establishment will continue to realize our anticipations, we cannot take leave of him without those feelings which are naturally

connected with a separation from a worthy brother and fellow-
laborer, who so well deserves the commendation of ' Well done,
thou good and faithful servant.' "

Of the work before the new superintendent, the president
speaks with remarkable discrimination. His suggestions are as
forcible and practical now as when embodied in this appropriate
charge : " The children you will have under your care are the
victims of vice ; not always resulting from their own depravity,
so much as from the negligence, the bad examples, and very
often the precepts of their parents, or of those from whom their
immature minds would receive character and impulse. It was
believed by the founders of this institution that many of these
might be reclaimed, and instead of being left to grow in vice as
they increased in years, that their young minds might be imbued
with the principles of virtue and religion, and the juvenile delinquent transformed into a virtuous, religious, and industrious
citizen. So far as we have had experience, we are warranted
to believe that such reformations may be effected—if not in all
cases, at least in such a proportion as will be an ample reward
for our exertions. But our success can depend on nothing so
much as upon the course pursued by those who may fill the
station you are about to assume. *It requires great kindness,
great patience, and great firmness.* The objects of your care will
understand from your attention to administer to their wants and
comforts, both in sickness and in health ; from your efforts to give
them religious as well as moral instruction ; from your making
them industrious, and giving them the means of gaining an honest livelihood, that you have no motive but their welfare. When
this impression is made on their minds, respect and obedience follow. If unhappily they should not, then punishment must be

inflicted. But this with you, I am persuaded, will seldom be necessary, and will be a last resort. It requires much less capacity, much less knowledge of human nature, to govern a child by his corporal than by his mental feelings. And therefore it is that the former are appealed to so often, and frequently so injudiciously. A child may be made quiet and industrious by beating, but it seldom happens, I believe, that kindheartedness, morality, and intelligence are induced by whipping. There can be no worthy sentiment in the apprehension of corporal chastisement; but an appeal to the understanding and affections will generally awaken feelings that soften the mind and elevate the character; no human being ever gave himself credit for doing right from fear, but every one feels a self-respect when he is conscious that he does right from reason. There may be, however, instances, and they are most likely to occur in an institution of this nature, where the painful necessity of resorting to punishment is inevitable. In such cases, I am convinced I need not say to one of your experience, that their efficacy, either for example or reformation, must depend on their being inflicted with firmness but with temperance, and with no more than a just severity."

Of the encouragements which might inspire the new incumbent as he entered upon his duties, he says: " The consciousness that by your assistance a number of your fellow-creatures are rescued from perdition, that the child who was hurrying from stage to stage in the progress of vice is turned to the paths of virtue, and instead of the hardened adult, becomes the virtuous citizen, must be a gratification not often enjoyed. But it is not only the individuals who may be here that will feel the advantages of this institution. Society at large has experienced

The Condition of the Children.

and will continue to feel its benign influence. Already has it greatly diminished the number of juvenile offenders who are brought to the bar of our criminal courts. Formerly there was no other mode of disposing of these than by sending them to the penitentiary or to the State prison. There they mixed with old and hardened offenders, and after having their vices confirmed, and received new instructions in wickedness, they were turned from the doors of the prison, without character, without food, and without a roof under which they could claim a shelter. What resource had these abandoned objects but to commit new crimes? And this they did with less reluctance because often they had not been taught the difference between virtue and vice." An additional consideration was to be found in the orphaned condition of many of the inmates. " Frequently an infant of tender years is left in our streets without protection by the death of a father or a mother. Some who might have been brought up virtuously and lived happily, had their natural guardians been spared to them, have no other recollections of their parents than are impressed on their minds by the agony with which a father or a mother bade them an eternal farewell, and left them unprotected and in poverty to struggle for an existence, and to encounter the temptations of the world. How many may there be among these poor orphans whose mother—

> ' Bent o'er her babe, her eyes dissolved in dew,
> The big drops mingling with the milk it drew,
> Sad presage of its woes in future years !
> The child of misery baptized in tears ! ' "

Mr. Hart's response was modest and appropriate. With a lively sense of his responsibilities, trusting in their wisdom for counsel and in the guidance of Him who prompted them " to

---

---

these praiseworthy acts," he consoled himself with the hope that
he should become "in a degree a father to the fatherless."
Addressing the children, he said: "I have sons and I have
daughters, and am enabled to feel for you. Often in my deal-
ings with the children of others I ask this question for my own
government, 'How should I like my child to be dealt with
under similar circumstances?' This rule shall govern me here.
As to government I have no doubt that many of these children
only require to know my wishes in order to obey them, but
others will require to be more closely watched. Virtue shall be
rewarded, while vice and immorality shall be promptly attended
to. . . . In my opinion, the most benevolent and humane
method for the management of children is, to require prompt
and implicit obedience."

Mr. Hart's first inscription in the daily journal was an additional sentence to the minute of Mr. Curtis, recording the
services of the day. "The exercises," says the new superintendent, "were made additionally interesting, while we witnessed the fond hearts of the children bursting forth in tears,
expressive of their tender regard for Mr. Curtis, when it was
announced that he was soon to take his leave of the House of
Refuge."

Until Mr. Hart's administration there had been no definite
code of regulations, marking out the particular duties of the
different officers of the House, giving a time-table to govern
the labor, instruction, and recreation of the day, and settling
definitely the character of the discipline of the House as to
rewards and punishments. Early in his connection with the
Refuge, Mr. Hart, who was of an organizing mind, proposed
the embodiment of the various suggestions, satisfactory experi-

ments, and final judgments of the Board of Managers, into a formal code.

There were two well-defined and well-understood unwritten commandments, which heretofore had been made, and which do really embody all the requisitions upon the inmates afterward established to be the law of the House : 1. "Tell no lies." 2. "Do the best you can." These commandments have never been repealed. Rules and regulations have been made, modified and rejected ; but these two golden precepts have remained the permanent, pervading common law of the institution. The last boy that entered the House was addressed very much as Mr. Curtis did the first : " My boy, we have but two rules in this place—tell no lies—do the best you can. You can keep these, can you not?" The last boy, like the first, smiled at their simplicity, but became amazed in a short time, as thousands have before him, to find himself met everywhere— in the yard, in the school, in the work-shop, in the chapel— with these simple but wonderful commandments covering all his conduct and stretching over all his time in the House. The French visitors, in 1832, noticed this. " When a young delinquent," they say, " arrives at the House of Refuge, the superintendent acquaints him with the regulations of the establishment, and gives him for the guidance of his conduct two rules, remarkable for their simplicity ; 1. Never lie ; 2. Do the best you can."

Only a short time since, a gentleman over forty years of age, who had not introduced himself to the superintendent, was sitting in the office, as some new-comers were questioned and taught the rules of the House. " Every thing besides the rules," said the gentleman, speaking to the superintendent,

" has changed since I was in the Refuge. The site has changed, for it was on Madison Square then. It is a very different building, and the officers are all strangers to me ; but I see you have the same rules. I have never forgotten them—tell no lies—do the best you can."

These rules have clung with remarkable tenacity to the minds of the inmates, and exercised a powerful influence over them. The third report records the story of a little English girl, received in the Refuge when she was thirteen years of age. She had repeatedly run away from her home, had been twice placed as a vagrant in the Almshouse, and had been guilty of stealing. She remained for two years in the House, and was then indentured in the country. The gentleman in whose family she found a home, after a period, wrote of her : " I should have written before, but thought best to delay until a sufficient time had elapsed to test her character. It affords me pleasure to say that, after six months' trial, I can bear testimony to the correctness of her conduct. The fundamental rules of the institution over which you preside appear to be indelibly impressed on her mind. I have never discovered any deviation from the truth in her, and as to the work allotted to her, she performs it as well as a child of her years can be expected to do. She expresses her gratitude to the managers and officers of the House of Refuge, for their interference in her behalf, in rescuing her from a vicious course. She does now, and I trust, by the blessing of God, will continue to do, credit to that best of charities, the House of Refuge."

For the general order of the House, carefully-prepared regulations were required. These were drawn up with great consideration and wisdom, and adopted by the Board at their meeting, January 2, 1827. It is remarkable how few changes have been made in them from that day to this. The system of grades and badges, which has been made to perform so excellent a service in the discipline of the House, although not so fully developed as at present, was then inaugurated. It causes a smile, to read over some of the forms of punishment established for minor offences. One was, " Sent to bed supperless at sunset ;" another was, " Gruel *without salt* for breakfast, dinner, and supper ; " and still another, which must have recalled " the bitter herbs " of the Jewish Passover, " Camomile, boneset, or bitter-herb tea, for breakfast, dinner, and supper." A child must have become peculiarly depraved to have chosen the latter as a " beverage." The time-table was carefully arranged, and the general regulations have, the most of them, been justified by the experience of nearly a half century.

The second anniversary was an interesting occasion, held in the new chapel of the House—a pleasant and commodious hall, constructed in the female department, and consecrated with appropriate services in the month of October, in the previous year.

The House now held one hundred and twenty-two boys and twenty-seven girls. A great interest had been awakened by the institution in the community, and, although the day was very unpleasant, a large audience was gathered on the occasion.

The *Evening Post*, in announcing the time of the meeting, remarked : " Among all the late establishments in this city for the benefit of society, this is to be classed among the very first, and we trust it will be regarded in this light by an intelligent and benevolent community."

The children were present, and added to the interest of the hour by their singing. Judge Irving read the report, which he had prepared, the second made to the Legislature and city authorities by the managers. It was an able paper, and full of encouragement as to the future usefulness of the institution.

During the early years of the Refuge, Nantucket and New Bedford afforded peculiar facilities for the employment of the older boys committed to its care. At this time the whaling-business was rapidly growing, and the demand for sailors more than equal to a ready supply. Some of the chief oil-houses in these cities were in the hands of members of the denomination of Friends, who were accustomed to meet at their Yearly Meeting with the respected and active members of the Board of Managers who were of the same persuasion. A wide opening for the discharge of the mature boys, who would be most likely to fall into their old habits if indentured upon the land, was in this way secured. During the third year alone, thirty boys were sent on whaling-voyages from Nantucket and New Bedford, apprenticed to captains or owners, many of whom took a great personal interest in the lads. Many fine sailors and officers were thus given to the country, who from time to time made honorable report of themselves to the House. Among others was Z. B. C., who had been a scholar in the Mission Sunday-school of Mr. Seaton, then and still, a Public-school Superintendent. His father was an intemperate man; his mother was a paying boarder in the Alms-house, then situated on what is now Twenty-seventh Street, she having a little property left to her. Z. was about fifteen years of age; he had a position as an errand-boy, but fell into bad company, and into the habit of stealing. He was finally indentured upon a whale-ship and afterward shipped on board a merchant-vessel, owned in London. The owner was an alderman of that city, and took quite an interest in Z. He soon rose to the position of first officer. During the English opium war with China he made three or four voyages with troops, and secured to himself a comfortable little property. He wrote to Mr. Seaton to learn about his mother, intending to return and provide for her, and in a corner of his letter he turned up the leaf and inscribed the place—" A kiss for my mother." But she had been dead seven years. Mr. Seaton was obliged to write to him that his kiss came seven years too late. Being acquainted with Mr. Bunch, the respected English consul in New York, Mr. Seaton requested him, through some friend, to make inquiries in reference to the young man. He wrote to Mr. Baring, of the great banking firm, who, instead of delegating the matter to another, went himself and made personal search for Z. He wrote a very interesting letter in return, saying that he found him to be a most worthy young man, bearing an excellent character. Z. afterward visited Mr. Seaton in the city, and bore himself with great modesty and propriety. He brought with him a handsome painting of his ship, which is still hanging upon the wall in the parlor of his old friend. He had then accumulated a fortune equal to his moderate desires.

Of the efficiency of the system of instruction and discipline, now well developed and in successful operation in the House, Messrs. Beaumont and De Tocqueville, as the result of their examination, say : " Now, what results have been obtained? Is the system of these establishments conducive to reform? And are we able to support the theory by statistical numbers? If we consider merely the system itself, it seems difficult not to allow its efficiency. If it be possible to obtain moral reformation for any human being, it seems that we ought to expect it for these youths, whose misfortune was caused less by crime than by inexperience, and in whom all the generous passions of youth may be excited. With a criminal, whose corruption is inveterate and deeply rooted, the feeling of honesty is not awakened, because the sentiment is extinct ; with a youth this feeling exists, though it has not yet been called into action. It seems to us, therefore, that the system which corrects evil dispositions and inculcates correct principles, which gives a protector and a profession to him who has none, habits of order and labor to the vagrant and beggar whom idleness had corrupted, elementary instruction and religious principles to the child whose education had been neglected ; it seems to us, we say, that a similar system must be fertile of beneficial effects. . . . Being desirous of ascertaining ourselves the effects produced by the House of Refuge in New York, we made a complete analysis of the great register of conduct, and, examining separately the page of each child who had left the Refuge, investigated what had been its conduct since its return into society."

The translator, Dr. Lieber, here remarks in a note : " All materials which could be of any use to us in this inquiry have been put at our disposal with the greatest kindness ; and, as we found ourselves in possession of original materials, we were enabled to form an exact opinion upon the conduct of all children after they had left the Refuge. Our inquiry extended to all the children that had been admitted."

The French report goes on to say : " Of four hundred and twenty-seven male juvenile offenders sent back into society, eighty-five have conducted themselves well, and the conduct of forty-one has been excellent. Of thirty-four the information received is bad ; and of twenty-four, very bad. Of thirty-seven among them, the information is doubtful ; of twenty-four, rather good than otherwise ; and of fourteen, rather bad than good. Of eighty-six girls who have returned into society, thirty-seven have conducted themselves well, eleven in an excellent manner, twenty-two bad, and sixteen very bad. The information concerning ten is doubtful ; three seem to have conducted themselves rather well, and three rather bad than otherwise. Thus of five hundred and thirteen children who have returned from the House of Refuge, of New York, into society, more than two hundred have been saved from infallible ruin, and have changed a life of disorder and crime for one of honesty and order." *

This examination embraced the period of the first five or six years. The processes of discipline were then new and experimental ; the first subjects were many of them very mature both in years and crime ; the first accommodations were poor ; the officers had enjoyed no previous training for their work ; and the time was not long enough to discover what would be the final choice of these young persons, or how strong, and redeeming, after all, the influences of the Refuge would prove. It has constantly occurred, that after a fall into temptation and a course of wrong-doing, the conscience, which has been awakened in the House, has lashed the fallen youth back again into the paths of duty and virtue.

On April 23, 1830, a large boy, named Charles Peterson, seventeen years of age, was committed to the Refuge, and after a year's training was indentured, but left his place and returned to the House. Some time after this he induced a number of the boys to join him in a conspiracy to attack the teachers and break away from the institution. He led off with a razor, but the oth-

---

* " On the Penitentiary System in the United States," p. 123.

ers did not follow him.   He wounded Mr. Terry, who was then
assistant superintendent, so severely, that his life was thought at
first to be in danger.   Two other officers were badly cut.   He
was tried for assault with an intent to kill, and sentenced to ten
years in Sing Sing.   The papers of the day were very severe
upon the young man, and rejoiced that a place for which he was
much better qualified than a House of Refuge, stood ready to
receive him.   But the wounded officers had not utterly lost their
labors upon even this violent young man.   During his confinement in the State Prison, he was penitent, well-behaved, and
expressed a hope that he had become a better man.   Eleven
years after he left the House of Refuge he was heard from, as
well married, a member of a Christian church, and doing well.

The ten years, between 1841 and '51, were afterward taken
in the same way, at the suggestion of the managers, and every
case was carefully examined.   The result was, that of the boys,
seven out of every ten were found to be living an honest and
self-supporting life ; the statistics of the girls were not quite as
favorable, but did not fall far short of this.

The succeeding year after the opening of the New York
institution (1826), a similar Refuge was established in Boston,
and called the House of Reformation.   Rev. E. M. P. Wells,
then a young Episcopal clergyman, was the first superintendent,
and to his extraordinary skill and magnetic power in the management of boys, its remarkable success with its inmates during
his administration was to be largely attributed.   While in the
New-York House the inmates were separated at night, in the
Boston House they were separated neither day nor night.   Upon
this the report from which we have quoted remarks : " We
have not noticed that in this " (the Boston) " House of Refuge

any disadvantage results from their sleeping together; but their danger is, in our opinion, not the less, and it is avoided in Boston only by a zeal and vigilance altogether extraordinary, which it would be a mistake to expect in general from persons the most devoted to their duties." The discipline of the Boston House was peculiar and somewhat complicated, but readily managed and pervaded with the enthusiasm of the man whose influence was felt in every department. The child's admission into the House was attended with peculiar ceremonies. " The establishment formed a small society upon the model of society at large. In order to be received into it, it was not only necessary to know its laws and to submit to them freely, but also to be received as a member of the society by all those who compose it already. The reception took place after the individual had gone through the fixed period of trial, if the candidate was not rejected by a majority of the votes of the little members composing this interesting society." The whole discipline was conducted much after the same manner. The translator of the French report remarks that the system appeared to him " to be planned with great wisdom, and to be executed with a profound knowledge of the human soul; . . . it appeared to us one of the most peculiar, most interesting, and most heart-cheering subjects which, in all our travels, has ever come to our knowledge, and which must be seen and personally inquired into, in order to be perfectly understood. We know of no instructor who has seen deeper into the human heart, and knows more thoroughly what principles in the human soul he safely may apply, than Mr. Wells."

In reference to all these elaborate systems, depending for their efficiency entirely upon one person of peculiar ingenuity, however pleasant they may be to look upon, the remarks of Beaumont and De Tocqueville, comparing the New York and Boston systems, are full of wisdom. " The system pursued in New York," they say, "though infinitely less remarkable, is perhaps better ; not that the Boston House does not appear to be admirably conducted and superior to the other, but its success seems to us less the effect of the system itself than of the distinguished man who puts it into practice. We have already said that the great defect of this House is, that the children sleep together ; the system, moreover, which is established there rests upon an elevated theory, which could not be always perfectly understood ; and its being put into practice would cause great difficulties if the superintendent should not find immense resources in his own mind to triumph over them. In New York, on the contrary, the theory is simple. The isolation during night, the classification during day, the labor, the instruction—every thing in such an order of things, is easily understood. It neither requires a profound genius to invent such a system, nor a continual effort to maintain it. To sum up the whole, the Boston discipline belongs to a species of ideas much more elevated than that established in New York ; but it is difficult in practice. The system of the latter establishment, founded upon a theory much more simple, has the merit of being within the reach of all the world. It is possible to find superintendents who are fit for this system, but we cannot hope to meet often with such men as Mr. Wells." The good sense of these gentlemen has been confirmed by later facts. With the resignation of Mr. Wells his system fell to the ground, and Boston has no reformatory where his plans of discipline are carried out ; while, on the other hand, Mr. Hart has been followed by four very different men, who have, in succession, had the charge of the House of Refuge. The numbers of the inmates have been constantly increasing. The difficulties and responsibilities of the position of superintendent have been, from the nature of things, greatly enhanced ; still the institution, without changing its simple form of discipline, has increased from year to year in its efficiency, and its records show that it has gained in moral power also.

The Philadelphia House of Refuge was opened in 1828, upon the same plan as the New-York House, and has continued its work with most encouraging success from that day to this. Its numbers, however, are only about half as large as those of its elder brother, and it has separated into a different department its colored children. The managers, who have kept careful records of their inmates, reported at the convention of 1857 that from sixty to seventy per cent. of their children were hopefully reformed by the discipline of the House.

On the 8th of October, 1832, a young candidate for the Christian ministry met, at the house of a schoolmaster in the German city of Hamburg, a number of friends, who, like himself, were " richer in faith and love than in silver and gold." A home-missionary society was formed, called the " Inner Mission," the influence of which, although its commencement was so humble, is now felt throughout Germany. " If the Kingdom of Christ," said these men of faith and earnest purpose, " is again to be established in our city, it is necessary among other things to found a house for the sole object of rescuing the children from sin and disbelief." Though without money or influence, they solemnly promised one another to give themselves no rest until their object should be accomplished.

In November, 1833, through the aid of providential gifts bestowed upon them, the leading spirit of this Society, J. H. Wichern (now Dr. Wichern), with his mother, entered into a large, old cottage upon a very rough farm which had been secured, and drew around him from the lowest haunts of vice and misery twelve of the worst boys of Hamburg. Here they were taught wholesome learning, the truths of the Gospel, and honest labor, by Wichern himself. This was an unquestioned family institution. Here were the house-father and house-mother—the beloved mother of the doctor and of the children—and here was only an ordinary family circle in size, differing from others at first, indeed, in the amazing depravity of the youths thus brought into an unwonted atmosphere of love and purity. The effect could but have been, as it proved, salutary in the highest degree. Either from the name of a former owner, or from the ungainly appearance at the first of the straggling old cottage, forming their afterward well-beloved home, they called it the *Rauhe Haus*, the rough house. Liefde, in his interesting work, "The Charities of Europe," gives another derivation of the name. The house, he says, was built a hundred years before, by a Mr. Ruge, and it had since been called "Ruge's house;" but as the *Platt-Deutsch* or Saxon word *ruge* is the same as the English *rough* and the Dutch *ruig*, it was translated by the corresponding German word *rauhe*. Mr. Ruge himself, however, was as little of a rough fellow as could well be imagined.

From time to time other cheap houses, more or less convenient for the accommodation of the same limited number of inmates, some for boys and some for girls, were constructed, until quite a considerable little village, with its church, school-

THE ORIGINAL RAUHE HAUS, NEAR HAMBURG.

house, and workshops, grew up in a garden of fruits and flowers, redeemed from the rough weed-sown fields.

All the time the children were being trained, another work was going on, which is constantly overlooked in this country, when this admirable experiment for the redemption of the most wretched children is spoken of. The great work of the " Inner Mission " was prosecuted at the same time. The house-fathers, teachers, shop-overseers, are all young candidates for the home-missionary work throughout the city and country. They offer their invaluable, devoted, and pious services for no other remuneration than their board and the training which they receive for their future and more extended labors.

Each family has in its home a number of these elder brothers pursuing their own education, and devoting themselves at the same time to the instruction and reformation of the poor children that have been gathered into the charmed circle of the Rauhe Haus. The female homes are as carefully and fully supplied with devoted Christian women. But the great inspiring heart of the whole institution, whose pulsations are felt by every brother and every inmate, who is daily met in the chapel and in their homes and shops, is the beloved Dr. Wichern.

" It is only when looked at in connection with this Inner Mission scheme of Wichern's, that the Rauhe Haus Brotherhood can be properly understood. Its foundation was the solution of the difficult problem how to form a band of well-trained, able Gospel laborers, who, while inspired by free Christian charity, would submit to the various conditions which the Inner Mission, according to Wichern's plan, would impose upon them. These were to be content with the humble work of evangelization among the lower classes ; to abstain from any attempt to raise or conduct a free religious movement, or to establish an independent mission work of their own ; to place themselves at the service of the Government, of the clergy, or of whoever should want them, without claiming any other title than that of being the servants of these parties for Christ's sake, or any other privilege than that of being permitted to do the work which other people had neither time nor fancy for. It is obvious that men of this kind, who would submit to such restrictions, are to be found chiefly among the artisan and peasant class, which is nearest to the lowest, and, respectable though it be, is accustomed to live in the service of others. . . . It is clear that to make up for their loss of liberty, and to guard them against the spirit of servility, which so easily creeps into the souls of men who are kept in constant subordination, they must be united into a brotherhood, in which, through mutual Christian fellowship and spiritual rivalry, strong enthusiasm would be maintained among them for their work, and high respect for their right of membership in such a body." *

It was this Protestant brotherhood, which Wichern himself trained for the work, supported by missionary funds, that afforded him the efficient assistants which he has always enjoyed in his great work. As the elder brothers left for responsible positions in the home-mission work in various parts of Europe, other young candidates, eager for the opportunity to secure the theological and practical training of this most singular but admirable theological school, would offer themselves for the work. For four or five years the children are retained under this remarkable training, until the boys have become perfectly versed in some trade, and are prepared at once to enter as journeymen

---

* "The Charities of Europe," by Liefde.

into the chosen business of their lives. A large amount of profitable work, such as printing and bookbinding, is done at the institution, going far toward meeting its own expenses. The proportion of the children redeemed from their evil habits under such discipline is, probably, very large; but in twenty years only about two hundred children have been sent out, as supposed to be reformed,—an average of ten a year.

Scarcely any impression would be made by so limited an institution upon the juvenile crime of a great city. Thousands would go down to ruin while one was being saved. It was Wichern's idea that he should be able, with God's blessing, to establish the practicability of efforts for the regeneration of abandoned children, which others would follow, and that numerous similar houses of redemption would spring up all over the land. And this expectation has been realized.

One very important element of the success of Wichern's system ought not to be overlooked. He remarks, in his report for 1843 : " Our surveillance of those who have left us is in no respect altered. It is no police superintendence, but a paternal oversight, exercised by the writer of this report, in coöperation with the resident brothers. If necessary, we visit the apprentices at their masters' houses *weekly*, but in the *ordinary* way only once a fortnight ; and every fortnight I assemble them on Sunday afternoon or evening in summer at the institution, in winter in the town. When on Good Friday seventy of us celebrated the Lord's Supper, there were among the number all our apprenticed pupils but one, who was hindered by no fault of his own. It is not to be expected that among so many young people no disorders should arise ; but a whole month frequently passes without any complaints of the apprentices ; and when such do occur

they are mostly of such faults as are common among all apprentices."

How much, even with his presence, depended upon the
character of his assistants, appears from his report in 1838.
" A change of assistants has caused much difficulty.   The
superintendent of the girls' house had left, and her place was
not immediately supplied.   The old sin quickly reappeared
among them, with a few consolatory exceptions.   All our regulations, and the efforts of three plain tradesmen's wives, selected
one after the other to superintend them, proved unavailing.   The
utmost that could be attained was superficial decorum, which
might have partially deceived me, had I not lived so entirely
among the children.   The girls' department was like a garden
from which the care of the gardener had been withdrawn.
Among other bad symptoms, were the gradual cessation of
songs, before so frequent ; and the extinction of all interest in
God's Word."

The effect of such a change upon the boys seems to have
been even more serious.   Such a result from the regular and
simple character of the discipline of the New-York House,
although officers are constantly exchanged, is never witnessed.
" Hypocrisy and mutual accusations are other features of the
picture, which became daily more gloomy.   Frivolity, shame-
lessness, grievous ingratitude, audacious perverseness, excessive
laziness, strife, and ill-nature, were the mere ordinary manifesta-
tions of the inward evil.   A certain satiety of bodily food even,
no less than the bread of life, prevailed, and we tried the experiment of enforced abstinence from both.   The experiment
succeeded to a great extent with a considerable number, but
only temporarily.   The crisis had not yet arrived.   Several

Evil of a Complicated System.

attempts at escape, false accusations, and a series of offences of the most scandalous character, gradually drew attention to two boys as the principal authors of the mischief. One, nineteen years old, had for *three years* abused our patience ; the other had been *four years* with us. Both finally made their escape, and fell into the hands of the police. From this time our community gradually recovered its moral health." Such an experience is unparalleled, certainly in the last ten years of the New-York House.

The same remark that was made in the French report of the plan of Mr. Wells, may be made of this—only Wichern can efficiently manage its very complicated details. It would be a vain hope to expect its marked success, without the aid of its body of trained and devoted assistants. It could only be worked with us when it naturally, from a very small beginning, should grow up around a magnetic man whose whole soul and life were consecrated to the work of juvenile reform. State and city institutions modelled upon such a basis, in our country, with such officers as we can secure, would certainly sacrifice all the benefits of a large institution with a simpler system, as to economy, regularity of discipline, and organized labor, without gaining the subduing and winning power of the family tie over the individual inmate. The true family reform school, with us, can only be the voluntary movement of one man, inspired with a passion for this work, aided, in a pecuniary way, by others, and receiving, perhaps, a small subsidy from the State ; gathering under his own roof and within the influence of his wife, as well as himself, a limited number of these outcast children to educate and train to labor. There cannot be too many of such institutions.

Mrs. Carpenter says, in her instructive work upon juvenile

delinquents : " Such schools or asylums, to effect the desired
end, must be under the guidance of enlightened Christian benevolence, sanctioned and mainly supported by government inspection and aid.   Since it is absolutely impossible that a
government, as such, can secure such guidance for these establishments, voluntary effort must be mainly looked to for the
infusion of the true reformatory element into these asylums,
and therefore must be encouraged, and, as far as possible,
called out by the Legislature ; which, granting the means and
the authority to carry out the work, will exercise inspection to
ascertain that these are wisely employed.   The State will thus
retain the authority it has taken from the parent, in consequence of his neglect of duty, and will place the charge in the
hands of those who can and will discharge it well."

The simple breaking up, however, of a large reformatory
into a dozen houses, with an entire separation of the sexes, and
a purely artificial life, would create no more of a feeling of
home in such an establishment, than the placing of a regiment
of soldiers in separate barracks for each company, but away
from mother, wife, or sister, would give to them a livelier home-
feeling than when dwelling in one continued block.

The whole training of a reformatory must be exceptional and
temporary, like the training of our own children in academies
and colleges.   We insist, properly enough, upon parental discipline there ; still it is not home even in what are called family
schools, but pupils are placed for months in somewhat monastic
seclusion, to prepare for the life before them.   Thus, after a
limited period of training, for the inculcation of good principles
and the establishment of correct habits, our criminal children (as
they cannot be so readily in Europe) can be placed in the

actual family, and be made to feel all the natural forces of a virtuous home drawing them in the right direction. The simpler the system, and the shorter the period required in the reformatory, the greater the probability that it will be properly carried out, and the better it will be for the child. Classification as to age and character may be very properly insisted upon, and can, by the arrangement of halls, be even more thoroughly secured in a large than in a small institution.

Of the impression made upon thoughtful men by the results obtained, even in its early years, by the New-York House, we need only quote from the introductory report to the new code of prison discipline, prepared by Edward Livingston, for the State of Louisiana. Referring to his plan for a School of Reform, he says : " In establishing it I have been guided by something better than the best reasoning. In the city of New York there is an establishment of this kind which can never be visited but with unmixed emotions of intellectual pleasure. It now contains one hundred and twenty-five boys and twenty-nine girls, for the most part healthy, orderly, obedient, and animated with the certain prospect of becoming useful members of society, who, but for this establishment, would still have been suffering under the accumulated evils attendant on poverty, ignorance, and the lowest depravity, with no other future before them than the penitentiary or the gallows. I ought not to omit mentioning here, that the female department is superintended by a Visiting Committee of ladies, who, at regular and frequent periods, examine the school, converse with the scholars, encourage the diffident, reprove the disorderly, reward the industrious, and inspire all with their own virtues. The code I submit invites a similar superintendence, from which the highest advantages, such as nothing but the benign influence of female character can give, are expected. . . . . Twenty-eight boys and fifteen girls have been indentured, and the most favorable accounts have been received of their behavior. Two having suffered what they thought ill-usage from their masters, left them and returned to the school, and only one has resumed his former bad habits. What renders the reformation of these children the more extraordinary is, that thirty of them had before been sentenced to the penitentiary from one to five different times."

The sixth annual report, offered in 1831, opens with cheerful views of the growing success of the experiment. " The short history," it says, " of our establishment has proved that it is possible to convert juvenile thieves and vagrants, gamblers and pickpockets, the most profane and abandoned, into honest farmers, good sailors, engineers, and faithful mechanics. It has also proved that a House of Refuge, while it effects these salutary changes in the character of its subjects, is nevertheless a house of improvement. It has thus gained for itself a name in the community, well known throughout the various ranks of juvenile depravity. Its name imposes a wholesome terror upon disobedient and vicious youth ; and it appears evident to the managers, from the small number of commitments which they now receive from the city Police and the Court of Sessions, compared with those of the commissioners of the Almshouse, that the influence of the Refuge is highly auspicious to the peace of the city and the security of our dwellings." How true is their next remark ; and how much light upon the great question of crime, its causes and its cure, the efforts of the friends of juvenile reform have thrown ! " It is an institution also," they say,

" which, with other concomitant circumstances, enables its managers to trace to their earliest effects the causes of those crimes which, in their punishment, occasion to the municipal and State governments so heavy an expense of time, and labor, and taxation ; and it must be by a judicious attention to facts, thus developed, that the criminal laws of a country can be made to approximate the most nearly to a perfect system of prevention and cure."

One cannot read the concluding pages of all the reports, containing selections from the incidents in connection with former inmates, which have come, during the year, to the knowledge of the officers of the House, without a feeling of astonishment and gratitude combined.   From the very depths of degradation children were raised to become useful and beloved members of society.   In 1832, Rev. David Terry, a Methodist clergyman, who was afterward a teacher in the Refuge, and finally succeeded Mr. Hart as superintendent, in writing to a friend in the city of New York, he being himself at that time in the country, says : " Please tell Mr. Hart that E. F. and G. H. are living in the circuit that I travel. I saw E. F. with his master ; he was dressed like a gentleman.   G. H. is all alive in religion, and I understand is very gifted—that is, he exhibits superior talents for a boy of his years."   This boy, Mr. Hart says, was brought up in the most dissolute part of the city (the Five Points).   His mother kept a brothel, and the child was suffered to run about the streets without restraint.   As he was active and cunning and had a pleasant address, he became the successful leader of a band of little thieves.   While in the Refuge, he became very much interested in religious things, and gave remarkable evidence, for a boy of his years, of the work of the Holy Spirit upon his heart. As his past life had been so perverted, it was thought advisable that he should have a long probation in the House, although the love the officers felt for him, and his amiable temper, recommended him to the superintendent and managers as a suitable subject for discharge to a proper home. After remaining over a year in the Refuge, he was placed in a religious family in the country. Good accounts had come from him from time to time, and now Mr. Terry's letter confirmed the confidence they had felt that the Refuge had left a powerful and permanent impression upon him.

These incidents fully justify the opinion of Sir H. L. Bulwer (who was the English minister in this country from 1849 to 1852), expressed in a work which he published at that time : " There are institutions in America where the experiment of instruction is made not merely on the boy whom you wish to bring up in virtue, but on the boy who has already fallen into the paths of vice ; and, singular to say, the education given in the Houses of Refuge to the young delinquents produces an effect upon them which education does not in general produce upon society. Why is this? Because the education in these houses is a moral education ; because its object is not merely to load the memory, but to elevate the soul, to improve and to form the character. ' Do not lie ! and do as well as you can ' ! Such are the simple words with which these children are admitted into these institutions."

It would be a natural fear that the Refuge would leave a prison-stain upon the character and on the consciousness of the inmates which would occasion a sense of humiliation in after-years, when filling honorable positions in life. Experience has shown that anxiety in this respect is uncalled for. A young merchant of the city, some time since, brought his wife to the House. He had lived some years after his discharge in Canada, where he married; the young lady was well educated, and had a very pleasing address. After going through the institution, she was asked what she thought of it: " It must be an excellent place," she said, " if my husband is a fair specimen of the men it sends out."

A lady and gentleman, connected with the same church in New York, crossed in the boat together. A little son of the lady was in the House, and as the gentleman was an officer in the Sunday-school where he had attended, she felt rather nervous at the idea of his discovering the fact that her child was now in the Refuge. She sat some time in the office, talking with her friend, hoping he would soon leave, and that she could see her boy alone. Finally, wearied with waiting, and having a mother's longing to meet her child, she said: " I do not know what you will think when I tell you that I have my little boy here."—" I shall think he is in a good place, for I was here once myself," was the very surprising and very comforting answer.

It is one of the well-confirmed incidents of the House that on one occasion, after a gentleman and lady had passed over the different departments of the Refuge, the gentleman turned to his companion, who was also his wife, and said, " I am going to tell you something now that will surprise you—I was once an inmate here."—" And I will tell you something that will surprise you," said the lady, in return; " I also was once an inmate in the female department."

It is not a tradition of the House simply, but a record in the daily journal, October 3, 1864, that " H. C. R., and his wife, Mary A. C., visited us. They were both formerly inmates and have been absent from the House for several years. At first they were in different localities, but about a year and a half ago fortune favored, and they concluded to form a partnership for life. They are a sprightly young couple, and are living happily together in the city of A., where H. C. R. is doing business on his own account."

The writer asked a young merchant, in the coal and wood business, in an adjoining city, how he would feel if it should be mentioned to the clergyman of the church with which he is connected, and who is a personal friend, that his active young parishioner was once a member of the Refuge congregation. " I have no objection," was the answer, " my character is established, and I cannot be harmed ; I should have been ruined if my father had not sent me when he did to the Refuge."

Of the great body of discharged youths, Hugh Maxwell, Esq., says, in the ninth report of 1833 : " We claim especially and emphatically that, having taken these children from the streets, highways, and market-places, and having instructed them, we have, in almost every instance, bound them out to respectable individuals who have taken them into their own dwellings, and placed them at the same table with themselves and their children. Previously to these children becoming inmates of the Refuge, they were shunned—all respectable people avoided them. But after being inmates of the Refuge, they are sought after ; the farmer and the mechanic take them from the institution in preference to all other places of confinement ; for when a convict has served out his time in any of our State prisons, who desires to employ him? Who will receive him into their families? If the fact of imprisonment be but known, no matter what his conduct while in prison, nobody is willing to employ him, and he may, and no doubt frequently does, suffer under temptation and want consequent on the above fact, almost beyond his control, and leading him as it were by necessity again to adopt his former vicious courses. This misfortune is not attendant on our youthful subjects, and it is most devoutly to be wished that such provision, if possible, may be made as will in this respect improve the situation of discharged convicts. A discerning public seek for children who have been disciplined in the Refuge, and take them from us as fast as we can provide for them. And while this demand for children from the Refuge exists, is it not to be regretted that a single child should be permitted to roam at large in delinquent courses until he becomes a confirmed criminal, and a fit subject only for continued imprisonment?"

In striking confirmation of the statement of Mr. Maxwell, the case of K. L. may be mentioned. He was about ten years of age when he was brought to the Refuge; he had lived in Catherine Lane; his father was a drunkard, and had deserted his family. He was one of the three white members of a gang of ten or eleven young negroes called the *Carlo Gang*, and he bore himself the singular *flash* name of *Ring-tail*. They frequently started in pairs in the morning in pursuit of booty on which they principally depended for support. They were always .n the lookout when a vessel was unloading old copper, lead, and iron. Their thefts of this description commanded a ready market at the junk-shops. They occasionally broke into the windows of toy-shops, and found an Englishman in Anthony Street who would purchase their ill-gotten spoils. Their depredations were often serious in amount.

When the boy was washed and clad in decent garments, all

were struck with his interesting appearance.   He did not know
his letters.   After enjoying the instruction and discipline of the
House he was indentured to a gentleman in Nantucket, who
had received several boys from the Refuge, and sent them to
sea.   Of K——, however, he wrote some time after :   " The boy
seems so nice that we have concluded *to take him into the family*,
and I flatter myself, at some future day, he will be a useful
member in society ; at any rate, if not prevented by his own
acts, I will give him a fair opportunity."

" Were a stranger to be taken into the Refuge blindfolded,"
the managers remark in their thirteenth report, " without previous information whither he was going ; were he to visit the
schools during the hours of instruction, the workshops during
the hours of labor, the chapel during the hours of worship on
the Sabbath, and the play-ground during the hours of exercise
and recreation, the last idea that probably would occur to him
would be that of a prison.   Nor, while watching the gambols
of the children, and sympathizing with their cheerful hilarity
when at play, or while looking in upon their sedate behavior in
the school-room, or when marking their grave demeanor in the
chapel, and perchance mingling his own voice with theirs in
hymning their Creator's praise, would a stranger be apt to suppose that those cleanly and healthy-looking groups, both of males
and females, had been gathered from the streets and highways
of the city ; from the abodes of rags, and wretchedness, and
crime.   In one word, though a prison to a certain extent, and
for certain purposes, the Refuge need not be thus considered
further than as a house of reformation ; nor can it be better or
more correctly described than it was some time since by one of
its inmates, a little girl, on going to a home in the country

When questioned as to what kind of a place the House of Refuge was, she replied : " It is a boarding-school for poor children." Such, in fact (with manual labor added), is the character in which it is the desire of the managers it should be viewed, as well by its inmates as by their friends.

From the beginning the institution has been favored with an extraordinary degree of health—but five children dying in the first ten years.   Death did not enter the House until more than three years had passed ; and this first case was of so singular a nature as to merit record.   The subject was a boy, seventeen years of age, who, in a fit of anger, took an ounce of the tincture of cantharides, supposing it to be laudanum.   He soon fell into convulsions of the most violent kind, but rallied under treatment, and after a few days appeared to be perfectly well.   Singularly enough, he was now seized with a strong presentiment, out of which he could not be reasoned, that he should die on the succeeding Sabbath.   He fervently exhorted his associates to reform their lives, expressing contrition for his own sins, and trust in the Saviour for mercy.   His convulsions returned, and he died on the day he predicted.   Quite singular physical phenomena attended his last hours : during the intervals of the convulsions, and after they had ceased, while he was in a state of perfect insensibility and volition entirely suspended, " his limbs would retain," says Dr. Stearns in describing the case, " for any length of time, the same position in which they were placed by any person present.   If they were placed in an erect or horizontal, or flexed posture, they remained so, perfectly motionless."

The prevailing good health and defence from malignant epidemics are to be attributed, under a Divine Providence, to the constant sanitary and hygienic suggestions of the well-known eminent men who yielded their valuable services to the House both as managers and physicians—Dr. John Stearns and Dr. Galen Carter. In later days, with larger numbers, the same high tone of health has been secured under the careful attendance of Dr. H. N. Whittlesey. When, in 1832, the cholera swept over the city with terrible power, and the hospitals lost a large number of their patients, out of ninety-nine cases in the Refuge but two proved fatal.

The death of children is always affecting; but some of the most touching scenes that the writer has ever witnessed have occurred in the hospitals, when, in the rare instances where disease has proved fatal, inmates have left us for another world. Whatever anxiety we may have had in discharging subjects to homes in the country or city; the gentle, forgiving, grateful, penitent, and devout tempers they have shown in the dying hour; the intelligent, humble, but confident trust in the Saviour; the peaceful and even cheerful anticipation of the final moment; the affectionate farewell, mingled with a thankful sense of what the Refuge had done for them, have removed all fears in reference to them and the life upon which they were about to enter. A short time before her death, a girl, eighteen years of age, who had shown marked results of the religious instructions which she had received, sinking under a severe form of typhoidal disease, at times delirious, broke the silence of the hospital, and brought tears to all eyes, by singing, with remarkable distinctness and pathos, the touching lines of Watts:

> " When I survey the wondrous cross
>   On which the Prince of Glory died,
> My richest gain I count but loss,
>   And pour contempt on all my pride."

HON. STEPHEN ALLEN.   p. 151.

In 1832, the removal of Mr. C. D. Colden from the city occasioning his resignation as president of the Board of Managers, Hon. Stephen Allen was elected as his successor. Mr. Allen was one of the founders of the Society and one of its first vice-presidents. He was a successful merchant and an honored citizen, sharing largely in the respect and confidence of the community. He was elected to the office of mayor of the city, and was a member of the State Legislature. Interested in all the public improvements of the day, his special efforts were directed, through the instrumentality of this Society, to the reformation of the criminal and perilled children of the city. He remained its president, always proverbially prompt and vigorous in its executive business, for a period of twenty years, until his lamented death in 1852. It is one of the well-preserved traditions of the Board, that he always called its members to order on the exact moment of an appointed meeting. If a quorum unfortunately were not present, he would adjourn the meeting, and although he met the slightly tardy managers upon the stairs, he never returned upon his steps. The result was that the meetings of the Board were attended with remarkable promptness, and the business was considered in regular order, and finished with the closeness of legislation becoming a deliberative body. He was one of the victims of that frightful catastrophe occurring that year upon the Hudson—the burning of the steamer Henry Clay.

It has been found, when the secret history of many such men has been revealed, that the constancy of their virtue and charity has not been simply a natural characteristic, or an accident arising out of their circumstances. In the pocket of Amos Lawrence, a copy of a series of resolutions for the government of his life and temper was found, and it had evidently been often and prayerfully perused.

When the body of Mr. Allen, then a venerable man, full of years and honor, beloved and esteemed by all who knew him, was recovered, in his pocket was found a printed slip, of which the following is a copy : " Keep good company or none. Never be idle. If your hands cannot be usefully employed, attend to the cultivation of your mind. Always speak the truth. Make few promises. Live up to your engagements. Keep your own secrets if you have any. When you speak to a person, look him in the face. Good company and good conversation are the very sinews of virtue. Good character is above all things else. Your character cannot be essentially injured, except by your own acts. If any one speaks evil of you, let your life be such that no one will believe him. Drink no kind of intoxicating liquors. Ever live (misfortune excepted) within your income. When you retire to bed think over what you have been doing during the day. Make no haste to be rich if you would prosper. Small and steady gains give competency, with tranquillity of mind. Never play at any game of chance. Avoid temptation, through fear you may not withstand it. Earn money before you spend it. Never run into debt unless you see a way to get out again. Never borrow if you can possibly avoid it. Do not marry until you are able to support a wife. Never speak evil of any one. Be just before you are generous. Keep yourself innocent if you would be happy. Save when you are young to spend when you are old. Read over the above maxims at least once a week."

These are golden sentences, and they were certainly embodied in the unblemished and useful life of their possessor.

" In the service of the institution," say his brother-managers, " he displayed in an eminent measure that energy of character, that straightforward honesty of purpose, that sagacious common- sense and indefatigable industry, for which he was so extensive- ly known in the various public offices and important situations he was called to occupy during his long career."

On the 1st of May, 1837, the institution was called to part with its excellent and beloved superintendent, Mr. N. C. Hart— " a man," as the managers say, " peculiarly qualified for the station, on the score alike of talents, habits, and disposition." His health breaking down under the exacting duties of his office, he was obliged to proffer the resignation of his place, and the managers as reluctantly to receive it. " He was an able disci- plinarian," they say in their report ; " possessed a happy faculty of securing the confidence, good-will, and even affection of the children ; was severe only when severity was necessary ; and was indulgent on all proper occasions. In one word, his delight was to do good, and his bosom was the abode of every generous and benevolent feeling."

CHAPTER VI.

BELLEVUE.

MR. HART'S successor was Rev. David Terry, Jr., who had enjoyed several years' experience as assistant superintendent and teacher under Mr. Hart. The managers add in speaking of the new administration, "That when they announce that the institution has not suffered by the change, they at the same time bestow the highest compliment upon Mr. Hart's successor."

In this report, the·thirteenth, the managers change somewhat the character of the selections of cases of probable reformation which accompany all their reports. " They have chosen," they say, " in some respects to vary their plan, by the selection of a few cases of both sexes in which the reformations effected have to a certainty been not only thorough but lasting. In order to bring out at once the strongest evidences of the great good that has resulted from the moral discipline of the institution, they have confined themselves to the histories of cases of long standing, in all of which the subjects have been reclaimed from the most vicious courses, have been married and comfortably settled in life, and are now worthy citizens and respectable heads of families."

They also remark that, in addition to the cases published in the Appendix, " they have it in their power to state that two

young men, formerly inmates of the Refuge, are now studying
for the Christian ministry—one of them in this State, and the
other in Pennsylvania." Of one of these young men they say,
he " dates his conversion during his residence in the House of
Refuge."

Most interesting and affecting records of seven young women,
formerly inmates of the House, at that time married, well settled in life, and the most of them known to be connected with
Christian churches, follow this report ; together with the story
of the history, equally satisfactory, of six young men. To such
cases the Refuge may turn as did the Apostle to his converts at
Corinth, and say, " Ye are our epistle . . . known and read of
all men."

An important era had now been reached in the history of
the House of Refuge. Population had been gradually expand-
ing the city toward the property of the Society, until it began to
break like a wave all around them. The long avenues stretching toward the north now ran parallel to the grounds, while the
projected cross-streets would pass through the property of the
Society. Twenty-fifth Street, for the laying out of which commissioners had been appointed, would destroy a large portion
of the buildings of the Refuge.

A committee appointed by the Board of Aldermen met a
committee of the Society to arrange the matter, and expressed a
willingness " to appropriate a portion of the corporation lands in
the upper parts of the city as a site to which the Refuge might
be removed." It is interesting to note the points then considered quite beyond the probable encroachments of population,
and favorable, from their isolated condition, for the establishment
of the Refuge. The three sites proposed were :—a block on

Murray Hill, between the Fifth and Sixth Avenues ; a block at Hamilton Square, between the Third and Fourth Avenues ; and the Bellevue Fever Hospital, with the block of ground between Twenty-third and Twenty-fourth Streets, and the First Avenue and Avenue A, opening out upon a fine and healthy river view. Upon careful consideration it was found that by the erection of a new edifice for the female department, and a wall, the buildings heretofore used as a hospital could be, without great expense, fitted up for the accommodation of the officers and inmates of the Refuge.

October 10, 1839, "At 8 o'clock this morning," says the superintendent in the daily journal, "we were safely and comfortably situated in our new home, at the foot of Twenty-third Street, on the East River side. The premises have been fitted up by our managers with great care for the comfort, convenience, and reformation of the juvenile delinquents committed to their charge."

During the period that the institution occupied the Arsenal grounds, about fifteen years, twenty-five hundred children had been received and sent back again into society. In view of this fact the managers remark : " The community supports this class of children partly in poor-houses, partly by charity at their doors, partly by larcenies on their property of a petty character, until they arrive at manhood ; then society supports them by grand larcenies, and suffers by their house-breaking, arson, and every other crime, and has in addition the immense expense of criminal courts and of all our prison establishments. In the Refuge the children are supported, schooled, furnished books, and clothed, on an average of about one year, and at an expense of about one dollar and twenty-seven cents per week, while an adult criminal is frequently a burden on the community for *life*, at a much greater weekly charge for support and guarding. Our statistics may not show the precise number reclaimed, but we venture to assert that, if the twenty-five hundred children which this institution has received and taught to read and write, and bound out to service, had been left in the idle and criminal courses which they had already commenced, society would have paid for and suffered in a tenfold proportion beyond the expense of teaching and indenturing these children. It is certain that setting fire to but one store or dwelling in each year, by any of these children, would have destroyed more property in value than the whole expense of the institution from its origin."

The success of the American Houses of Refuge already established, awakened not only much interest throughout the States, but much correspondence and many inquiries from Europe. In 1837 M. de Metz, a judge of the Court of Assize, at Paris, was appointed on a commission to visit and report upon the prisons of the United States. In pursuing his inquiries, which were embodied in a valuable state paper, he was peculiarly struck with the Houses of Refuge in New York and Philadelphia. His own feelings had been deeply roused heretofore, by the number and character of the youths brought into his court; as he remarked a few years since, in a speech in England, "Many of these were no higher than my desk, and as there were at that time no establishments for the reformation of juveniles, I was obliged to consign them all to prison." By the French law, when a crime was charged upon a youth under sixteen, it was permitted to the court at its discretion to acquit the criminal as having acted *without discernment*, and to deliver the youth to his natural guardians, or detain him for education, a period not exceeding his twenty-fifth year. This detention came practically to amount to their incarceration in jail with older offenders, and by their depraving influence, to the ruin of the young delinquents. In these American institutions he found exposed and criminal children trained and educated with good results. He resolved to devote himself to the work of rescuing the young *détenus* (as they were called) of France from the ruin which he had so often witnessed in his judicial office. He at once determined to resign his position and sacrifice the prospects of worldly advancement before him, to accomplish the new mission upon which he was about to enter with so much zeal. Upon his return to Europe he pursued his inquiries among the institutions for juvenile reform that had been already established in Belgium and Germany, and was particularly impressed with the remarkable success of Dr. Wichern at the Rauhe Haus in Hamburg. His active, originating mind at once devised a plan combining the German and American systems, and engrafting upon them a military discipline, peculiarly adapting it to the taste and character of his own country. He retained the strict order, the constant labor, the regular daily hours of school instruction, and the close supervision of the American House of Refuge, but broke his institution up into small three-story buildings, capable of holding forty boys with their officers. The military discipline supplied the absence of walls and bars, in connection with the high moral tone of feeling which the noble and admirable chief directors were enabled to awaken in the minds of their young convicts.

The first work of De Metz was to secure the coöperation of influential minds throughout the empire; and by his personal influence he succeeded in establishing the " Paternal Society," having for its object a benevolent guardianship over all children accused of crime, and acquitted on the ground of having acted without discernment, and who might be committed to their care by the magistrates. The objects of the Society would be, to secure for these children a moral and religious training, together with elementary instruction ; to have them taught a trade, and then to place them in the country as apprentices to tradesmen and farmers. A second office of the Society, whose members were scattered throughout the empire, was to keep an eye upon the conduct of these children, and to assist them by acting as their patrons for three years after their leaving the institution which it was proposed to establish. Thus the English, American, German, and French systems of juvenile reform, grew out of the voluntary benevolence and coöperation of eminent Christian philanthropists in their chief cities.

An old school-mate of the judge, M. le Vicomte de Courteilles, who, though he had been in the army, had paid much attention to the subject of criminal discipline, and had just published a work on " Convicts and Prisons," became at once enthusiastically interested in the new movement. He owned an estate at Mettray, four miles from Tours, and one hundred and forty-eight southwest from Paris, on the Loire. This he at once devoted to the undertaking, and, what was of even greater service, he devoted himself, and remained on the ground, literally engaged in the work, until the moment of his death. He was attending the sick-bed of a youth who had, to all appearance, become thoroughly hardened, when the latter, for the first time since his admission into the colony, exhibited some sign of contrition. The joy which the pious Vicomte experienced on the occasion reminding him of an extract from a sermon which he had inserted in his work on prisons, he went for the volume, and was reading the passage to his friends that were around him, when the book dropped from his hands ; he was dead ! In his will was found this touching and prophetic sentence, which was also inscribed upon his tomb : " I have wished to live, to die, and to rise again with them " (the boys of the colony).

Before De Metz and the Vicomte took a boy or laid a stone, they drew around them *twenty* men, the most of them young men respectably connected, to become their staff of instruction and discipline. They secured also a chaplain (a Catholic) to assist them in religious instruction. The judge, soldier, and priest, then devoted themselves for *six months* to the training of their twenty officers. Five houses were first constructed in the space of five months ; in ten months they were able to receive one hundred and twenty children ; five other houses, a chapel, punishment-wards, stables, barns, a complete farm-house, and a dwelling for the Sisters of Charity, who became the nurses and matrons of the institution, were successively completed. The buildings were severely plain and economical in their construction. The ground floor was used as a workshop, and each of the upper floors served in turn, during the twenty-four hours, as a sleeping, eating, and school-room, for twenty boys each—the hammocks for beds, and the tables for meals, were swung from the sides or lowered upon the centre posts of the building as the time for their use arrived. Each house has two carefully-trained officers—a chief and a sub-chief—together with two subordinate officers, holding office for three months at a time, appointed from the trained and best-behaved boys themselves, called *elder brothers.* The institution is styled " The Agricultural Colony of Mettray,"

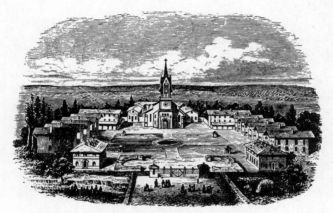

AGRICULTURAL COLONY AT METTRAY. p. 160.

avoiding, thus, any term that might of itself affect unfavorably the reputation of a former inmate, although, as it is generally understood what class of youths become the subjects of its training, the ruralness of its name would in no measure propitiate a person so uncharitable as to distrust a young man who had been an inmate of a house of refuge. It has an average of six hundred lads; about one-half of whom are employed upon the farm, and the others in various forms of mechanical labor.

"Mettray," says De Metz, "has first for its basis religion, without which it is impossible for such an institution to succeed; secondly, the family principle for a bond; and thirdly, military discipline for a means of inculcating order. The military discipline adopted at Mettray is this: the lads wear a uniform, and they march to and from their work, their lessons, and their meals, with the precision of soldiers and to the sound of a trumpet and drum; but as the sound of the trumpet and the drum leads men on to perform acts of heroism, and to surmount the greatest difficulties, may it not reasonably be employed with the same object at a reformatory school, where, in resisting temptation and conquering vicious habits, true heroism is displayed, and a marvellous power of overcoming difficulties must be called forth."

Every possible effort is made, by public notice and disgrace, to awaken a keen sense of pride and personal honor. "The system of De Metz," says the *London Quarterly*, "is an elaborate use of the passion (for so we must call it) of emulation. A French writer (M. Cochin) describes it as a kind of alliance between vanity and the conscience, and remarks that 'the founders of Mettray, in addressing themselves to this quality, have shown a remarkable knowledge of human nature, and of the French nature in particular.' The list of honor, as it is called, is a general one for the whole institution, and is displayed in the class-room, which is their common place of meeting. Mr. Hall was struck by this manuscript, which contained the names of three hundred and five colonists, who, during three months, had given no occasion for punishment. Out of the list, forty-seven had been struck, showing that these had given no occasion for punishment since the preparation of the list. A similar list is exhibited weekly in each family, and it is a mark of distinction to each family to be able to display what Mr. Hall calls a clean bill of health, i. e., a list, showing that no member had been punished in the preceding week. When this is the case a flag is hoisted, and the insignia of the house (consisting of presents made by former inmates) are displayed, all of which are removed as soon as an offence is committed by a member of the family." This makes the boys exceedingly watchful of each other, and so keen is the emulation between the houses, that cases have occurred where families have petitioned for the expulsion of an incorrigible member, on account of his keeping down the character of the house. The appeal to the sense of honor is, after all, not the highest motive; and, although with French children it may have been quite successful, we should doubt its wholesomeness or even practicability to accomplish its object as a general principle. It may excite to fierce competition, engender strife, awaken pride, and foster selfish affections. An appeal to honor does not change the heart, nor fortify the soul against the approaches of temptation in after-life; it makes good soldiers, perhaps, and among some of the bravest in the Crimea were found the graduates of Mettray; but whether this discipline will develop a quiet, harmonious Christian life and

temper, may at least be considered a question. Miss Dix, the
American philanthropist, did not receive as pleasant an impres-
tion of the colony as many of its visitors. The military spirit
of the place and the manifest tendency of its discipline to divert
the minds of the inmates from the labors and sacrifices of a
peaceful life to the ambitions and fields of war, did not strike
her favorably. Out of 856 youths that had left Mettray, 223
had entered the military service. She also thought the inmates
appeared under-fed and overworked, exhibiting a depressed
rather than a cheerful appearance. Feeble health now retains
the excellent founder in Paris, and the institution lacks the magnetism of his presence. An American friend, personally connected
with a reformatory institution, modelled somewhat upon the
plan of Mettray, has lately returned from a tour in Europe,
and rather confirms the views of Miss Dix. He noticed a
marked lack of tidiness about the premises.

We have noticed this institution at some length, inasmuch
as several of the later reformatories which have been established
in this country have been modelled somewhat after this plan,
and at the present time it stands rather as the representative of
the advanced line of progress in this direction. In simplicity
of management, in arrangement of buildings, and in the general
spirit of the institution, we have no doubt that our family reform
schools (so called) have improved upon their model. But in one
respect they can hardly ever hope to equal Mettray—in the band
of carefully-trained and permanent officers. After all, it was
not so much the system as it was M. de Metz and the Vicomte,
that exercised such an influence over the young *détenus*, and
their absence will never cease to be felt. As De Tocqueville
said (already referred to), it is too complicated a plan for ordinary

minds to grasp and wield. Instead of having one powerful
mind to be felt throughout the institution, almost equally powerful reformatory minds are required in each house of forty inmates. The moral, intellectual, and economical statistics, are
not of a character to give this interesting colony, which has become the model of hundreds of others in Europe and several in
our country, any marked advantage over the one visited in New
York, in 1837, by its truly venerable and devoted founder, and
which seemed to have awakened in his mind the first practical
thought as to the reformation of juvenile offenders.

It is this simplicity of plan, administered with a Christian
spirit, and with an even and constant discipline, that called out
from Captain Basil Hall, who was, as all know, by no means
a laudatory observer, during his tour in this country, published
in 1829, the remark, "I have rarely seen in any country an
institution containing less admixture of speculative quackery, or
better calculated to remedy acknowledged evils, by getting at
their source and checking their growth. A bounty on virtue, in
short, is offered to these young people by showing them, while
their tastes and habits are yet ductile, the practical advantages
of good conduct."

Whatever visitor honors the House with his presence is
sure to find its inmates engaged in their daily duties. They are
never called away from their tasks or from their schools to make
any . exhibition of themselves or of their attainments. In all
visits from persons high in office in this or foreign countries, the
regular order of the day has remained unchanged, and they have
enjoyed what they could but appreciate, as did Captain Hall,
the sight of the institution in its undress, engaged in its legitimate work. Only upon holidays is this order interrupted, and

then the freedom of the inmates is as unrestrained as can consist with the largest wholesome indulgence.

It cannot have escaped the notice of the reader that, in many of the instances given of the favorable influence of the institution over the character and life of its subjects, the persons were committed after their sixteenth year. With all these grateful facts, it was the conviction of the managers and officers of the Refuge, that the probabilities of reformation were greatly decreased after sixteen years of age, in the instance of both sexes, and that the presence of these older children was seriously prejudicial to the younger girls and boys. The managers of the Philadelphia Refuge had gone so far as to say, that " experience has shown that after fifteen or sixteen years there is little hope of reformation." The New York managers say, in 1843, in reference to this sentiment: " Without meaning to indorse it to its full extent, our own general experience, although individual cases may occasionally present exceptions, strongly impresses us with the wisdom of the limitation in the act of April 10, 1840 (amending the Revised Statutes), which provides that ' whenever any person, *under the age of sixteen years*, shall be convicted of any felony or other crime, the court, instead of sentencing such person to imprisonment in a State prison or county jail, may order that he be removed to, and confined in, the House of Refuge.' "

They found, however, this limitation almost constantly transgressed. The year before, a young woman, evidently above eighteen years of age, the limit at that time of their retaining the custody of girls, had been sent to them for a serious offence, and had scarcely arrived when her husband appeared and claimed her as his wife. The mildness of the discipline of the

Refuge, the avoidance of the disgrace and ruin of the prison, and the hope of an early discharge, induced friends often to urge the courts to send mature youths to the Refuge.

From its origin it has constantly demonstrated the necessity of some other place of confinement for young criminals, no longer children, but still not beyond the hope of reformation. As the Refuge was constituted, both upon Madison Square and at Bellevue, having no opportunity for separation, according to character or age, in either the male or female departments, it was more exposed to the injurious influences of mature youths of either sex. As now constituted, with two divisions of boys and two of girls, it can, without peril to the inmates, and with much greater success, attempt the important work of the reformation of boys and girls whose age and experience in crime might seem at first to forbid much rational expectation of their recovery to the paths of virtue. The second division of boys and girls now present an appearance of maturity that is to be found in few reformatories, either in this country or Europe. The result is very encouraging. A greater proportion, indeed, of this class than of the younger children will return to their old vices and crimes, but a large majority of such inmates, particularly boys, have done well.

The Daily Journal of the institution, which had been faithfully kept from the first, has become by this time (1843) peculiarly interesting. Almost every day records the visit of former subjects, now grown to manhood. There is a great variety in them, some of them recording sad failures, giving satisfactory assurance of the truthfulness of these annals. "D. G.," says the record of April 17th, "one of the first fifty we received into the Refuge, came to see us, saying: 'I desire to see my old home once more.' Whilst he was an apprentice, we had satisfactory accounts of his conduct, and so we have had since. He is now a member of a religious society, the father of three children, keeps the yard (for tanning) his master formerly occupied, and feels encouraged with his prospect of securing a comfortable provision for his family."

How interesting and significant the record of the 22d of July of this year: "M. D. E., now a school-teacher, formerly under our care, makes application to have a girl indentured to him to assist in his family. He has a wife and three children."

"S. D. A., who left the institution ten years ago, called on us this day. He served his time faithfully, got a thorough knowledge of his trade, which he is now pursuing on his own account on a pretty large scale. He employs several hands, is respectably married, and has two children. He is so much respected by his neighbors that they voluntarily gave the place in which he resides his name, with *ville* at the end of it. His object in calling was to get a girl, and, having an order for one from one of our Indenturing Committee, he was promptly supplied with the best we had."

"W. H. W., who, eight years ago, was indentured to J. B., a farmer in New Jersey, called to see us this day in company with his master. He was well dressed, intelligent, and manly in his bearing, and Mr. B. seemed as proud of him as if he had been his own son. He takes his master to tarry the night with his mother in the city; returns with him to-morrow, and will take his farm on shares in the spring."

Sometimes we hear indirectly from the old inmates: " A man from Connecticut, who had one of our boys, visited us to-day, and said that E. A., who was some twelve years ago indentured to a farmer, served his time faithfully to within one year; that year he bought of his master, who, confiding in the integrity of the lad, trusted him for an indefinite period, or, until he should be able to pay. E. then bound himself for a given time to a mechanic, served his time out, got a good trade, paid his first master, started in business, got married, and is now reckoned among the most promising of the citizens of his age and circumstances in the place in which he lives."

The failure of a child indentured in a family is by no means a fair measure of the influence of the institution over him. In many cases, perhaps nearly one-half of the failures, this may be attributed to the lack of wisdom and knowledge of human nature, or of Christian, or even natural kindness on the part of those receiving the child. The homesick and lonesome boy or girl is often rather spurned than drawn to the hearts of his now legal guardians, and made to feel that they are rather his natural enemies than his friends. We are speaking now of the cases of failure, which form but a small minority of those indentured, and we make the statement more confidently, for the sad story of the child has been often confirmed. The rejected boy or girl, and often the runaway, has been immediately indentured in another family, and proved to be unexceptionable. The great majority of those placed at service have found good homes, and have amply returned the kindness that has been bestowed upon them.

Although quite a long letter, it is such a capital one, from a gentleman who had taken a boy, in answer to the requisition of the indentures that he should report every six months in reference to his health, conduct, and progress, that we introduce it unabridged. We select it particularly for the eminent good sense contained in the close of the letter. All persons having in hand the discipline of young persons may learn a lesson from it:

"B—— J——, *Nov.* 11, 1843.

" Agreeable to request (of circular handed to me and accompanying the indenture of Sandy) I address the institution, and be assured it affords me a great pleasure to be able to give so good an account of Sandy. He has the general work of a farm to attend to, viz., to assist to milk six cows, and feed and fodder them and the cattle and calves; clean a span of almost white horses and feed them before breakfast; and, much to Sandy's credit, he takes delight in keeping and making his horses look a little better than any other team in the neighborhood. He feels quite proud when I am detained in town over night and come back with the horses all stained up from under the charge of professed hostlers who do not clean the team as well as he does. After breakfast there is wood to chop and split, water to draw from the spring, etc., at all of which Sandy is as good as I am. Of our farm-work, he can hoe potatoes and corn, husk the latter, pull beets, etc., as well as I can. Next summer he thinks he can cut as much grass as I can. I shall give him a scythe and let him try. He expects to make considerable next harvest as raker and binder; last harvest he was hardly strong enough, except to bind some very light oats. In hunting cattle, and we have a great deal of it to do, as our pasture is so large, being nothing more nor less than a large prairie, Sandy beats me all to pieces, for he is an excellent horseman. We ride bareback. He delights to get his cattle up when no other boy in the neighborhood can, which he has frequently done in very dark nights.

I have sometimes feared he was lost; but he says there is no danger of that, for you can't lose the horses, and he can stick to the horse, he knows.

" When we arrived here Sandy was very sullen and saucy, and I was obliged to flog him; and after about six months he, in company with one of my neighbor's boys, ran away. We, however, found them at night about nine o'clock camped in the woods with a good fire, probably left by some travellers. Brought them home, gave Sandy a severe flogging, and then *resolved never to do the like again.* I have taken an entirely different course to bring him up. I commenced by appealing to his feelings and talking to him; giving him encouragement in various ways, and making him have confidence in himself. In hurrying times such as haying, harvesting, and cleaning up grain, I made a bargain with him, and he has earned enough in that way by extra work to pay a part of his winter clothing, and he has also a fine calf. It is my intention to turn his earnings into stock, and in the course of a few years he will have quite a smart chance of cattle. *I don't think I shall ever flog again,* I am well convinced it does no good. Sandy now has a regard for me and takes an interest in things; flogging would only make him do what he was compelled to through fear. *One cheerful hand is worth a dozen grouty ones.*

" You would hardly recognize Sandy, he has grown so. He is about as large as I am except in height, and is healthy and strong as a young giant. In fact I hardly know what or how I should do without Sandy. We commence our school again in a few days, and I intend Sandy shall write you before spring, perhaps about New Year's. My long delay in writing has been to give a good account of the boy, which I am now able to do.

In hopes to hear from you occasionally, particularly if you could communicate any thing to the interest of the boy,

"I am yours,   E. P. D."

In 1844 Mr. Terry resigned his position as Superintendent, having for about eight years fully sustained the high reputation which the Refuge had won under his predecessor. Mr. Terry, filling an important station in the Missionary Board of his church, still lives to mark the widening influence of the institution, to which he devoted so many of the best years of his life.

His successor, Mr. Samuel S. Wood, had for some time filled the position of assistant superintendent in the House, and was familiar with the duties and responsibilities of the place. He had many qualities of mind and temperament peculiarly fitting him for his new position. The managers remark of him in their twentieth annual report, "The experience acquired by him in the position he formerly occupied, justified the managers in the belief that under his superintendency the institution would lose none of its efficiency. In every respect the opinion of the managers has been fully sustained by the zeal and ability of Mr. Wood."

The previous year, 1843, had been peculiarly fatal to the friends and managers of the institution; during its months, Colonel William L. Stone and Samuel Stevens, both active, earnest, and greatly-respected members of the Board, were removed from its management by death. At the close of the same year, by a very sudden and afflicting providence the Society was deprived of the valuable services of John R. Willis, one of the noble company of Friends so interested in the charitable institutions of the city. He was chairman of the Indenturing

Committee, and ably fulfilled its exacting duties down to the close of his valuable life. " He took," says the twentieth annual report, " a benevolent and active interest in every thing calculated to promote the comfort and happiness of the unfortunate children of the Refuge, and with unsurpassed fidelity devoted his time and exertions in the cause of public and private charity. By his experience and wise counsels, he gave energy and efficiency to the action of this Board. . . . His name," they add, " will long be remembered by those who were the witnesses of his benevolent and disinterested exertions in promoting the good of society."

In the second annual report, we find among the managers the name of Robert C. Cornell, a highly-esteemed merchant, and a member also of the Society of Friends. From the first he was one of the most active and efficient managers of the Refuge. For the last twelve years of his life he held the office of vice-president, and when he fell by the stroke of death in 1845, his brother managers say of him : " His eminent public services, his devotion to the cause of public and private charity, his enlarged and liberal spirit of philanthropy, and his fidelity and zeal in promoting the interests of the various institutions with which he was connected, render his name and memory worthy of our highest respect and veneration." The earliest managers never lost their interest in the institution over which they had watched with so much anxiety in the years of its first experiment in the field of juvenile reform. Removal or death only changed the names upon its Board. It was natural that when death began its work the venerable founders would follow each other in rapid succession.

The succeeding year marked the decease of their admirable

treasurer, Cornelius Dubois, Samuel Downer, and John R. Townsend; and, from among the lady managers, they are called to mention the departure of Mrs. Sarah Hall, wife of the late highly-respected editor of the *Commercial Advertiser*, Francis Hall. "For many years," say her companions, "connected with this charity, and with associations of a kindred nature, she devoted her means and energies to the cause of philanthropy. She was in frequent attendance at the House, and took a lively interest in the advancement of the moral and religious condition of the female inmates."

This year, 1846, commissioners from Massachusetts, appointed by the Legislature for the establishment of a State Reform School, visited and carefully examined the House. This institution, originating in a large donation (some $70,000) from one of its honored citizens, Hon. Theodore Lyman, was probably the first Reform School established either in this country or Europe by the State, and governed by trustees appointed by its Executive. The institution went into operation in 1848. Its buildings were first constructed to accommodate five hundred and fifty inmates, much upon the plan of the New York House. By a disastrous fire some years since one-half of the main edifice was destroyed, and instead of rebuilding upon the same plan, several small houses have been constructed near the principal edifice, each accommodating about thirty inmates.

As a marked improvement upon the French institution, each house is placed under the charge of a gentleman and his wife, giving much of the character of a home to the administration of its discipline. It is certainly a very pleasant innovation upon the congregate system; but it will be seen at once that every new house requires for its head a person quite equal himself to be the superintendent of an institution, and on this very account less fitted to fill a subordinate position.

For the short period that these youths should be detained in such institutions before trying the experiment of placing them in actual families, and in view of the constant, earnest discipline of labor indispensably requisite for the training of such vagrant and idle children, it may be questioned whether the results gained compensate the additional expense and the greater risk to the harmony of the establishment, arising out of so many subordinate, but, in some measure, independent authorities. There is nothing in the reported results of the experiment that give it an advantage, as to moral and economical statistics, over the New York House. Since the opening of the State School at Westborough, other State and municipal institutions have been constituted, with Boards of management appointed by Executive authority, which probably afford a confirmation of the experience of the Massachusetts school in this respect. It has been managed by some of the foremost men of the State, and, undoubtedly, with the most painstaking care and integrity; yet it has been so unfortunate as to come into collision with the Executive Department of the government; expose its Board to abrupt changes and its officers to sudden removals; and, what is more serious still, has brought upon the institution itself the distrust of the community—a lack of confidence which, from considerable personal knowledge of its affairs, we think to be undeserved.

The experience of the half century fully confirms the wisdom of keeping such institutions from the perils of our changing politics. They should be committed into the hands of those whose intelligence, benevolence, enjoyment of the public confidence, and personal interest in the work, will secure for them a constant and faithful supervision, and be subject simply to the careful periodical examination of some proper officer of the State.

During the same year, commissioners from the city of New Orleans, and of our own State, visited the House in view of the erection of similar institutions. A House of Refuge was opened in New Orleans in 1847, and the Western House of Refuge, as a purely State institution, went into operation in 1849.

The Refuge at Rochester follows the system of the New York House, except that it was arranged for boys solely. By an act of the Legislature, juvenile delinquents, from the first, second, and third judicial districts, were to be sent to the latter House, and from the remaining five districts were to be sent to the former. Girls from all parts of the State were still to be sent to the New York House.

The two institutions, although from year to year other establishments of a municipal, voluntary, or denominational character, have been opened, have found their large accommodations required for the increasing neglected juvenile population, chiefly occasioned by the enormous immigration annually entering the country through our State.

Nearly all the later institutions have been constructed on the principle of separating the sexes, not merely in different buildings, shut off by high walls, but by placing them in institutions in different portions of the country. It was thought by many that the attempts which it was supposed would be made to hold intercourse with each other would interfere with the discipline and result in mutual contamination. It was also feared that the knowledge they might acquire of each other's presence in the House would become a temptation, or an occasion of disgrace, in after-times. The debate is still upon a living question, and intelligent men differ widely in their views. As a matter of fact, since the New York institution has been located in its present buildings, near each other, but entirely separate, and each enclosed by its own wall, no difficulty of the nature suggested has been experienced. There are no attempts at correspondence; no signalling with the eyes or hands in public service, and no irritability and desire to gaze upon each other are displayed. The curiosity that would become morbid for lack of gratification loses its power by constant repetition, and our children sit in their capacious and beautiful chapel with as much quiet propriety as any audience in the land. It is the conviction of the officers and managers that the morbid excitement which attends the entire separation of the sexes is greatly modified by their daily intercourse in hours of labor and devotions in the presence and under the eyes of their appropriate officers. No instance of demoralization has been brought to the knowledge of the Superintendent arising from an acquaintance formed between the sexes in the House.

The beneficial results are many. Both departments have forms of labor incident to their daily necessities requiring the services of the opposite sex. In purely male institutions this work is done by the boys, while in female institutions it is performed by hired men. In the New York House each sex has its appropriate form of labor. The making, mending, and knitting form the employment of a portion of the younger girls, together with the washing and ironing of the whole institution. The boys thus relieved from their inappropriate services are enabled to enter upon trades that afford better discipline for their minds and moral faculties, and secure for them a better opportunity after their discharge from the House.

The experience of the writer, connected as he has been with a separate institution for girls, is, that the girls, as a whole, are as cheerful, more readily managed, as well fitted for the stations they will be called to fill, as much under the influence of moral restraints and influences, in the united institution as in the separate. There was an opportunity certainly afforded in a school, where but thirty were gathered in a house, for a teacher to draw some particularly interesting girl nearer to herself, and to inspire her with higher motives and mould her by her own powerful influence over her. Nearly the same results, however, are gained by the subdivisions into classes of the same number, and, after all, the great thing to be accomplished is, with the shortest possible training to secure the awakening of the moral faculties, to place these girls in good families, where the undivided care of a Christian woman will be devoted to their instruction and nurture. The results of a personal examination of a large number of girls indentured from the House in surrounding States, were peculiarly favorable, both as to the character of the families that had taken them, and the condition in every respect of the girls themselves.

Our chapel is so constructed, that the girls sitting in the gallery, and the boys in the body of the room, are invisible to each other; but, when repairs in this building required us to find some other place of assembly, the whole institution met together on the same floor—the girls separated by a simple passage-way from the boys. It was the universal testimony of officers and managers, that, during the Sabbaths in which our worship was thus conducted, not the slightest exhibition of impropriety, or even curiosity, was observed.

The sexes were intended to be educated together, and it is

of no ordinary service to have the proprieties connected with the intercourse of men and women practically taught and illustrated, in the presence of pure persons of both sexes.

The opening of the new institution, at Rochester, requiring an experienced Superintendent to preside over its organization, Mr. Wood, who had enjoyed, during his connection with the House, the entire confidence of its managers, and had brought its discipline into an admirable condition of efficiency, was requested to inaugurate the internal management of the new establishment, and felt it to be his duty to accept the responsibility. This station he retained, with great credit to himself, and benefit to the thousands of lads who have passed through the halls of the Western House, until the present year (1868). His memory will ever be cherished in the hearts of these reclaimed young men.

Up to this period four thousand six hundred and sixty-three inmates had been received into the House of Refuge since its establishment, and it accommodated at this time about three hundred and fifty. Of the condition of the institution at this period we have the testimony of the grand jury, at the head of which was the ex-Mayor, Hon. James Harper, rendered June 23, 1848: "In happy contrast," they say, in referring to certain penal institutions, "is the House of Refuge, at the foot of Twenty-third Street. Here, for nearly a quarter of a century, has been in active and successful operation one of the noblest and most beneficent reformatory systems ever devised by human philanthropy. The physical, moral, and intellectual redemption of thousands who were almost lost, has been achieved, and still the good work is going on faithfully and efficiently under the intelligent administration of the Society for the Reformation of

Juvenile Delinquents, and of the various officers to whom the
execution of its design is intrusted.   There are now in the
Refuge two hundred and fifty boys, and sixty girls, chiefly supplied from the city, though small additions are made from other
parts of the State.   The inmates are carefully instructed in the
useful branches of a plain English education, and are, besides,
usefully employed in various handicrafts, qualifying them to fill
reputable and advantageous stations in society, when they are
fitted to return to its duties and privileges.   A great step to such
a return is effected by the system of binding out those whose
conduct in the Refuge proves them worthy, to such employers,
residing in the country, as are willing to take apprentices from
the institution.   The Records abound with proofs and illustrations of the happy agency exerted in this way by the Refuge.

  " The best evidence that can be afforded of good and humane
management on the part of those having the charge of these
youthful candidates for reform, is the fact that, notwithstanding
the unfavorable influences among which their childhood was
generally passed, naturally tending to sow the seeds of disease,
the grand jury found only two girls, and not one boy, on the
sick list.   Equally strong testimony to the moral care employed
is presented in the established certainty, that about three-fourths
of those who enter the institution, leave it thoroughly reformed.
Visits are continually received from such, now become prosperous and respected members of society.   About one-third of the
expenses is defrayed annually by the proceeds of the boys'
labor; the residue is met by grants from the State, and by the
license tax on theatres, etc.   The physical condition of the
Refuge appears to the grand jury all that could be desired.
Cleanliness and order were strictly observed throughout, and the

whole system of government is manifestly a happy combination of firmness, kindness, judicious control, and mild persuasion."

John W. Ketchum, Esq., was elected Superintendent, in place of Mr. Wood. He had been for years at the head of one of the finest public schools of New York, and for several years had faithfully administered the office of Police Judge in the city. He was a man of commanding presence, of a ready address, with a fine, searching eye, fond of children, with much personal magnetism drawing them warmly to himself—altogether a man eminently qualified to take the institution, at the point of progress it had reached, and to carry it forward.

Every year now the reports contain the touching memorial tributes of the managers to their deceased members. The noble men that laid the foundations of the House were rapidly falling away, and leaving its increasing responsibilities to be borne by their successors. Captain James Lovett, whose name had never been out of the record from the appointment of the first Board, in 1824, has a significant star placed against his name in 1850. He was " an attentive and valuable member of the Board," say his companions, "and of its committees, so long as age and health permitted, always an earnest friend. . . . . He has been added," they remark, " to the number of those good and thoughtful men whom Providence has removed from earthly duty, after prolonging their lives until the efficiency of an institution, founded by their wisdom and liberality, has become widely known, and until its success has caused the foundation of other refuges for the same end, and conducted upon the same principles as their own."

Daniel Seymour, Esq., one of the most cultivated and intelligent men whose presence ever graced the Board, and who had been for several years upon the Indenturing Committee, left all earthly service in the same year (1850). "To a mind of high order, improved by travel and extensive observation, were united habits of indefatigable industry, and an unwearied zeal in the cause of benevolence." His attention became directed in a special manner to the wants of the institution, and all his energies were enlisted in devising and carrying out measures for increasing and extending its usefulness. A vice-president of the Board also, David C. Colden, Esq., son of the first President, fell this year. He was "for many years a manager, zealous and untiring in its cause, as he was wherever philanthropy and charity were invoked. In the various positions he held in the Board he gave constant proof of the thoughtful and active benevolence to which his life was devoted, and for which his memory will long be cherished by the poor and friendless, by the stranger and exile."

While these good men were resting from their labors, "their works were following them." The Daily Journal is full of the most satisfactory assurances that their labors have not been in vain. It is difficult to make selections, or to restrain the pen in copying :

"John M. N., who was indentured from here about seven years ago, called to see us to-day. He remained about two years at his trade, when his master's shop was burned, and he gave up the business. John was intelligent and of a studious turn of mind, and, having connected himself with a Christian church, he secured friends and influence, which enabled him to get a collegiate education. Only a few months remain to complete his course, when he will go, under the auspices of the church of which he is a member, as a missionary to the heathen, and a preacher of the Gospel. His early history was not promising."

"J. S., a lad of eighteen years of age, who was indentured to a trade one year ago, called on us, having been permitted by his master to come to the city to visit his parents. We have had several flattering accounts of this lad's conduct, and have great confidence that he will make a respectable man. He has united with a Christian church, and shares the confidence of all who know him. He is very active at his trade, and is earning from six to seven dollars per week for his master. What a transition from *picking up rags in the street for a living!*"

"A. McD., who was indentured two years ago, visited us to-day, having served her time out faithfully, and brings an excellent letter of commendation from her employer. She comes well clad, and is quite an interesting girl. She has engaged to return in a few days and remain with the family on wages. Poor child! she has literally been snatched from ruin. Her father is a miserable inebriate; her mother is in the penitentiary; a sister is in the almshouse, maimed, and another sister is a wretched outcast. This family presents a sad picture, and most sadly does this poor girl weep over it. She feels that a providential hand directed her to the Refuge."

"J. McC, who was permitted to ship in the United States service seventeen years ago, called on us. During several years past he has been employed in the merchant service as a mate of a vessel. He has a wife and four children, whom, by prudence and economy, he has not only supported comfortably, but he has accumulated some property. He is now thirty-four years of age, and will emigrate to California with his family in a few days."

Clothed, and in her Right Mind.

" Your letter of inquiry relative to Sarah E. W., indentured to me in 1846, has been received. In reply, I am happy to say she is still a member of my family, is honest, industrious, and improved in education. She is a regular attendant on the Sabbath-school, and ambitious of future respectability and usefulness. She has been hopefully renewed by the Divine Spirit, and was one of twenty-three who made a public profession of their faith in Christ, in the First Congregational Church in this town, a short time since. Her heart glows with gratitude to God for the way in which she has been thus far led, and she is anticipating the time when she can appear in person at the House of Refuge, and thank yourself, the managers, and the matrons, that she ever saw that institution, and left it for the quarter that she did."

Such instances might be indefinitely multiplied. They form the most assuring evidences of the reformatory power of the Refuge, and of the kindness with which its discipline has been administered; the inmates, like children of a family, reporting their sorrows and their successes to their well-remembered and beloved home.

CHAPTER VI.

RANDALL'S ISLAND.

As early as December, 1848, Mr. David C. Colden, in view of the crowded condition of the institution, three hundred and fifty-five inmates being present in the House at the time, moved the appointment of a committee to consider the best mode of providing accommodations for the increasing number of subjects and also for their better classification. A committee was appointed, and the discussion of these two important questions was commenced.

The opening of the Rochester House, in 1849, delayed for a time the report of this committee, as it was deemed expedient to learn what relief it would bring to the crowded halls of the New York Refuge. But the Western House at once justified the wisdom of its erection by developing the need of its provisions for the northern and western counties of the State, and it was able to afford hardly a perceptible relief to the older institution. The river counties, Kings and Queens, and New York City, as the influence of the House became more and more appreciated, overran the accommodations at Bellevue.

In January of 1850, Mr. Seymour, of this committee, made a report, which was accepted, urging especially the importance of securing the means of classification and the separation of the more vicious inmates from the others, recommending a change of location and increased accommodations, and the appointment of a committee to confer with the city authorities in reference to the exchange of the property of the Society then held, for a more eligible site. This committee was also to apply to the State Legislature for aid to erect the new buildings. The recommendations of the report were followed.

Mr. Seymour was placed at the head of a committee appointed for the purposes specified, and secured from the corporation of the city a prompt response, authorizing the Society to sell the property held at the foot of Twenty-third Street, and to appropriate the proceeds to the purchase of another site, and the erection of suitable buildings. About ten and a half acres of land on the southern shore of Ward's Island, nearly opposite 102d Street, a very secluded site, and one that would not be likely to be intruded upon for purposes of business or commerce, were first purchased.

Owing to an objection of Governor Fish, to some of the provisions in the bill which passed the Legislature of 1850, empowering the Society to remove their House, and granting them an appropriation toward its construction, no further steps were taken until the succeeding year.

Upon consideration, the difficulty of access to the site upon Ward's Island, and other objections, induced the Society to propose to the city government an exchange of this property which they had purchased, for some thirty acres of rocky and marshy land, forming the southeastern point of Randall's Island. This proposition was accepted, and the building committee commenced its important work.

Nothing could have been more unpromising than the origi-

nal appearance of the place. Few sites are more charming
now than the noble buildings, surrounded with their hand-
somely-arranged grounds and fruitful gardens—a very happy
symbol of the work upon which the Society for half a century
has been engaged. Her grounds have been recovered from
stony wastes, and from low and unwholesome marshes, and are
now both beautiful and useful. The inmates of her Houses have
been often the hardest and most unpromising children of the
land, taken from the lowest haunts, and themselves noxious
members of the community. Many of them are now an honor
to her culture, and to the State that has generously offered the
means both for the physical and moral changes which have been
wrought out here.

Of the place the committee say: "The Cemetery, or Pot-
ter's Field, occupied nearly all the best land, and the remainder
was either swamp or rock. On the western front the shore was
indented by a cove, where the tide at high water came up
nearly to the spot now occupied by the steps of the main entrance to the Boy's House; while, on the north, there arose a
considerable rocky elevation, covering a portion of the ground
upon which now stands the entrance of the north wing, the
termination of this rock being immediately upon an extended
swamp. To the south, there was another mass of rock occupying a great part of the space now covered by the building of
the Girl's Dwelling, reaching to a height nearly equal to some
of the buildings afterward erected thereon."

The estimated expense of grading and preparing the grounds
for the buildings was so heavy ($20,000), that the committee
would not move forward until they had submitted it to the consideration of the Governor, Washington Hunt, who from the

ROBERT KELLY, Esq.

p. 187.

first, manifested a lively interest in the undertaking, and to the State Comptroller. "Go forward," said the Governor, "and I will stand by you."

The act of the Legislature, appropriating $50,000, required that provision should be made for one thousand inmates. Three hundred dollars were offered for such a plan of the new buildings as might be selected by the committee, and eight competitors presented their designs. That of Messrs. Dwight and Bryant was accepted.

These well-known architects had made such generous provisions in the dimensions and arrangements of the immense buildings, that several of the committee, although reluctant to disturb the admirable proportions, became alarmed at the great cost which would be entailed upon them. Finally, Mr. R. G. Hatfield, of this city, was instructed to reduce the plans to meet the views of the majority of the committee, and was appointed architect for the construction of the buildings.

This year (1852) the honored president of the Board, Hon. Stephen Allen, closed his active and valuable life in the terrible catastrophe heretofore mentioned. The Society had been singularly fortunate in its two presiding officers, in securing men of remarkable executive ability, of great persistence of purpose, and sharing in a very large measure the confidence and respect of the community. It was equally successful in the election of the successor to Mr. Allen, Robert Kelly, Esq. He was the son of a successful merchant of this city, entered Columbia College at the head of his class, retained the position through his course, and graduated with the highest honors in 1826, when he was but eighteen years of age. His father died a year before his graduation. At the urgent solicitation of his brothers, a few years older than himself, he entered into business with them, rather than upon a profession. "During his commercial career," says E. S. Van Winkle, Esq., in a published tribute to his memory, "he was distinguished for perseverance and untiring industry, for extraordinary attention to detail, for great decision of character, and for an integrity and sense of honor which no temptation could reach. No misrepresentation, however slight, on the part of his clerks, was ever allowed to pass unrebuked. By the establishment of just and inflexible rules in every department, he acquired for himself and the house a reputation for integrity and fairness never excelled."

Ten years of business life conducted upon these principles, commenced, indeed, with a considerable capital left him by his father, endowed him with an ample fortune, and he retired from active connection with business before he had reached his twenty-ninth year.

During his active life he had kept up his scholarship, and become master of the French, Spanish, Italian, German, and Hebrew languages. Upon leaving business he did not simply return to his beloved studies, but while he was able to devote more time to them, he gave his best years and ripened powers to the various public societies and charities that eagerly availed themselves of his rare abilities. He became a trustee of the New York and of Madison Universities, and was the president of the Board of Education when the Free Academy, now New York College, was established—an enterprise in which he was peculiarly interested. "The success of the scheme," says Mr. Van Winkle, "both of study and discipline, is enough alone to stamp his name as one of the most enlightened and judicious among the friends of education." The portrait of his fine, intelligent face, of which our engraving is a poor representation, hangs in an honored place upon the walls of the hall of the Board of Education. Mr. Kelly recommended the establishment also, after a few years of experiment with the institution for males, of an academy of equally liberal scholarship for the other sex. He died before he could initiate so praiseworthy an enterprise, and the undertaking still awaits the "man and the hour."

He became connected with the management of the House of Refuge in 1839, and from that time until his death the institution retained a remarkable hold upon his sympathies. His biographer says: "He regarded this charity with more favor than any other, because he believed it to be the most useful of all the truly benevolent institutions which adorn our city. He would often, with trembling voice, tell of cases of reform, where the vile had been reclaimed by its influence and had become good and virtuous citizens." * He was peculiarly fitted for the place and the circumstances, when called to be the president of the Board of Managers upon the death of Mr. Allen. He was a remarkable presiding officer. "As a presiding officer," says Mr. Van Winkle, "over deliberate assemblies or public meetings, he will be long remembered as being almost unequalled. Having complete command of temper, a dignified and most courteous manner, with perfect fairness toward those who differed from him, and a keen sagacity and prompt decision, which enabled him to forward business and give the proceedings a practical direction, he earned a reputation in this respect second to no man in the State." But he became the head of the institution at an hour of peculiar responsibility. The Board had just entered upon an

---

* "A Tribute to the Memory of Robert Kelly," by E. S. Van Winkle.

undertaking involving great pecuniary liabilities, and these were to be met by its success in convincing successive Legislatures of the necessity and economy of the large appropriations required. Mr. Kelly took broad, manly, and hopeful views, and never for a moment distrusted the good sense, honor, or generosity of his State. He entered upon his duties with the laying of the corner-stone of the new buildings, and closed them with his eloquent dedicatory address.

As president of the Board, " he was the principal instigator and mover of an extensive reform in its management and discipline." No man's mark is more deeply impressed upon its regulations than his. He was, indeed, a martyr to his interest in the institution. Delaying into the evening of April 27, 1856, that he might attend an examination of the schools, and crossing East River in an open boat, he was seized with a severe cold. He never recovered from it. Although no danger was apprehended at first, the attack increased in violence until he peacefully departed, fully sustained by the grace of the Gospel, of which, from his youth, he had been an humble and faithful disciple. " He died in the midst of the community in which he was born and reared; in the midst of which he had displayed his remarkable qualities; in which his virtues were known, and by which they were appreciated. Seldom has the death of a private citizen been followed by such universal regret. With the public acknowledgment of his worth," says his memorialist, " by the civic authorities, and by the numerous scientific, political, financial, and benevolent bodies he was connected with, we have mingled ours " * (the " Column," of which social and literary club he was an honored and beloved member).

---

* " Tribute to the Memory of Robert Kelly."

His colleagues say of him, in the report that announces his decease: "We regret to be obliged to record the great loss the institution has sustained in the removal by death of its late president, Robert Kelly. For years he had taken a great interest in this institution, and had devoted much time, and thought, and labor, to put it upon a firm foundation. In the midst of a variety of pressing duties, he always placed his judgment and influence at its service, and our buildings on Randall's Island will be a lasting memorial of his lofty ambition to be useful. The good which he has done will outlive those whom he benefited. Our institutions profited largely by his life; his departure at this period seems most unfortunate. He had exerted himself with great perseverance to procure the funds necessary to pay our debts and complete our buildings, and our success in these particulars in his lifetime would have crowned one of his favorite labors."

The corner-stone of the main building of the boys' department was laid upon the 24th of November, 1852, in the presence of the officers of the Society, the mayor and corporation of the city, and a large number of guests. After the usual introductory services, Hon. A. C. Kingsland, mayor of the city, was introduced and made an appropriate address. "The occasion," he remarked, "on which we are assembled is one of no ordinary importance and interest—importance in view of the influence which the labor this day commenced is to have upon the rising generation, and interest in view of the truly noble and philanthropic motives of those associated in the enterprise. We are not here merely to lay the corner-stone of a public edifice with imposing ceremony; we are here to commence the foundation of a building which may in time send forth to the world wise, good, and virtuous citizens, whose influence and example will be felt and acknowledged far and wide. . . . . The youth growing up in our midst in vice and ignorance, without moral restraint, may be placed within the reach of proper care and culture, through the medium of such an institution as this; habits of industry and discipline may be acquired which will follow them into the world and render them good and useful citizens. And many, who otherwise might find a home in a prison-cell, or end an ignominious career upon the gallows, may live to bless the day in which they were thrown under the kind and paternal influence which this association seeks to impart.

"I am very happy, gentlemen, to have the honor, as chief magistrate of this city, of taking an official part in these ceremonies; as a private citizen, my warmest sympathies have ever been enlisted on behalf of the association, whose members now surround me, and I am glad to lend my official coöperation to a measure which will tend to enhance so greatly its usefulness and enlarge the sphere of its operations, the gratifying results of which must cause a thrill of pleasure to every heart."

The mayor then proceeded to perform the ceremony of laying the corner-stone, the secretary of the Building Committee, J. W. C. Leveridge, Esq., having deposited in a cavity of the stone all the published documents relating to the history and discipline of the institution.

At the close of these ceremonies, Mr. Kelly, as president of the Board, delivered a very interesting and impressive discourse. Opening with a full outline of the history of the Society from its origin, describing the close relation of the Board to its management, and referring to the sources from which the institution derived its support, he adds: "It will thus be seen that the Society is a private corporation, employed by the State as the care-taker, educator, and reformer of its juvenile vagrants and offend-ers. But though a private corporation, it is completely under the control of the representatives of the people. All the inmates it admits it receives by law through regular commitments by judges and police magistrates, and when it shall be found not to fulfil its objects properly the law can take away all its subjects and put an end to its operations. It is an organization for the enlistment of a body of volunteers devoting themselves to a be-nevolent task, giving a full account of their action, accumulating a store of experience in their work, and continued in their trust until their services shall be no longer required.

"The position of the Society toward the State was presented with characteristic force and eccentricity by the late reverend and venerable Dr. Stanford, so long the chaplain of our public charitable institutions, in a sermon preached in the House of Refuge, on the first Christmas-day after its opening. 'Take this child away and nurse it for me, and I will give thee thy wages,' was the text. The daughter of Pharaoh represented the State, and this Society was the nurse into whose arms the child was *committed.* The good doctor did not forget the ap-plication, which he urged with great zeal, that the nurse's wages should be punctually and liberally paid. The Managers of the Society will feel it their duty at the present juncture, in view of the heavy expenditure they are compelled to undertake, to repeat the *application* to the city and State authorities."

Of the result of the labors of the Society, continued at that time for more than a quarter of a century, he remarks: "It is not easy for us to estimate the good that has been accomplished in the House during the twenty-eight years that it has been in existence. A very large majority of its five thousand graduates, of both sexes, have been saved without doubt, whereas the greater part probably would otherwise have been lost to themselves and others, ruined for time and eternity, and fated, by the law of their moral natures, to spread, wherever they should go, the leprosy of evil. One of the pleasantest circumstances connected with our labors is the evidence we are constantly receiving of an entire change of character that has taken place in children who have been under our care, as shown by letters from them, by information from those with whom they are living, and occasionally by visits at the House of men who introduce themselves as former refuge-boys, and express their gratitude for what the institution did for them."

Having been twice disturbed in the sites selected for the House, by the encroachments of a rapidly-increasing city, he congratulates his audience upon the assured prospect of permanence. They were now "safely, conveniently, and admirably located, where streets cannot cut through the premises, and the tide of the city's population can never dash against its walls." Of the Commissioners of Charities and Corrections, who had the charge of the nurseries connected with the Almshouse department, at the upper end of the island, he says: "We mean to be good neighbors, only we intend to compete with them in the supply of apprentices, and gain, if we can, the reputation of furnishing the most useful and best-behaved children. Our formidable wall of enclosure will protect our children from the contamination of theirs, or *vice versa*, as the case may be."

He closes this admirable address with these eloquent sentiments: "We have now, upon one of our isles of the unfortunate, laid the corner-stone of a temple of humanity. This range of beautiful islands seems to have been set on purpose to be a moral rampart around our great city. The towers which shall be erected upon them, unlike the fortresses which encircle the cities of the Old World, are not for our defence against foreign enemies, nor to overawe our own peaceful citizens, but for the protection of the destitute, and for a defence against crime and depravity. There is something peculiarly appropriate in such a site for the purpose of our institution. The unfortunate and erring youth who shall be gathered upon this Isle of Refuge, separated from the city by yonder silvery channel, and breathing the pure air of heaven, will look, within a short period, upon a dense mass of buildings, homes of comfort and domestic happiness, reared by industry, and tenanted by thrift, with churches and school-houses scattered among them, and will see what labor and virtuous endeavor, the restraints of law, and the influence of education and religion, have done for the great body of that vast population.

"I have called our House of Refuge a temple of humanity; and, when I think of its purpose, to receive the young within its shelter, reclaim and restore them, teach them the duties of the present life, and tell them of the life herafter, it seems to me to be, in its spirit and object, an embodiment of that beautiful expression of the Saviour of mankind—' *Suffer little children to come unto me.*'"

We have seen how suggestions received from one continent become the seeds of abundant harvests of good in another. As early as 1820, while the great Scotch divine, Dr. Chalmers, was the minister of the Tron Church, in Glasgow, with an outlying parish of ten thousand souls, he became deeply impressed with the slight benefit received by a large portion of these thousands from the Christian truths uttered in the house of God.   He saw and felt the impossibility of drawing the poor, intemperate, miserable criminal population, which, of all others, most needed the Gospel, to the public services of the sanctuary.   They will not come to the church, but the Master has sent the church to them: "Go ye into all the world, and preach the Gospel to every creature."

Dr. Chalmers determined to institute an experiment.   Having secured the services of the afterward deservedly celebrated Edward Irving, at that time just ready to enter upon the office of the ministry, a man eminently devoted, with all his eccentricities, he commenced the work of evangelizing the whole district, calling in as additional laborers the deacons of his church; day-schools and Sunday-schools, lectures and public Sabbath services, were held in the humblest accommodations, and near to the residence of the most neglected portion of the population.   The experiment was peculiarly successful, and the interest excited by it never left the mind of the great preacher.

Long after, when a theological professor, resident in Edinburgh, in 1845, at the age of sixty-five, he determined to organize another movement for carrying the light of Christian truth into one of the most abandoned portions of the city.   The scene of this most successful and encouraging experiment was a part of the city in much the same moral condition as the worst portions of the Fourth and Sixth Wards of New York, or as the Five Points before its redemption.   "The locality selected," says Dr. Hanna, in his interesting biography of his father-in-law,* "as the scene of his projected enterprise, was the West Port; a part of Edinburgh to which, a few years pre-

---

* Memoir of Dr. Chalmers, vol. iv., p. 388.

viously, an infamous notoriety had been attached by those secret murders (by a person named Burke), the discovery of which sent a thrill of horror through the land." The population here seemed lost to all the decencies of a civilized life. The children were growing up in ignorance of any thing useful, but nurtured in vice. "The physical and moral condition of this community was deplorable; one-fourth were paupers on the poor-roll, and one-fourth were street-beggars, thieves, or prostitutes."

The doctor was again successful in finding a pious and laborious co-worker, Rev. Mr. Tasker, who entered heartily into his grand idea of changing this barren waste, with God's blessing, into a fruit-bearing Christian field. When Mr. Parker "made his first visits to some of the filthiest closes, it was no uncommon thing for him to find from twenty to thirty men, women, and children, huddled together in one putrid dwelling, lying indiscriminately on the floor, waiting the return of the bearer of some well-concocted begging letter, or the coming on of that darkness under which they might sally out, to earn, by fair means or foul, the purchase-money of renewed debauchery. Upon one occasion, he entered a tenement with from twelve to twenty apartments, where every human being, man and woman, were so drunk that they could not hear their own squalid infants crying in vain to them for food. He purchased some bread for the children, and, entering a few minutes afterward a neighboring dram-shop, he found a half-drunk mother driving a bargain for more whiskey with the very bread which her famishing children should be eating ! He went once to a funeral, and found the assembled company all so drunk around the corpse, that he had to go and beg some sober neighbors to come and carry the coffin to the grave. It was a formidable enterprise—to many it would

have seemed altogether hopeless—to come into close quarters
with such a population. Aided, however, by that band of
zealous associates which his public lectures and many private
interviews by which they were followed up, had gathered around
him, Dr. Chalmers went hopefully forward." *

The great problem was, to aid this wretched community to
help itself, and not to perpetuate its pauperism by simply carrying them food and improving their homes; to inspire *them* to
seek for their children the advantages of an education, and the
privileges of the house of God, and not merely build school and
meeting houses for them. A school-room was hired " at the end
of the very close down which Burke and his associates decoyed
their unconscious victims. Fronting the den in which those
horrid murders were committed, stood an old deserted tannery,
whose upper store-loft, approached from without by a flight of
projecting wooden stairs, was selected as affording the best accommodation which the neighborhood could supply. Low-roofed
and roughly floored, its raw, unplastered walls, pierced at irregular intervals with windows of unshapely form, it had little
either of the scholastic or the ecclesiastical in its aspect, but
never was the true work of school and church better done than
in that old tannery-loft of the West Port." *

A nominal sum to awaken a feeling of independence on the
part of parents, was charged to secure the advantages of the
school, one of the best teachers that could be found in the
country having been obtained for the position. Within two
years, through the aid of Christian friends, and always securing
the small contributions and consequent personal interest of the
people themselves, a comfortable church and school-room had

* Memoir of Dr. Chalmers, vol. iv., p. 395.

Dr. Chalmers's View of the Experiment.

been built, a model tenement-house constructed, and the tone of the community wonderfully raised. The great preacher did not live to see the full result of his experiment, but in his last circular, issued before his death, he anticipated it. "We have long thought," he said, "that the failure of every former attempt to reclaim the masses of our population is due to the insufficiency of the means which have been brought to bear upon them; and while deeply sensible that means alone will prove of no effect without the blessing from on high on the devotedness and conscientious labors of those into whose hands they are intrusted, yet we hold it irrational to look for any great or sensible result with so slender an apparatus as that of Sabbath-schools and prayer-meetings, and rare occasional visits from house to house, under the conduct, it may be, of a few missionaries for the whole of a large town—each sinking under the weight of the many thousands who have been committed to his care, and dispirited by the want of any such visible fruit as might serve to satisfy both himself and his employers that his efforts are not wholly dissipated or lost, to all observation at least, in that mighty aggregate of human beings wherewith he has to deal. It is under this conviction that we have long advocated the concentration of commensurate efforts and means on a small enough territory. What cannot be done in bulk, and all at once, let us try in separate portions. . . . . The very essence of our scheme lies in the thorough operation of what we have called the territorial principle. We limit our attention to a single district or locality, itself split up into sub-districts, having each a Christian agent attached to it; so that not a home or family which might not be frequently and habitually visited by one having the charge of not more, if possible, than twenty households. By this busy internal missionary process a vast amount of direct good might be done."

All these visits were made to tell upon the economical and spiritual well-being of the population, and especially upon the constant attendance of the children upon school, and of all upon the public services of the Sabbath.

In five years after the far-seeing and devoted originator was in his grave, the ripe fruit of his early sowing began to appear. The whole character of the locality was changed. Between four and five hundred children that, except for this truly Christian movement, would have been the abandoned outcasts of the streets, were in daily attendance upon the schools ; " *nor was it known that there was a single child of a family resident within the West Port who was not at school.*" Well may the biographer of Dr. Chalmers remark : " Of what other like district in this country could the same be said, and by what other instrumentality could it have been accomplished ? The most commodious school-room might have been built, and the ablest teacher salaried, and the education offered gratis to all the families, and yet hundreds of these children have remained untaught. It was the district visiting, and the zeal especially of those ladies by whom a special oversight of the children's regular attendance at school was undertaken, by which this great achievement has mainly been accomplished."

Such an experiment never stands long alone. It becomes like the prophetic handful of corn sown upon the mountain, the harvest of it soon " shakes like Lebanon." Every large city has its West Ports—poverty, and vice, and crime, naturally concentrate in local centres, and become the more terrible by this very aggregation. These plague-spots, however, do not confine their corrupting influence within their own limits, but poison the whole atmosphere. When, a year or two since, our city was threatened with the ravages of the Asiatic cholera, there were certain quarters, crowded with overflowing tenement-houses, and reeking with filth, where it was well understood that the fatal plague would make its first appearance, and from whence, if it were once permitted to gather head, it would spread over the whole island. Prompt and energetic measures were taken to purify these predestined seats of disease, and so efficient were the sanitary applications in these unwholesome quarters, that even they were defended from the pestilence, and the whole city was saved. There are the same well-known and well-defined centres of vice and crime; indeed they are the same filthy localities where all forms of physical disease are bred.* The mala-

---

* Mr. Oliver Dyer thus describes a New York tenement-house: "A person who has never seen a New York tenant-house can form no idea of these structures. Some of them are eight stories in height, including basement, and are built two to a lot (25 by 100 feet), one in front and one in rear, for economy's sake. The basement is usually crowded with families; and sometimes the cellar underneath, lying below high-water mark, and frequently flooded by the tide, swarms with squalid women and children, burrowing in miasmatic lairs. A hall, about three and a half feet in width, usually runs through the centre of the building, dividing it into two tiers of apartments on each floor, from basement to attic, and these apartments are subdivided into front, middle, and rear, making six suites on each floor. The first-floor fronts are often used as low groggeries, with the families of the owners living in the rear of them, and the remainder of the building is packed, six families to a floor, clear to the roof. These houses are sometimes built twice and even thrice as deep as the one we have been describing, with six and even eight suites of apartments on each side of the hall, making from twelve to sixteen suites to a floor.

"The expression, 'suites of apartments,' will be certain to mislead the reader as to the real character of the rooms in which these people live without a special statement on the subject. They should really be called *sets of dens*. They usually consist of two rooms, a living-room and a sleeping-room.

rial influence of these localities poisons the whole city.   It is an impressive saying of Mr. Oliver Dyer, *that no child is safe so long as any child is neglected.*   Five or six little girls, all of them under fifteen years of age, were taken from one of the lowest haunts of the city and sent by the Police Court to the House of Refuge.   Their parents were in good circumstances, and very respectable persons.   They were quite overwhelmed to learn what had occurred.   They had sent them every day to school or to their work, and they had never been absent from their homes at night.   They could not believe *that the testimony against them*

the first being about eight feet by ten, and the second seven feet by ten, and averaging seven feet in height.   The bed-room has no ventilation except what it gets by the door opening from the living-room ; and the living-room, when in the centre of the floor—that is to say, when it is not a front or rear room— has no ventilation or light except what it gets through the door and a window opening into the narrow hall.   The so-called living-room is used to cook and wash in, and is also frequently used as a shoe-shop, tailor's shop, or for other manufacturing purposes.

"Not unfrequently two families—yea, *four* families, live in one of these small sets of dens ; and in this manner as many as 126 families, numbering over 800 souls, have been packed into one such building, and some of the families taking boarders and lodgers at that.   And worse yet, all around such tenements, or in close proximity to them, stand slaughter-houses, stables, tanneries, soap-factories, and bone-boiling establishments, emitting life-destroying exhalations.   Nor have we yet reached the climax of these horrors. *One* such nest of pest-pits would be bad enough, even if planted on a wide-spreading prairie ; but, here in New York, we have scores of them, towering in such close proximity as to shut out the air and sunlight from their inmates—with noisome, stench-reeking alleys leading to the rear houses, with yawning cesspools and privies in the areas, and steaming garbage-boxes on the sidewalks, and gutters running with festering filth, altogether forming a conglomerate mass of indescribable nastiness, from which ceaselessly go up such rank-smelling odors as might well cause the Man in the Moon to hold his nose as he passes over them.

"Persons who have never applied their noses to this matter may think that these expressions are rather strong ; but they do not begin to be as strong as the smells."

was true ; but the little girls confessed to their personal partici-
pation in the frightful vices of the place where they were found.
They had been beguiled into it during their intermissions from
school or work, and had always been careful to reach home at
the proper hour. It is the poison of the streets that occasions
the constant surprise we feel in learning that so many of the
children of our reformatories have been religiously trained, and
enjoyed the affection and counsels of Christian parents.   In
leaving so many neglected children in the streets we peril the
safety of all the others.

Christian women in our city, encouraged by these successful
experiments in Scotland, impressed with the truth that vice and
crime could only be cured by going to the fountain-head, and
deeply moved by the appalling moral condition of certain portions of the city, were the first to determine to put forth practical efforts for their regeneration.

As early as 1848, the ladies of the Home Missionary Society
connected with the Methodist Episcopal Church had fixed their
eyes upon the Five Points, which was then the most abandoned
and frightful portion of the city, as a sphere for their operations.
" We all feel," they say, in their report for that year, " that this
is emphatically *mission ground.*   We plead for the children—
the children, because through them we hope to reach the
parents—the children, because ere long they will hold the des-
tiny of our city within their hands."

There were some features that rendered this field more difficult of cultivation and hopeless than West Port, in Edinburgh.
In the latter the great body of the miserable population was of
a common nationality, and the question of a religious belief
would have hardly occasioned a serious discussion.   In the Five

Five Points as Charles Dickens saw it.

Points almost every nationality under the heavens was represented, and bitter sectarian prejudices greatly embarrassed the progress of the work. But to faith nothing is impossible!

A low valley, between Broadway and the Bowery, once the site of a pond of water, with a depth in the centre of fifty feet, on which the first boat sailed ever propelled by steam,* gradually filled up, but badly drained, the angles of the narrow, dirty streets, running to and through it, forming five corners around an irregular and indefinitely deep mud-hole in the centre—such was the physical geography of the place in 1850. Of the general aspect of its tenements, and the moral character of its population, that wonderful artist in descriptions of wretchedness and crime, Charles Dickens, has given us the picture to life, as it struck his eye a few years before the ladies commenced their work of redemption. "Let us go on again," he says, in his "American Notes," "and plunge into the Five Points. But it is needful first, that we take as our escort these two heads of the police, whom you would know for sharp and well-trained officers, if you met them in the great desert. . . . This is the place; these narrow ways, diverging to the right and left, and reeking everywhere with dirt and filth. Such lives as are led here bear the same fruit here as elsewhere. The coarse and bloated faces at the doors have counterparts at home and all the wide world over. Debauchery has made the very houses prematurely old. See how the rotten beams are tumbling down, and how the patched and broken windows seem to scowl dimly, like eyes that have been hurt in drunken frays. Many of these pigs live here. Do they ever wonder why their masters walk upright in lieu of going on all fours! and why

* Chart of John Fitch, 1793.

they talk, instead of grunting. . . . So far, nearly every house is a low tavern, and on the bar-room walls are colored prints of Washington and Queen Victoria, and the American eagle. . . . What place is this, to which the squalid square conducts us? A kind of square of leprous houses, some of which are attainable only by crazy wooden stairs without. What lies beyond this tottering flight of steps that creak beneath our tread? A miserable room lighted by one dim candle, and destitute of all comfort, save that which may be hidden in a wretched bed. Beside it sits a man; his elbows on his knees, his forehead hidden in his hands. 'What ails that man?' asks the foremost officer. 'Fever,' he sullenly replies, without looking up. Conceive the fancies of a fevered brain in such a place as this! Ascend these pitch-dark stairs, heedful of a false footing on the trembling boards, and grope your way, with me, into this wolfish den, where neither ray of light nor breath of air appears to come. A negro lad, startled from his sleep by the officer's voice—he knows it well—but comforted by his assurance that he has not come on business, officiously bestirs himself to light a candle. The match flickers for a moment, and shows great mounds of dusky rags upon the ground, then dies away, and leaves a denser darkness than before, if there can be degrees in such extremes. He stumbles down the stairs, and presently comes back shading a flaring taper with his hands. Then the mounds of rags are seen to be astir, and rise slowly up, and the floor is covered with heaps of negro women, waking from their sleep, their white teeth chattering, and their bright eyes glistening and winking on all sides, with surprise and fear, like the countless repetition of one astonished African face in some strange mirror. Mount up these other stairs with no less caution (there are traps and pitfalls here for those who are not so well escorted as ourselves) into the housetop, where the bare beams and rafters meet over head, and calm night looks down through the crevices in the roof.   Open the door of one of these cramped hutches, full of sleeping negroes.   Bah ! they have a charcoal fire within, there is a smell of singeing clothes or flesh, so close they gather round the brazier, and vapors issue forth that blind and suffocate.

"From every corner, as you glance about you in these dark streets, some figure crawls, half-awakened, as if the judgment-hour were near at hand, and every obscure grave were giving up its dead.   Where dogs would howl to lie, women, men, and boys slink off to sleep, forcing the dislodged rats to move away in quest of better lodgings.   Here, too, are lanes and alleys paved with mud knee-deep ; underground chambers, where they dance and game, the walls bedecked with rough designs of ships, and forts, and flags, and American eagles, out of number ; ruined houses, open to the streets, whence, through wide gaps in the walls, other ruins loom upon the eye, as though the world of vice and misery had nothing else to show ; hideous tenements which take their name from robbery and murder ; all that is loathsome, drooping, and decayed is here ! "

Thus forbidding, in only a passing visit, did this locality appear to Mr. Dickens.   But this is only a faint picture of the reality.   "It was a God-forsaken place," says one of the reports of the House of Industry, "where neither education nor religion was permitted to enter, and the respectable inhabitants of New York, though then living not far from the scene, were callous of, and indifferent to, the fearful degradation which there existed.   Certainly as no spot of ground on this continent had the reputation of having been the witness of more crime, so no spot had such repulsive features or exhibited want and woe in darker colors. Every house was a brothel, the resort of persons of every age, sex, and color, every store a dram-shop, where, from morning until evening, the thieves and abandoned characters of the town whetted their depraved tastes, and concocted future crimes and villanies."

Into this waste of sin and wretchedness went these heroic and devoted ladies, accompanied by their minister appointed by the New-York Methodist Conference, Rev. L. M. Pease, a man of remarkable magnetic power, and having many endowments peculiarly fitting him for this work. A hall was hired and it was filled on the first Sabbath, and seventy scholars were formed into a Sunday-school. The obstacles in the way of these pioneers were appalling, but they were successfully overcome from the first. An advisory committee of Christian gentlemen, practical business men, was selected, who cordially yielded their advice and pecuniary aid in carrying forward the undertaking. In 1852, having long felt the need of sufficient room, one of the ladies, who had been a ward visitor of the New-York Clothing Society, proposed the purchase of the Old Brewery— a name which it bore from the business once carried on in it, but at this time inhabited by hundreds of the most depraved characters—as offering a favorable site for a mission-house, and abolishing at one blow one of the most terrible resorts of crime and vice, embraced in the field of their labors. A daily paper, describing the place as it then stood, says: * " An alley extends all around the building; on the north side it is of irregular width, wide at the entrance, and gradually tapering to a point.

* As quoted in the "Old Brewery," p. 47.

The Old Brewery.

On the opposite side the passage-way is known by the name of
'Murderer's Alley,' a filthy, narrow path, scarcely three feet in
width.   (Another portion of the alley was called the Den of
Thieves.)   There are double rows of rooms throughout the
building, entered by the alley-ways on either side. . . The dark
and winding passage-ways, which extend throughout the whole

building, must have afforded a convenient means of escape to
thieves and criminals of all kinds; there are various hiding
places recently discovered, which have also, no doubt, afforded
the means of escape to offenders against the laws.   In the floor
in one of the upper rooms, a place was found where the boards
had been sawed; upon tearing them up, human bones were

found, the remains, no doubt, of a victim of some diabolical murder. Our way was explored by the aid of a single lamp, in company with two gentlemen and a guide; besides these, were a number of rather rough-looking customers, who appeared as much interested as any one else. But it was not until one of the gentlemen complained, in one of the dark passage-ways, of a strange hand in his pocket, that their characters were suspected. Then our guide informed us, in an undertone, that we were surrounded by a gang of the most notorious pickpockets and thieves of that section, and that we must take good care of our watches, or we should lose them. . . . The basement of the building is even worse than the upper part. In a lower room not more than fifteen feet square, twenty-six human beings reside. A man could scarcely stand erect in it. Two men were sitting by the blaze of a few sticks when our company entered; women lay on a mass of filthy, unsightly rags in a corner, sick, feeble, and emaciated; six or seven children were in various attitudes about the corner, and the smoke and stench of the room were so suffocating that it could not long be endured."

The announcement of such a site for a mission was received with surprise, but further consideration showed the wisdom of the proposer. The property was purchased; the old walls, that had long resounded with curses, were demolished, and the corner-stone of the new edifice was laid by Rev. Bishop Janes, with the impressive words: " For the promotion of education, of virtue, and of religion, and to promote the best interests of men, and the glory of God, we now lay the corner-stone of this edifice, in the name of the Father, and of the Son, and of the Holy Ghost." Where was once the foulest haunt in the city, is now to be seen a plain and substantial structure, containing within its ample walls a chapel, parsonage, school-rooms, bathing-rooms, and tenements for twenty families.

During the eighteen years since its organization the Society, enjoying the aid of a succession of excellent ministers, by domiciliary visits, by sermons, by lectures, by temperance associations,

by day-schools, and Sunday-schools, has been operating upon the individual members of this wretched population. The result may be stated in figures, and may be seen by the eye in the entire physical change of the vicinity, and in the increased value of property, but the chief results can only be measured by the

Divine eye—the hearts that have been redeemed and made
happy, the thousands of young lives that have been snatched
from courses of sin, the inspiration that has been given to hundreds of others in different parts of our land and England to
"go and do likewise"—the full measure of these results God
only knows.   Each one of the original band of ladies entering
upon the work still survives, to enjoy the wonderful success that
has followed their humble commencement.   Rev. J. N. Shaffer
has been for a number of years their missionary, entering heartily, and with great prudence and devotion, into the various opportunities afforded him for the execution of his truly evangel-
ical mission.

About a thousand destitute children have been placed in
good and permanent homes in the country.   Although originated and managed by members of the Methodist Episcopal
Church, it has been generously sustained by different denominations, and has been conducted in the most catholic and unsec-
tarian manner.

The first missionary, Mr. Pease, conceived from the beginning
of his work a broader scheme than the constitution of the Mission or the funds at the command of the ladies justified.   De-
siring to redeem the adults, as well as the children, if possible,
he saw that nothing could be done without providing forms of
honest remunerative labor for them.   His widely different views
soon separated him from the original organization, and hiring
several houses upon his own responsibility, he and his wife with
extraordinary self-denial and diligence devoting themselves to
the work, he filled his rooms with the former occupants of the
wretched dens around him, provided them with work, disposed
of their manufactures, opened schools, and conducted religious

services, until his strength began to yield under the burden. The community became greatly interested in his movements, and aid in the form of money and personal assistance was freely offered.

In 1854 the Mission was surrendered into the hands of a body of trustees, formed under an act of incorporation from the Legislature, Mr. Pease still remaining Superintendent. Through munificent bequests and donations, an immense edifice, adapted

to all the purposes of such a mission, and known far and wide as the Five Points House of Industry, was erected, nearly opposite the Mission-house of the ladies.

In the thirteen years of its existence, in addition to its charitable work in the House and out of doors, and to the opportunities for labor which it has supplied, the House of Industry has gathered within its walls 18,087 children, and has, as is also the case with its neighbor at the present time, between four and five hundred pupils from the vagrant class in its schools.

A farm was purchased in Westchester, for the employment of the boys, to which Mr. Pease retired upon the failure of his health in 1857. This farm eventually came into the hands of a Lutheran association, under the direction of Rev. Mr. Passevant, who proposes the establishment of orphan-houses, upon the plan of Wichern in his Rough House at the Horn, in Hamburg.

Mr. Pease was followed by able successors : Mr. Talcott, now of the Providence Reform School ; the beloved, devoted, and martyr Barlow, who fell a victim to his self-denying zeal ; and the present Superintendent, S. B. Halliday, than whom, perhaps, no one is more familiar with the poverty, misery, and crime of the city, or has more judicious views of the best agents and agencies to meet the existing condition of things.

The trustees of the House of Industry have of late taken another advance step toward the abatement of social crime, on the part of exposed young females in the city, by opening a large and well-arranged boarding-house, on Elizabeth Street, called "The Working-Women's Home," where neat accommodations and wholesome food, with the privileges of a Christian family, can be secured at a very low price per week.

In 1855, Rev. W. C. Van Meter, a young Baptist clergyman, having just graduated from a seminary at Granville, Ohio, on his way to visit New York, fell upon Solon Robinson's touching story of "Hot Corn," founded upon incidents gathered in the mission-work at Five Points. A man of ardent temper, of the tenderest sensibilities, with a peculiar love for children, and earnest in his devotion to the cause of his Master, his soul was set on fire by the irresistible pathos of the story of the little redeemed outcast. Among the first places he visited in the city was the Ladies' Mission. He united with them in their religious services. His heartiness, his tenderness, his simple and affecting eloquence, drew attention to him at once, and arrangements were made to secure his services to present the claims of the work to the community, and to discharge the duties of a missionary. His acquaintance with the West, its wants, and its opportunities, suggested to his mind the expediency of removing the poor friendless children from the city, and placing them in families that would eagerly receive them and bring them up as their own. In May, 1855, he took the first delegation of the children of the street, and transported them westward, attracting much attention by the way.

He had left the service of the Mission, for a Bible agency, in 1861, when, being struck with the terrible moral condition of the Fourth Ward of our city, with a tenant population packed in at the rate of two hundred and ninety thousand to the square mile, almost destitute of Protestant instruction, with as many rum-shops as tenements, with the vilest dance-houses and dens of infamy in the city, and swarming with neglected children, he said to himself, " This is my field of labor ; here I can distribute personally and most effectually the Word of God." Starting out like Müller, of Bristol, in simple dependence upon a Divine Providence, he hired rooms, resolved not to go in debt, and not to turn a destitute child from his door. He called his house " The Howard Mission and Home for Little Wanderers." He sought not the aid of the Legislature nor of the city authorities, but threw himself upon the charity of the religious community, not of this city only, but of the land, as the whole country, in a degree, is affected by the moral condition of the city.* His faith was justified by the results. During seven years he has been able to make provision for seven thousand five hundred and eighty-one children, of clothing, food, instruction, and, where it has been required, of suitable homes in the country. After working alone for three years, he surrendered the work into the hands of an incorporated Board of Trustees, by whom he is employed as the Superintendent of the Mission.

Upon the expiration of the lease of the buildings, which he had hired, last year (1867), the trustees, sustained by a generous community, secured lots on the opposite side of the street, and are erecting a suite of edifices adapted to the various benevolent

* Mr. Oliver Dyer thus presents the claims of the city upon the country : " Our country friends must help us, not only for our own protection, but for theirs also. In some respects the evils which result from the present condition of things in this city fall more heavily on them than on us. The statistics of vice and crime show that their ranks are more largely recruited from the families of the State at large, than from the native families of this city. Young men and young women are constantly coming hither from other parts of the State to seek their fortunes, and too often they find them in a felon's cell, or a castaway's grave. The minions of vice and debauchery go forth from this city to the utmost bounds of the State, seeking whom they may lure into the ways which lead to death. There are keepers of houses of ill-fame in this city who have daughters at country boarding-schools, under assumed names,—whether sent there as decoys, or to escape their mothers' shame, we cannot tell ; but, in any event, what virtuous mother would not shudder at the thought of her daughter's sharing the room and bed of one of these children of sin and infamy !

" A faint notion of the result of all these things may be conceived by considering the fact that, at the last investigation of this matter, made a few months ago, there were one hundred and eighty-three families living in the State at large, represented among the abandoned women of this city. That is an average of over three families to a county, and more are coming all the time. Not a week passes that the railroad trains do not bear hither, from other parts of the State, fugitive daughters fleeing from homes which shall know them no more forever."

operations of the Society.   The effect of this mission upon this
dark quarter of the city, especially upon its exposed childhood,
is manifest.

The site which Mr. Van Meter had previously used has been
bought by the Roman Catholics, and a very handsome edifice,
under the care of the Society of St. Vincent de Paul, has been
erected, called the St. James's School.   It is intended to offer the
same opportunities to neglected Catholic children that the Home
for Little Wanderers has offered to all indiscriminately.   It also
serves as a house of detention for the Catholic protectorate at
West Farms, and, in this capacity, receives an annual appropriation from the city.

These positive preventive movements, instituted within those
precincts of the city where heretofore juvenile crime has been
nurtured, have been eminently useful in decreasing the vicious
and perishing classes, and have excited much attention and interest throughout our country and Europe.   In Boston, Philadelphia, Chicago, Cleveland, and other cities, similar missions
have been instituted, and in our city, among both Protestants
and Catholics, other enterprises somewhat similar have been
undertaken.

One of the most interesting of these is the St. Barnabas
House and Chapel, under the auspices of the Protestant Episcopal Church, and intimately associated in its mission work with
the House of Mercy and the Sheltering Arms.   These several
institutions, in different parts of the city, receive and administer
to all forms of want, weakness, and exposure, of both sexes and
all ages.   The chief duties in the truly benevolent work of these
institutions, under the direction of clergymen, are performed by
a body of intelligent Christian women, voluntarily associating

themselves under the title of the Protestant Sisterhood of St. Mary. Since 1866 the officers of the St. Barnabas House have instituted a "Midnight Mission" among the abandoned girls of the city, which has been attended with quite encouraging success.

In the commencement of the half century which we have been considering, the minds of thoughtful men were drawn to the injudicious multiplication of eleemosynary institutions, and to the evil effect of an unwise administration of charity in the encouragement and nurture of pauperism. In 1842–'43, this same condition of things again attracted the attention of thoughtful men. It was found that there were in the city " between thirty and forty benevolent societies in operation for the relief of particular classes of the indigent, and which united moral objects with the relief of physical want. It had become evident, however, from the results, that their modes of relief were defective. For, even with this enlarged provision, in addition to the supplies of legal charity, while every class of the indigent appeared to be provided for, the streets were still filled with mendicants, the benevolent harassed with applications, and importunate impostors constantly obtaining the aid which was designed only for the needy and deserving." *

A consideration of these facts resulted in the formation of the " New-York Association for the Improvement of the Condition of the Poor." Under the judicious administration of the Corresponding Secretary and General Agent of this Society, Robert M. Hartley, Esq., the whole system of public and voluntary charity in the city has been greatly simplified, directed to legitimate objects, a harmony of action between different asso-

* Eighth Annual Report of the New-York Juvenile Asylum.

ciations secured, and a residence in the work-house made the involuntary condition of the sturdy beggars that heretofore infested the streets.

No association for the improvement of the poor can proceed far in the inquiry as to the cause of pauperism without being confronted with the fact that juvenile vagrancy and truancy form the great fountain of supply for mendicancy, intemperance, and criminality. This association found itself forced to consider the fact that many thousand children, without proper guardians, were wandering in the streets and prowling around the markets, docks, and public resorts, constantly tempted, and falling into a criminal life. They found their number was so large that the Refuge could not accommodate them if any serious effort were made to relieve the streets of their presence; and they considered their characters to be still so unhardened and hopeful, that, after a short training of perhaps three or four months, they might be safely removed into the country. Thus, with the same accommodations, a very much larger number of youth might be instructed for a season, and then be placed away from the temptations of the city.

Public attention was drawn to the matter by able articles in the daily and religious prints, and very general interest among benevolent men was excited. In October of 1849, a committee of the Association, consisting of Joseph B. Collins, Thomas Denny, Frederick S. Winston, Apollos R. Wetmore, and Robert M. Hartley, was appointed, to consider, among other things, the subject of making some effectual provision for the benefit of the depraved children of the city. To this committee were afterward added Benjamin F. Butler, Luther Bradish, and Horatio Allen. After entering upon their work, the committee learned, through the mayor of the city, Hon. Caleb S. Wood-hull, that another company of gentlemen were engaged in the consideration of the same question. These persons—Dr. John D. Ross, who became the first superintendent of the institution which grew out of this movement, Solomon Jenner, James H. Titus, and Isaac Hopper—were invited to a common meeting at the mayor's office, and, after the discussion of various proposi-tions, a sub-committee was appointed to present the subject to the State Legislature, and to secure an act of incorporation. The result of their efforts was, that the State Legislature, for 1851, constituted twenty-four well-known and benevolent mer-chants of the city as a body corporate under the title of the "New York Juvenile Asylum," for the purpose of receiving such children, between the ages of seven and fourteen, as might be voluntarily intrusted to their care by parents, or be committed to them by competent legal authority. By an equal voluntary subscription and appropriation from the city Super-visors, the ample and handsome structures for the House of Re-ception, in the heart of the city, and the Asylum, near High Bridge, were constructed.

The annual expenses of the institution are borne by the sub-scriptions of individuals and the city government; its Execu-tive and the president of the Council are *ex-officio* members of its Board. Two hundred thousand dollars have been con-tributed by private benevolence for the purposes of the institu-tion since its establishment.

In its House of Reception all vagrant children of the street can be placed, and, if proper guardians do not appear within ten days (notice being given, if they can be found), the child becomes the ward of the Asylum, to be trained, discharged, or indentured through its minority, at the discretion of its managers.

The institution has been admirably conducted, and has been an object of deserved pride to its managers and to the city. Its schools have been efficiently sustained, and the moral influence of the Asylum has been excellent over the characters of its young protégés.

Its Board has very thoroughly organized the work of sending children to the West, employing a permanent and intelligent agent, who makes his residence in Chicago, and becomes, by personal examination, familiar with the most favorable portions of the country for the distribution of the children sent from the institution. Within a short period arrangements have been made to open a House of Reception in Chicago, to receive any child that may be returned by the party taking him, as unsuitable or incorrigible. A very important addition this is to their other facilities for placing these children in Western homes. Their agent is expected, also, to make periodical visits to the children, and keep up a correspondence with the families where they are placed. More than two thousand eight hundred children have already been sent to Western homes.

The managers have the power, of which they avail themselves, of committing incorrigible subjects to the House of Refuge. In the period of sixteen years its Board has had, for a longer or shorter period, under its control, nearly thirteen thousand children (12,942).

Their two Houses are now in an admirable condition of neatness and efficiency, and are filled almost to their utmost comfortable limit. The Superintendent, Dr. Brooks, is an intelligent and skilful physician, and a gentleman of large experience in the

NEW YORK JUVENILE ASYLUM

175 ᵗʰ St. near 10 ᵗʰ Avenue

1856.

government and training of neglected children, having been Superintendent for a number of years of the Farm School connected with the State Almshouse Department, in Massachusetts. The Asylum near High Bridge, with its five or six hundred boys and girls, is an honor to the city, and is making a manifest impression upon the vagrant children of New York.

Ragged Schools, as they were called, some years before these American missions among the perishing classes of the community, had been organized and prosecuted with encouraging success in England.

These collections of the lowest and most vicious of the street children in various cities of Great Britain originated in the interesting experiment of a poor shoemaker, in the town of Portsmouth. Through an accident which happened to him in the dock-yard, where his father was a sawyer, when he was fifteen years of age, John Pounds was crippled for life. The sad condition of a little nephew, who was a cripple, like himself, awakened his sympathies. He adopted the lad, and, as he was not in a condition to pay for his education, he undertook it himself. To make study more agreeable to the boy, he sought in the streets, among the outcast and poorest of the children, companions for him. Becoming greatly interested in the work, he continued and enlarged it, when the boy for whose sake it was first established no longer needed his instructions. Finally, the school gathered within his humble shop consisted of forty scholars, including twelve girls.

These children were the most destitute and degraded in the town. He called them his "little blackguards." "Many a time he has been known to go out upon the public quay and tempt such as these, by the offer of a roasted potato, or some such simple thing, to enter his school. There is something in the voice and manner of an earnest, truthful man, which is irresistible; it is an appeal made to that divine image of which there is some trace still left in the most corrupted heart; and it was seldom, therefore, that the summons of John Pounds passed unheeded; and when once at the school, his scholars seldom needed urging to come a second time, for their master taught them not only ' book-learning,' as he called it, but his trade; if they were hungry, he gave them food; if ragged, he clothed them as best he could; and, added to all this, he joined in their sports." * It is certainly no matter of wonder, that when he died, suddenly, in 1839, at the age of seventy-two, " the poor children who then formed his class wept, and some of them fainted on hearing the news."

The success of this individual experiment in Portsmouth attracted many eyes in Great Britain and in this country. A society was formed soon after the death of John Pounds, in the Scotch city of Aberdeen, under the leadership of Sheriff Watson, for the purpose of supplying instruction to all the vagrant children of the city, in connection with wholesome meals and industrial occupation.

" The police were instructed by the magistrates to convey every child, found begging in the streets, to a large room, which also served as a soup-kitchen; and thither, on the 19th of May, 1845, seventy-five children, boys and girls, were taken. The scene which ensued was almost indescribable: confusion, uproar, quarrelling, fighting, and language of the most horrible kind, were to be encountered and vanquished. The task was a hard one, but the committee, before the evening, succeeded in estab-

---

* Philosophy of Ragged Schools, p. 43.

lishing something like order. The children were then told that this place was open for them to return to daily, and they were invited for the morrow, but were, at the same time, told that, whether they came or not, they would not longer be allowed to beg, since food, no less than instruction, was offered to them there. The next day the greater portion returned, and the committee of managers were able soon to report the most gratifying results. 'Whereas a few years since,' they say, 'there were three hundred and twenty children in the town, and three hundred and twenty-eight in the county of Aberdeen, who, impelled, by their own or their parents' necessities, to cater for their immediate wants, prowled about the streets, and roved over the country—cheating and stealing their daily avocation—now a begging child is rarely to be seen, and *juvenile crime* is comparatively unknown.' " *

This example was soon followed with very encouraging, if not equally successful, results, in various parts of the kingdom. The effect upon juvenile and adult crime was noticeable, and the Christian spirit and effort called forth by the missions among the abandoned classes powerfully impressed even those who had been trained in vice. A notorious thief said to one of the missionary teachers in London, who visited him in prison: "I always considered religion all humbug, and the persons humbugs who were paid for praying and preaching, but, when I see people taking young thieves, who are following in my steps, out of the streets to save them from ruin, this is something like Christianity."

Just about the period of the establishment of the Juvenile Asylum, a young man from Litchfield, Connecticut, was pur-

---

* Philosophy of Ragged Schools.

suing his theological studies in the Union Theological Seminary, in this city. Seeking opportunities for usefulness on the Sabbath, he offered his services in aid of Mr. Pease, in his mission among the wretched children of the Five Points, to the public penal and charitable institutions, and to the singular meetings which were instituted a little before this time among the Arab boys of the streets and docks by Mr. A. D. F. Randolph, then connected with the American S. S. Union, and others, called "Boys' Meetings," the first and most remarkable one being held on the corner of Hudson and Christopher Streets. Upon finishing his course at the seminary, Mr. Charles Loring Brace (for this was the young theologian's name) in company with his friend Olmsted, author of "Walks and Talks of an American Farmer," travelled, on foot, over Great Britain, and a considerable portion of Europe. He gave his attention especially to the consideration of the condition of the lowest, the vagrant, and criminal classes, and the measures taken for their elevation and reformation, in the countries he visited.

Upon his return, while engaged in the preparation of the various volumes in which he has embodied the results of his observations and studies, he devoted himself to a more thorough personal investigation of the most wretched portions of the city. He was appalled by the multitudes of neglected children, growing up amid the powerful and constant temptations of the streets, which he met in his inspection of the lower portions of the city. He immediately commenced a series of very vigorous and stirring articles in the religious and secular prints, calling the attention of the community to facts that came under his personal observation. He felt much as did Wichern, that, if New York were ever redeemed, some positive and wide-spread measures must be instituted for the rescue of the thousands of exposed children filling the city streets.

After more than a year's trial of voluntary labors on the islands among prisoners, and at the Five Points, he says, in his interesting introduction to his "Sermons to the Newsboys:" "I became convinced that no far-reaching and permanent work of reform could succeed among these classes. It was right that those who loved humanity in its lowest forms should labor for the forlorn prostitute and the mature criminal. But, on a broad scale, no lasting effects could be produced to society from such efforts. The hopeful field was evidently among the young. There crime might possibly be checked in its very beginnings, and the seeds of future good character, and order, and virtue, be widely sown."

He drew into conference with each other a number of benevolent and intelligent men, who had been interested in the boys' meetings, such as Judge Mason, B. J. Howland, W. L. King, W. C. Russell, and J. E. Williams, and finally a Society was formed in February, 1853, called the "Children's Aid Society," of which he has been, from the first to the present time, the inspiring agent in its multifarious measures, and its able secretary. Calling out the best talents of the leading Christian gentlemen and ladies of the city, the Society has established industrial day-schools, sixteen of which are now in operation, providing clothing and food, as well as industrial and intellectual instruction, for the children, and Sabbath-schools, in various portions of the city, where the moral degradation of the children rendered the work the more urgent.

The most interesting field of the Society's operations has been among the little street merchants, bootblacks, and newsboys, and the homeless girls of the city.   In 1854, over the *Sun* office, on Fulton Street, Mr. Brace inaugurated the first " Newsboys' Lodgings," where, for a few cents, a clean berth, a good bath, and a meal could be obtained by the homeless boys of the streets.   A house was afterward opened for the girls, and other similar lodgings have been constituted.   By moral instructions, the economy of a Savings Bank, and Sabbath services, these very popular institutions have been rendered of incalculable benefit to the wandering youth of the metropolis.

The great work of the Society, however, is, by monthly companies, to gather from all these depositories—lodgings and industrial schools, from almshouses and the streets—neglected children, and to transport them to the far Western States, to be distributed in the families of farmers and mechanics.   In fifteen years the Society has sent out fourteen thousand eight hundred and seventy-nine persons—a large proportion of them boys and girls.

All these important and interesting movements for the prevention of juvenile crime were going on while the stately proportions of the House of Refuge were rising upon their foundations.   The Divine Spirit inspired the movers in these benevolent schemes, and a Divine Providence brought them to an efficient condition.   With all their combined efforts we have hardly kept pace with juvenile crime, and the immense capacity of the Refuge has already been fully tested.   The good work of training its unfortunate children went quietly on in its crowded halls at Bellevue during the years the new edifice was in construction.

On the first of December, 1853, the Chaplain for nearly a quarter of a century, Rev Thomas S. Barrett, M. D., a lay minister of the Methodist Episcopal Church, died in great peace. Of him the managers bear the kind testimony that, "without any brilliant qualities, or any pretensions to extensive learning, he had much that was of more importance in his sphere. He had a heart warmly interested in his work, a manner that caused his hearers to be interested in him and his teachings, and a way of making great doctrines level to the comprehension of the anomalous audience to which it was his duty to minister."

Forty years ago there was no name more familiar to the childhood of the land than that of Mahlon Day. As the printer and publisher of the juvenile literature of the times, his name became a household word. He was a man of fine presence, with a most benignant countenance, becoming in his manner the plain dress of the Friends, of whose Society he was a member, and rendered the more impressive himself by it. Very fond of children, his presence was welcomed with delight, especially by the younger members of the institution, when his radiant face appeared in the yard. His wife, Mary Day, was one of the lady visitors. Like Zacharias and Elizabeth, "they were both righteous before God, walking in all the commandments and ordinances of the Lord blameless." In the calamitous loss of the steamer Arctic, by a collision with another vessel while crossing the Atlantic, they met a common and solemn death (but one for which they were undoubtedly well prepared), with nearly three hundred other passengers. It is said that Mr. Day was near one of the boats crowded with rescued passengers. They proposed to take him in, and even urged him to permit them to lift him into the boat. He saw it was full; he feared his additional weight would peril other lives. He declined to avail himself of possible salvation at another's risk. Calmly bidding them all farewell, he unclasped his hands from the boat and sunk out of sight. "The care of the youthful outcasts, gathered within the House of Refuge," say the managers, of Mahlon and Mary Day, "enlisted their sympathies and united their labors in the same work. Their friendly counsels to the children, imparted with almost parental kindness, exerted the happiest influence upon their susceptible minds, and have left, without doubt, wholesome impressions on many a heart. Mr Day had been a manager for about ten years, during several of which he had discharged faithfully the arduous duties of a member of the Indenturing Committee. The companion of his life was a member of the Ladies' Committee. Death summoned them together from a career of active usefulness."

While earnestly contemplating the hour when the new buildings would obviate the present crowded condition of their halls, the managers speak with great confidence of the character and permanence of the work they were effecting. "Of the six thousand children and youth," they say, "who have been inmates of the House, it is but fair to presume that the greater portion would, but for the intervention of the Refuge, have been inmates of our prisons, and that but a comparatively small portion of them have become such, gives an incalculable value to this establishment."

The sale of the property on Twenty-third Street secured for the managers the sum of $172,625. The remainder of the amount necessary to complete the two large edifices for boys and girls, with their appropriate out-buildings, schools, kitchens, and shops, was supplied by successive annual appropriations from the State. The ultimate cost of the completed establishment was $470,000. Of this amount the building committee remark:

"We can say with entire confidence that no part of this large sum has been misapplied or expended in useless experiment, or inappropriate ornament. The House of Refuge, as it now stands on Randall's Island, complete in all its various departments, while presenting a fine and imposing appearance in its structure and architectural arrangement, at the same time gives no evidence of extravagant and needless expenditure."

The several committees of the Legislature before whom members of the Board annually appeared to present the estimates for building for the ensuing year, in addition to the current expenses, always received them with the utmost courtesy; and the long history of faithful management had so effectually won the confidence of the community, that these vast sums of money were unhesitatingly committed to their discretion, subject to the review of the Executive and the Comptroller of the State.

It was a work of ten years before the whole plan was brought to a successful conclusion; entered upon in 1851 by the Board, it was near the end of 1861 before the Building Committee closed up its accounts.

As the main building, which for some time was occupied by both sexes, approached its completion, arrangements were made to remove from the old site. It was an important era again in the history of the institution, and was fully appreciated by the managers. "Its removal," they remark, in the thirtieth annual report, rendered January, 1855, "to a site distant from the residences of the managers, has rendered it necessary to review the whole plan of conducting the business, the chief part of which has been transacted hitherto through the Acting Committee. This committee has met once a week regularly, since the establishment of the New-York House of Refuge, and every item of business, whether relating to contracts, to ordering supplies, to the payment of bills, or any matter connected with the internal management, has been considered and acted upon with scrupulous care and diligence.   Precise punctuality has been their rule, and it has been a rare event for a single failure to occur in the meetings of the committee in the course of the entire year. A visiting committee, appointed by them, has been charged with the duty of examining the institution once a week.   A sub-committee from the Ladies' Committee has performed the same duty for the female department.   This service has been in addition to the visits of the Indenturing and School Committees, in the discharge of their functions.   The whole financial business of the Acting Committee will now be transferred to the whole Board of Managers, who will alone authorize the payment of bills.   An Executive Committee of three will meet at the House once in each week, to transact such business relating to the management of the institution as may come before them.   They will perform the duties of the Visiting Committee, and in part those of the former Acting Committee.   The Ladies' Committee will provide for a visitation of the female department once in two weeks. The Indenturing Committee will hold stated meetings at the same interval, in lieu of their weekly sessions.   The School Committee will perform their service as heretofore.   It is believed that the scheme, in its various details, will be found manageable and efficient.   [All this it has fully proved itself to be.]   The Board of Managers have also revised the entire organization of the establishment, and adopted a new set of rules and regulations for its government and management.   The enlargement of the institution, the character of the location, the extent of the premises, and the arrangements rendered practicable by the improved plan of the buildings, demanded many changes. The principal of these refer to the classification of the inmates. The boys and girls are to be divided respectively into two distinct grades. The boys assigned to the higher moral grade will be subjected to a more lenient discipline, and enjoy superior privileges. (As a matter of fact, however, excepting the additional hour of labor, there is no variation in the discipline of the two divisions.) A separate time-table for each will distribute six hours of labor in the day to the one class, and from seven to eight to the other." The grounds of distinction between the divisions they state as follows: " Those who, from their previous career, may be deemed disposed and likely to contaminate their companions, or who may exhibit an intractable disposition, either before commitment or during their residence in the House, shall occupy the north wing. Those of a less depraved character, and more liable to be injured by the corrupting companionship of hardened offenders, shall occupy the south wing. The age of the vagrant or delinquent shall not be conclusive, nor even his good conduct in the institution, in determining his position; but the danger of imparting or receiving contamination shall constitute the main consideration."

The same provision was made for the classification of the girls.

On the last day of October, 1854, the inmates of the Refuge, now numbering about four hundred, were removed to the new building on Randall's Island, and on the 24th of the following November it was formally opened by very impressive public services. There were present among the guests, Hon. Horatio Seymour, Governor of the State, members of the State Legislature, the Mayor and Council of the city, and a large number of distinguished citizens. The religious services were conducted by Drs. Adams and Cuyler. The singing was by the children, under the lead of Julius Hart, Esq.

The opening speech of President Kelly was remarkably appropriate and eloquent. Referring to the fact, that the New-York Refuge was a pioneer institution, and that succeeding institutions had been largely modelled after its plan, he remarked, that the fact " that experience has shown so little to amend in the original scheme, and that so few changes have been introduced in the various places where these institutions have been established, affords the highest testimony that can be offered to the enlightened and practical judgment of the founders of the New-York House of Refuge. The improvements that have been introduced were generally anticipated by them, and the principle of separation into grades seems to have been recognized at an early period. The importance of this principle, with respect to females, was particularly and constantly noticed by the managers and the Ladies' Committee, under whose special charge, as to moral discipline, the Female House has always been placed. New York may, therefore, justly present a claim of precedence in this important department of benevolence and reform. . . . .

" For several years past the institution has received annually about four hundred children of both sexes. This process of absorption, going on constantly, is rendering an important service to society. It is like the abstraction of so much poison . . . The whole number admitted since the commencement is 6,269 ; the number now in the House, 401, namely, 331 boys, and 70 girls, leaving 5,868 as the number who have passed from under its care, including those who have been surrendered to their friends, and not deducting the few deaths that have occurred.

There is satisfactory evidence that a large proportion of these children have been saved to society, to become industrious and orderly men and women.

" This institution blends the characteristics of a private, a city, and a State institution. The management of charities by associations of citizens, devoting themselves, from benevolent and disinterested motives, to the task, is a strictly American invention, and has been found in practice a highly economical and advantageous system. There are some charities, and among them schools of reformation, which perhaps could not be conducted at all except under such a system, or some arrangement which would secure in the service citizens of the same character and qualifications. If abuses arise, there is, of course, power enough in the public authorities to interfere."

Of the subjects of their reformatory work, Mr. Kelly uses these admirable words : " A divinely-imaged soul lies wrapped up in the life of each one of these children, and the moral lineaments of his heavenly birth may be restored. They are sufficiently impressible to lay aside old, and to put on new habits. Past deficiencies may be remedied by instruction and discipline. Their false idea of the constituent elements of human happiness may be removed by implanting true views of life, with its duties, its responsibilities, and its retributions. Their conceptions of their own position in the world may be transformed into earnest and hopeful aspirations. The love of vicious excitement may be superseded by purer tastes and higher motives. This is the spirit which should pervade the whole scheme of reformatory discipline for the youthful vagrant or offender. Who of us, that has never been exposed to the temptations that have surrounded these children, and has been trained, from infancy almost, in the knowledge of the Scriptures, and in all that is wholesome, and pure, and true, can put his hand upon his heart, and declare that he is, by nature, any better than one of them? Who of us dare to say, that if he had been exposed to the same influences, he would have preserved his integrity, and come out of the fiery ordeal unscathed? The sight of such a group of children as is collected in those seats, and in yonder gallery, should fill us with humility, and teach us lessons of mercy. . . . .

"It is no degradation to the children that they have been confined in this House; on the contrary, it is a progressive step in their elevation to the rank and character of respectable citizens. And happily, it does not act as a process of degradation upon them. Instead of impairing their self-respect, it tends to awaken a sentiment of dignity by the reflection and conviction that there is nothing now to prevent their rising. When they are ready to leave the institution, they go forth with a fair education, and with habits of industry adequate to provide for their wants. A sense of independence, therefore, accompanies them. The fact, that there has been no cessation in the demand for apprentices since the commencement, is an evidence that others do not regard our children as reprobates. The moral, mental, and industrial training they have received makes them valuable as apprentices. And when they enter upon the new course of life, after graduating from the House, there is no stigma branded upon their characters, rendering their intercourse with others embarrassing or disagreeable. Those who conduct with propriety acquire the esteem of the families where they live, and of the acquaintances they form, and gradually rise to a perfectly independent and respectable position. . . .

Has become a "City of Refuge."

"The House of Refuge has, at length, a permanent resting-place, capable of any extension that may be found necessary hereafter, on a location uniting in its advantages nearly all the conditions that could be desired. Fifteen years has been the term of its occupation at each of the former sites. There is no reason to doubt that it will remain here for centuries; for we cannot hope that the time will ever come when it will not be wanted. In view, therefore, of the future, and the important character of the work, it is the part of sound wisdom to project the material arrangements upon a liberal scale, and to provide in the structure every thing likely to conduce to the object in view. A House of Refuge, worthy of the City and the State of New York, should not be restricted in the means and appliances that are necessary to develop a perfect system of juvenile reform. . . . This is no longer a House—it is a City of Refuge. The managers have fully realized the magnitude of the undertaking. . . . It is now seven years since the project was started, and it has taken all that time to surmount the various obstacles that were to be overcome. The honor of initiating the movement belongs to one whose name is recorded on the tablet in the vestibule, but is, we trust, recorded on the imperishable tablet of an eternal mansion, David C. Colden. Foremost on the roll of the first Board of Managers of the Society stands the name of Cadwallader D. Colden; foremost let the name of the son be placed, in connection with the foundation of the latter House. Next in order, but second to none, in the value of his services, in his devotion to the cause of benevolence, in his talents and unrelaxing energy, ranks another, whose name has also disappeared from our list of managers, David Seymour. . . . Of the present managers, I will content myself with giving you the names of the Building Committee, under whose charge the building has been erected: Charles M. Leupp, Linus W. Stevens, Elias G. Drake, Joshua S. Underhill, J. W. C. Leveridge. I must allude particularly to the service of one member of the committee, for I know his colleagues will be dissatisfied with me if I fail to do so. Randall's Island bears a twofold testimony to the labors of Linus W. Stevens, in the service of benevolence. That gentleman served upon the successive committees of the Common Council, under whose charge the Nursery Buildings, at the north end, were erected, and now his name is honorably associated with the temple of charity that adorns the southern end."

Mr. Kelly then presents a comprehensive summary of the various educational, charitable, and reformatory institutions of the city, and closes with these eloquent sentences: "How beautifully this belt of islands encompasses the city as with a girdle of charity! The cestus of Venus did not add more grace to the queen of beauty than does this chain of beautiful islands to the queenly city. Every new edifice erected upon them is another gem set in the zone. I never visit these islands without a sentiment of admiration, excited by the beauty of their position and adaptedness to the purposes to which they have been appropriated. There they lie, stretching along for miles, face to face with the city, and in view of the population, with their penitentiaries and workhouses and almshouses, and hospitals and refuges and nurseries and public cemetery, teaching no mean lesson of the value of home, the blessings of independence, and the duties of men in the various relations of life. How fortunate that they have not been parcelled into lots, and occupied with improvements of the transition period! . . . Far more are they to be admired with these institutions of blessed charity scattered upon them, than if a nation's treasures had been expended to fit them for the residence of a monarch, spanned the intervening streets with royal bridges, and filled them with palaces and galleries like another Versailles, or Oriental luxury had decked them for the summer seraglio of a sultan, with terraces, and garden alleys paved with precious marbles, fountains casting their spray upon the perfumed air, and minarets rising in graceful majesty from the midst of the luxuriant foliage."

After singing, interesting addresses were delivered by two of the original managers, Hon. Hugh Maxwell and James W. Gerard, Esq., whose emotions on this occasion, as they recalled the "day of small things," can be more readily imagined than described.

Governor Seymour then delivered a happy address, remarking in its course that during the previous two years he had been compelled to act upon more than two thousand applications for pardon. "It has been," he says, "my daily and painful duty to listen to the entreaties of those who sought to turn away from themselves or their friends the consequences of their guilt; I cannot, therefore, but feel the deepest interest for an institution which converts the very errors of youth into a blessing rather than a curse. While, upon those who enter the walls of an ordinary prison, the door of hope is closed, the portals of this institution open up to the offender the path to happiness and to virtue. The ordinary execution of the laws of the land impresses an indelible stigma upon the future fame of the offender, while here all stains are wiped away; early delinquencies are obliterated, rendering the offender in his future life a good citizen. Those who have occasion to engage in the legislation of our

country, or to watch the execution of its laws, are daily taught
how utterly inadequate are all statutes to restrain vice or to enforce virtue.   In the discharge of my official duties, I have frequently felt the inadequacy of man's wisdom, and have been
made grateful that there were higher and more reliable influences upon which we might safely rest our hopes for the amelioration of our social condition.   The chief value of this institution consists in this—not that it constrains, but that it edu-
cates—not that it strikes the vindictive blow, but evolves and
cultivates the better sentiments and feelings of our natures.
A comparison between this asylum and its influence upon those
confided to its care, with the ordinary prisons of our land and
their wretched inmates, will teach us to feel the beauty and the
truth of the sentiment of the philosopher, when he said that
' the unwritten laws of religious nurture, of moral culture and
of virtuous education, will ever be found a sure dependence, and
will constitute the very bonds and ligaments of the States, when
the enactments of the legislator shall be found vain and inef-
ficient.' "

Thus opened auspiciously the new era of careful classification
and enlarged facilities for discipline, labor, instruction, and moral
training.   But one building, however, was yet completed, and
the girls occupied a portion of one wing of the boys' House.
It was not until the Twenty-sixth Annual Report, for 1860, that
the managers were able to say, " the completion of the House
for the girls has at last enabled them to institute the long-desired
and fundamental system of classification.   One division of boys
now occupies the south wing of the main building recently
vacated by the girls.   A complete separation is thus made in all
the departments of the House.   The girls are divided in the

OLIVER S. STRONG, Esq.

same manner, each division occupying their own appropriate wing of the House for females. From the immediate effects observed, the managers feel encouraged in the prospect of a very marked improvement in the order and other beneficial results of the system."

April 28, 1856, the Society was called to mourn the loss of its very efficient third president, Mr. Kelly, who was succeeded by the present occupant of the chair, Oliver S. Strong, Esq. Mr. Kelly was permitted to see the great work nearly completed, in which he had taken such a lively interest, and to which he had largely contributed by his personal efforts and influence. He was followed in a few years by another, whose place, in the sadness of the first hour of his sudden and peculiarly afflictive death, it seemed difficult to supply. He had been one of the most active members of the Building Committee, and contributed much, by his zeal, wisdom, and business tact, to the successful issue of the great undertaking upon which the managers had entered. Of Mr. Charles M. Leupp the managers say, in their Thirty-fifth Annual Report, " In the death of this gentleman have been sundered ties cemented by long periods of active duty and coöperation in behalf of the interests of the House of Refuge. His services were freely and cheerfully rendered in the labors of some of its most important committees during the course of nineteen years. In its favor he incurred large pecuniary responsibilities, and profoundly sympathized, with the ardor of a warm and generous nature, and as a good citizen, in its large and beneficent public aims."

In August, 1856, an interesting experiment in the work of juvenile reform was inaugurated in Lancaster, Mass. The State Legislature, moved by numerous petitions and a voluntary subscription of twenty thousand dollars for the purpose, made provision for the establishment of an Industrial School for girls; boys only being admitted into the State Reform School at Westborough.

The site selected was an old brick mansion, in the ancient town of Lancaster, situated upon a fine, high lawn, embowered in elms, and surrounded by a farm of one hundred acres (since increased to one hundred and forty), sloping downward to a branch of the Nashua River. The lawn was increased in size and made symmetrical by the generous gift from the town of the old common, or training-field, that laid unimproved in front of the estate.

The large, square "Stillwell Mansion," by the outlay of a few thousand dollars, was made to answer, quite conveniently, for one of the family houses. From the adjoining mountain water was brought down in pipes, in sufficient quantity, and of an adequate "head," to meet all the wants of the institution, and to be distributed in every portion of it. The site was every thing that could be desired, and was secured at a comparatively small price. To the indefatigable labors of Colonel Francis B. Fay, who deserves, for many reasons, the title of "father" to the institution, the State owes the admirable location of the school, and the marked economy attending its establishment.

After a careful examination of the plans of the more prominent European and American institutions for the reformation of juvenile offenders, and calling to their aid the practical thinkers and writers upon this delicate question, the commissioners reported to the Legislature a system of organization and discipline, called, to distinguish it, the "family plan," following quite closely the arrangement of the institution for boys at Mettray,

The Family Plan inaugurated.

in France, which was at that time attracting more attention among the friends of reform than any other in Europe or America. Heretofore every public institution of the kind in this country had been upon the "congregate plan," constructed very similarly to penitentiaries, but made more comfortable, and wearing no penal aspect in their discipline. Greater indulgence than is permitted in a penitentiary has always been allowed in passing in and out of the limits of the reformatory, on the part of the children, and the officers are expected to hold a parental relation to the inmates, but still these institutions have been included within walls, and the dormitories are closed by locks and bolts.

But the commissioners proposed that, at Lancaster, separate buildings should be constructed, capable of accommodating thirty girls in each, and that each house should be a separate family, under its appropriate matron, assistant matron (who should also be the school-teacher), and housekeeper. All the work and study of the family, it was arranged, should go on under its own roof. No walls enclosed the village of homes that it was proposed to erect, and no fastenings defended the windows of the sleeping-rooms from offering their facilities for the escape of the inmates. It is an interesting fact that only two girls have succeeded in escaping from the school since its establishment, and these during the first six months of its history. In each house it was proposed to distribute a portion of the older and of the younger girls—thus keeping up the idea of a family and securing the easier performance of the housework. The older girls were to have separate rooms, while the younger slept with a monitor in an open dormitory. The work proposed for the girls was housework, the making of their own garments, knitting, and such plain trades as skirt-making and straw-braiding. From these sources, in the experiment of ten years, the time of the children has been fully occupied, when not engaged in school or in their necessary recreations.

The only change in the manner of committing subjects to the school from that pursued at Westborough, in the same State, was the particularly happy arrangement to avoid the disgrace and taint of the court-room by appointing special commissioners to hear the complaints against the children, and constituting judges of probate, *ex officio*, commissioners for this purpose. By this means, also, the institution, it was thought, through the more careful supervision of special officers, would be saved from being overrun by a class of hardened and hopeless criminals, or by diseased and idiotic children.

Girls were permitted to be sent to the institution between the ages of seven and sixteen, and were, at first, committed until eighteen years of age. Since its organization, the trustees have received power from the Legislature to retain, under certain circumstances, the custody of their subjects until they are twenty-one. As in other institutions, the trustees were empowered to indenture the girls, after having bestowed upon them sufficient training in the schools, to good families in the State, or beyond its borders.

The institution was publicly dedicated, and the first house opened, August 27, 1856, and was, in a few months, filled with inmates of various ages, and a large proportion of them of American parentage. This somewhat remarkable fact, although the proportion has sometimes varied, has continued to characterize the subjects of the school until the present time. The new houses were constructed of brick, two stories in height, very neatly and conveniently finished, at an expense of about twelve

STATE INDUSTRIAL SCHOOL, LANCASTER, MASS.

thousand dollars each. By April, 1857, the third house had been opened, and, in January, 1860, the fourth. In 1861, the fifth, and last house, a wooden dwelling-house, fitted up for the purpose, was provided to meet the constantly-increasing demand for accommodations. From the opening, the capacity of the school has always been fully taxed, and there has been scarcely a month when the rooms have not been uncomfortably crowded, and applications from commissioners declined. A convenient house, already on the grounds, formed a pleasant residence for the Superintendent, and another for the Farmer. A neat, white village church, standing unoccupied, was removed at small expense, and placed upon the lawn; and thus, five homes, capable of receiving one hundred and fifty inmates, two family residences, and a pleasant chapel, were secured at an expense of but little over sixty thousand dollars.

In October, 1866, there had been received into the school 464 inmates; there were present at that time, in the different homes, 132, and 234 had been returned to friends, or completed the term of their indentures. The remainder had been removed to hospitals or almshouses, or discharged as unsuitable.

Without doubt, a large proportion of these girls are now living honest and pure lives. Some of them are filling quite conspicuous positions as teachers or matrons in similar schools, who seemed, at the time they were sent to the institution, predestined to a life of sin and sorrow. Many have not fulfilled the expectations excited in their behalf, and are now wandering amid the retributions of the life of a transgressor.

The close and beautiful relation existing between three Christian women and thirty young girls, sitting at the same table, and forming one circle in family prayer, and in all domestic and social duties and enjoyments, must have, as the experiment has proved, a powerful and redeeming influence.   It is possible that the Industrial Home may have been so pleasant and so light in its exactions upon the girl, that sometimes she has turned away dissatisfied from a somewhat rough and exacting country home; or an ambition has been aroused for other employments than housework, and, in the failure to gratify this newly-awakened taste, the temptation to turn aside to the paths of sin may have been awakened afresh.   It may also have happened that the difficulties attending the indenturing of the girls have induced the retaining of children too long in the school.   All institution-life is, as we have occasion often to remark in this volume, unnatural, and no child should be confined in any one, however improving, longer than is indispensable to prepare it for the natural home in a family, where it must, certainly, ultimately live. We should never weary of the experiment of placing the child in a home.   If it fails in one, it may find a congenial atmosphere in another.

All these tendencies and open problems are constantly in the thoughts and discussions of the cultivated and benevolent gentlemen that watch over the interests of this favorite institution of the State, and the highest success that wisdom can secure for it will be their earnest and constant endeavor to attain.

To the writer, it would seem an improvement upon this system, to have one larger building, where all the inmates should be at first received, and afterward be detailed to the various homes. This building might admit of some restraint, as all attempts to escape are in the first weeks of a child's connection with the institution.   In this building might also be the rooms of the Superintendent's family and the public offices.   Here also accommodation could be provided for girls returned from their places, or sent back by the commissioners after their discharge. Such girls often exercise an unhappy influence over one of the families, by the stubborn tempers or vicious habits which they usually bring back with them.

It would be better, the writer thinks, not to have separate schools in each family, but to have one school-house, and all the children attend there, as they meet in chapel. This would admit of better classification and instruction, and break up, in a measure, the somewhat monastic character of the institution-life.

But, take it altogether, there probably is not a public institution of reform in the world better subserving the great purpose for which it was established, or bringing more honor or satisfaction to the State which has given it birth, than the State Industrial School at Lancaster.

The school is particularly fortunate in its present superintendent, Rev. Mr. Ames, who is also its chaplain, and in the excellent ladies who, with much personal sacrifice, have devoted themselves to this noble work of reforming the tempted children of their own sex.

The writer of this volume, who had the honor of first carrying out, as superintendent, the intentions and wishes of the benevolent and intelligent founders of this beautiful reformatory, may be permitted to state, as a matter of fact, that with all the outward indulgence possible in a school for one sex only, and the charming scenery of the place, with the limited number in each house, and the homelike appearance of the buildings, the girls, although contented, were not more cheerful than are the occupants of our girls' department in the New-York House; they were not more readily approached with moral motives, nor more powerfully assimilated to the characters of their officers, nor more generally satisfied with their position when discharged from the institution, than are the girls gathered under the care of our Society.

At the commencement of 1858 a similar institution for boys was opened in Lancaster, Ohio. It has five houses, capable of holding from forty to fifty boys, with suitable offices, school and chapel accommodations. It is situated in an agricultural country; and the boys are chiefly employed in farm labors. Considerable attention has been paid to the cultivation of vines and small fruits; but the results have not been very encouraging in a pecuniary point of view. The head of the institution, Mr. Howe, is a man of rare ability, and he has succeeded in infusing his own spirit in a good degree through the somewhat complicated and difficult system of discipline which has been instituted in this interesting forest reformatory. The moral influence of the place is represented to be eminently wholesome, and the statistics of those that have been discharged are encouraging. The school is an American copy of the French Mettray, with the modifications rendered necessary by the impossibility of securing the number of carefully-trained and devoted officers which the Catholic and Protestant brotherhoods of France and Germany yield to the institutions of these countries.

These are interesting and attractive experiments; and at this hour they are particularly arresting the observation of commissioners of States, in whose limits institutions of reform have not yet been established. There is nothing, however, in the results that are to be attributed to the systems of discipline rather than to the successful reformatory agents that have been happily secured to work them, and the more complicated the system the

The Reformatory simply prepares for a Home.

more difficult it will be to find men to run them. We are never
to forget that all institution-life is simply a necessary evil, and
the great work is to prepare the child, by moral cultivation, by
the habit of industry and the rudiments of learning, to find a
better home and a fair beginning for life in a respectable Christian family. If a boy, through great moral weakness or per-
versity, cannot be trusted in the community, then some other
place besides a reformatory should be furnished by the State to
receive him, and to secure the expense of his maintenance from
his productive industry.

CHAPTER VIII.

THE CONGREGATE SYSTEM IN REFORMATORIES.

ON the 12th of May, 1857, and at about the same date in 1859, conventions of the managers and superintendents of Houses of Refuge were held in the city of New York, and a very general attendance from all parts of the country was secured. A valuable correspondence was also held with the most prominent friends of juvenile reform in Great Britain and France.

Almost every question relating to the care and cure of youths, vagrant, orphaned, and criminal, was fully considered, and the various experiments under trial throughout the civilized world were presented and discussed. The novelty and interest with which the family and separate systems were invested made them, on the whole, the favorites among the friends of reform. The peculiarly attractive accounts of the German and French reformatories, and the successful experiment in Lancaster, Mass., just about to be repeated in a town of the same name in Ohio, with the other sex, gave a marked prominence to this form of organic effort for the rescue of criminal children. It naturally led to a thorough revision of the whole question.

Since that time the Massachusetts Board of State Charities has, through some of its members, such as Dr. Howe and its

Young Criminals cannot safely be intrusted to Families.

cultivated first secretary, Mr. F. B. Sanborn, given much consideration to this question.   The leaning of this Board seems to be rather to the opinion that no large institutions should be established, but that vagrant and criminal children should be boarded and disciplined at the expense of the State in individual families.   This, indeed, without much expense to the State, is the work that Children's Aid Societies are constantly doing for the vagrant youths of the street.   But young criminals, now numbered by thousands, require more energetic treatment than any private family could be expected to bestow.   Many of these have fallen into crime, not through the want, as we have seen, of excellent homes, but through peculiar weakness or corrupting influences.

Orphan and half-orphan asylums, magdalen and temporary homes—all deserve the aid they receive from the community, and more; for they are doing the work of Christ upon the earth, and affording their supporters the opportunity of learning the truth of that saying of the Master, that "it is more blessed to give than to receive."   Small voluntary reformatories, newsboys' lodgings, and the deporting of homeless children to the broad farms of the Western country, are accomplishing an untold amount of good; but, after all these agencies have reached the limit of their possibility, the words of prophecy will still be illustrated in reference to all dense communities: "And the streets of the city shall be full of boys and girls *playing in the streets thereof.*" *

The immense importation of the poorer and lower classes of Europe, the most destitute portion of which lingers in our East-

* Zech. viii. 5.

ern cities, greatly increases the statistics of exposed and criminal children.   Poor blood, low moral culture, the pinch of poverty, the habit of indulgence, predispose this class to early crime. After all the institutions we have named, and many others, have sifted out from this sad mass of childhood their appropriate subjects, from the remainder, the police officers and courts are constantly gathering up large numbers of young criminals from the streets, but leaving many more behind and winking at their first offences.   The latter, as well as former, must be cared for in some way, or the fruitful streams that supply adult crime will not be closed.

Of those arrested, there will be boys of sixteen, often of eighteen, but still wearing a youthful aspect, and giving some promise of redemption, under wholesome influences; some of twelve and fourteen, also, who have committed quite serious crimes, such as grand larceny, burglary, arson, forgery, and assault with dangerous weapons.   To send these boys to the penitentiary is to deliberately give them over to ruin, and to entail upon the community the frightful tax of a life of crime. No family would receive such a boy at once into its bosom, and the defenceless door of a family school, if any considerable number of such were received, would be an irresistible invitation to them to escape, until such time as would be required for the silver links of moral chains to be forged and drawn around the heart.   Family institutions defend themselves by refusing this class, or only receiving them in very limited numbers, and at intervals so long that they may be morally digested.   Positive restraint at once removes the irritability caused by the hope of escape, and prepares the way for the discipline of labor, education, and piety.   The arrangement of various divisions, readily

Effect of Training upon Mature Boys.

secured in large establishments, defends younger and softer boys from the possible injury of contact with those more confirmed in criminal habits.

Here, then, we approach the measure of the moral power of large congregate institutions. It becomes a question of fact with a long list of witnesses. Many of the boys, described above, undoubtedly go forth from such a congregated refuge as the New-York House to a life of crime and to the suffering of its penalties. But the overwhelming majority of even these mature boys, as shown by the experiment of nearly fifty years, turn out well. The boys themselves, by their letters, or by their verbal testimony, and their friends also, attribute their reformation and their success in life to purposes suggested and formed when under the discipline of the House of Refuge.

The files of the House are full of letters, and its daily journal of recorded visits, of individuals of this class, who, having reached manhood, have voluntarily given expression to their belief that the Refuge was their moral birthplace.

Another very considerable portion of juvenile offenders not finding legitimate discipline in other institutions, are, as has already been suggested, boys about the same age, from fourteen to eighteen, who have quite respectable parents, and have been brought up in indulgent homes. They are easily influenced, often very capable, and have been drawn into temptation and positive crime by vicious companions. They have been sent away to school, removed to friends in the country, placed in good situations for business, but have baffled every effort of parents and friends to secure a reformation from ruinous habits. The humble garb, the plain fare, the daily labor, the daily school, the positive discipline—all so different from home, have, in a large number of such instances (and these are very trying cases), to our personal knowledge, been exceedingly efficacious.   At the end of a year or more of such training, with constant moral influences operating upon the mind, and the love of home expressing itself, from time to time, in visits and affecting letters, we have often found that a permanent reformation has taken place.

The parental relation should not be sundered when there is considerable promise that it will be a shelter and a comfort to the child.   Such children the State does not need to remove entirely from friends, nor to send beyond its limits, but only to discipline awhile, and then return to their natural guardians.

We find this same interesting and difficult class of subjects in the other sex.

While this volume is passing through the press, a father from the city of Albany accompanies his daughter to the House. She has enjoyed every opportunity that money could provide to secure an education.   Her parents are church-members, and she has been connected from her childhood with a Sunday-school. She has just passed her sixteenth birthday—a bright, fine-looking girl.   No language can do justice to the agony, shame, and anxiety she has brought into the hearts of her parents.   She has, in a fit of passion, thrown a fifty-dollar bill into the flames; several times she has set the house on fire, so that her father could not renew his insurance, and, most terrible act of all, she left her indulgent, Christian home, and was found in a house of ill-repute in the city of New York.   The interview between the child and her father, when they separated at the Refuge, was affecting in the extreme.   The girl had no complaint to make of her home, had by no means lost her sensibility, but bitterly blamed her-

self for her conduct. This, her father assured us, she had done
many times before. Now, what, in a private family, or in a
small, undefended family school, could be done with such a
girl?

Another and great class, affording subjects for the congregate institution, is the foreign childhood that floats along the
streets and docks of the city; vagabondish, thievish, familiar
with the vicious ways and places of the town; in rags, living in
dirty and often vile resorts, having no education, knowing no
Sabbath, and with lips friendly to oaths, but strangers to
prayers. Families in the country will not take these children
in this condition; and if they would, these little Arabs, the next
night after their country adoption, would take the turnpike or
railroad-bed, and beg or steal their way back again to the city.
"Their name is legion." They pass the nights, many of them,
in boxes and old sheds, and wherever they can find a shelter.
We had one little fellow who had not slept in a house for more
than six months. The money they earn or steal is expended in
low theatres or in drinking-saloons; and boys of a most immature age are found bearing the marks of vices that seem only
possible to adults. Something more than shelter is necessary.
Two-thirds of our city boys have, at some time, availed themselves of the opportunities of the newsboys' lodgings. Family
institutions cannot be multiplied with sufficient rapidity near
dense populations, to meet the requisitions of this class. These
form the breeding-sources of crime; but when these festering
rags are shaken up, after a period of discipline, often, bright,
capable, and reliable boys are found to have been in them. Now,
these boys, in twelve or eighteen months, will show their true
character and promise for the future. In some instances they

are found to have mothers that need their assistance, and a little effort often secures for them, after the training of the Refuge, a position where they can obtain good wages, and rescue a parent from the almshouse. Many of these boys have no relish for farm-life: if sent into the country they will run; but, placed at a trade in the city, will do well. But the majority, after this preliminary discipline, are distributed over the country, and placed in the very best institutions on the family system—i. e., a farmer's family, with this one boy to be trained in it.

If the moral influence of such an institution as we are considering is unwholesome, it must appear in the experiment of years, upon these classes. If conspiracies are formed in them, which are developed after the boys are discharged, the fact would soon become patent. The records of the largest institution in the country, and probably in the world, whose inmates have all been received through the courts, show that the number of those known to do well after their discharge, far exceeds the number that do ill; and what is particularly significant, is the fact, that at this time, when its numbers are nearly fifty per cent. greater than heretofore, there are more perceptible evidences of the presence of a strong moral influence among the inmates, than for many years since. In all this time there is no recorded instance of one dating his ruin to intimacies formed in the House, or of combinations to commit crime after discharge. This plainly shows, that what may be considered the incident evils of a congregate institution may be very largely controlled.

Before considering two or three of the positive advantages of a large institution, especially near a city population, it may be pertinent to the subject to remark, that our experience and observation do not confirm the opinion that a very long period

Should be retained in House but a Short Time.

at any institution is desirable.   In the European establishments the inmates are expected to learn the trades that they will afterward follow, and many forms of business, such as printing, book-binding, carpentering, and the different handicrafts, are taught and followed for the support of the reformatory.   In the crowded communities of the old country, it is much more difficult to find positions for untrained children; therefore more must be done for them before they can be sent forth in a condition to earn an honest living.   With us demand for labor, even unskilled, presses closely upon supply.   With a fair rudimental education, long enough training in regular labor for the habit of industry to be somewhat formed, and with a good moral purpose developed, the children in our communities may be safely intrusted to the farmers and mechanics that stand ready to receive them.   Especially may this be safely done where the institution exercises a supervision over its indentured subjects, and has room and facilities for receiving them again, when it is discovered that they have been sent out prematurely.   In instances where boys or girls prove somewhat intractable, a long period in the institution will rarely cure the difficulty.   Evil tempers and habits become confirmed, and the child settles down into a sullen despair of improvement.   When such a child has been returned from a family, after a short period of discipline, another trial, in a family of a different class, should be afforded; and the child will thus have a new opportunity to commence life under encouraging circumstances.   Repeatedly, in our experience, the experiment has proved safe and successful.

In an institution of an adjoining city, serious charges were brought against the superintendent—a man that had borne an unblemished reputation—by a combination of girls that had

been connected with it.   Whatever grounds any one had to believe that there was the slightest foundation to the story, all
were convinced that it was wickedly exaggerated, and, in all
essentials, totally untrue.   These girls had been connected with
the institution, some of them for seven years, and they had been
treated as the daughters of the family, receiving the evening kiss
from the house father and mother when they retired for the night.

It is not a natural condition of things at the best; and even
the family system, so called, is, after all, a "make-believe"-
family, differing from the congregate only in the limited numbers gathered together.   If the introduction of a step-father or
mother into a family circle so often breaks its power of love
over a child, we can readily see how almost impossible it is, by
any artificial arrangement, exactly to renew the natural relation.
Institution-life of every description should be as limited as it
can be consistently with the results it seeks to accomplish, and
then the children should be sent forth singly into the best homes
that can be obtained for them.

We do not wish to make institution-life so desirable, that it
should be preferred to an ordinary Christian home.   We are
chagrined when a child from a decent home, where the work is
not too severe, and common affection and sympathy are shown,
comes crying back to the shelter of the Refuge, complaining of
his fare and his labor; but proud, when, having wrought
bravely and well, the boys, after their first personal successes,
come, with glowing faces, to tell us what they have accomplished, and to receive, what they so eagerly expect, our hearty
commendations.   As Daniel Webster said of New Hampshire,
the House of Refuge should be a good place to emigrate from,
and a delightful place, afterward, to visit.

As in the case of the children filling our common schools, we consider that there are many benefits resulting, with some serious but controllable evils, from their being educated together; so when they need to have their moral faculties developed and trained, while there are apparent perils, there is not nearly as much danger as is supposed, under proper supervision, in permitting this work to go on in companies; and there are some marked advantages. It is not possible for the boys, in such divisions as those arranged in the New-York House, working, studying, playing, in the company of mature and observing persons, constantly brought in contact with the strongest moral forces, to have such an influence for evil upon one another as the children of decent families, spending their days between the school and the street; for how powerless for good, in most instances, are the average homes in which city children live!

The positive advantages of a large reformatory in a dense community may be thus set forth:

I. It is in a condition, from its extensive resources—sanitary, educational, industrial, and moral—to receive a large number, at any given time, within its halls, so that a great diminution of juvenile crime and evil influence may be secured in the vicinity. It allows of a better classification, just as large grammar-schools have this advantage over small. From its organization and the incident demand of its numbers it must have better discipline, as a public school has the advantage in this respect over a small private academy; and strenuous discipline, and an idea of the sanctity of law, are the peculiar necessities of these children. It admits of an earlier distribution of its inmates; because if the experiment of their discharge prove unsuccessful, it has room enough to receive them again. This is a felt evil in small establishments. Their rooms are generally filled, and they have no reserved resources to meet the exigencies of returned children; besides, they are much more embarrassed, in limited families, by the influence of a returned child over the other inmates.

The object of a Reformatory is not to send forth a class of highly-educated and polished young persons, but to raise up out of the dust hundreds now festering in sinful homes and vicious societies; to hold them near the truth until their minds shall be impressed with it; to teach them the use of the personal implements with which, in most cases in the humblest walks of life, they will secure an honest living; and then give them a fair start, with hard labor and an honest purpose, to create for themselves a comfortable home. The congregate system, near large cities, with the wide facilities of our new and vast country, presents an opportunity for doing this work, with much promise of success, on a large scale.

II. It was well remarked, in the very able report of the Massachusetts State Board of Charities for 1865, that few persons have the reformatory power—that strong, magnetic, spiritual power of awakening, with the Divine blessing, the latent manhood and the latent conscience in a boy's heart. When such a person is found, it is therefore the more desirable to give him a wide field. Numbers do not necessarily destroy this power. Sheridan had that same magical influence over a division that was apparent when he commanded a brigade. Indeed, these magnetic men multiply their power by the numbers they touch. Is the influence of the great preacher of Brooklyn weakened, because more than three thousand constantly hang upon his lips? But these reformatory minds are not always either executive or economical. We know a superintendent who has this marvellous power over children, but is not blessed with the ability to arrange details and organize the discipline and economy of his institution.   It was happily said of it, by one who had been connected with both, that his Refuge was more like a newsboys' lodgings than any thing else.   In a large institution you can secure both descriptions of ability and the highest order of them.   You may make mistakes in your men, but you command the resources to obtain the right persons when they providentially appear—the clear-headed, executive business mind, and the nervous, impulsive, warm-hearted, generous moral instructor and cure of souls.

Now, neither trees and flowers, nor working in the earth, nor collecting a few children together in a pleasant home, nor singing and playing, will reform these boys.   Neither walls nor barless windows can do this.   It is that sanctified power with which God endows His chosen instruments that awakens the inward being, that enthrones conscience above the passions, and suffuses the whole nature with the love of its Saviour, that radically reforms.   There is no power on earth so much to be coveted as this.   Some have it in a large measure.   Surround them with proper concomitants, and then give them a wide field for its exercise.   Large institutions have also the power of throwing this influence over their indentured subjects as a shield of defence against temptation and abuse.

III. But the great advantage of the congregate system is the opportunity it offers for systematic labor.   Almost without exception, the best boys, so called, and the worst that are sent to the Refuge, are lazy.   They have lived truant, vagrant, and vicious lives.   They hate work.   They take hold of a hoe or a spade, when they come, rather as slaves than as free boys, as if intending to show how little work can be done in the longest time.   They are sluggish in school and unable to render proper attention to moral instruction.   Farm-work is not sharp enough as a counter-irritant in the majority of these cases.   It is not sufficiently electric.   It does not wake the boys up.   But the shop, with its carefully-adjusted stints, with its delicate labors, requiring constant and absorbing attention, with its daily recurring duties always demanding faithfulness, has an amazing power over their minds.   The first work with a child of a feeble mind is to catch and hold the attention; when this is done, the rest of the work is comparatively easy.   The well-organized shop never fails in this, and for this reason the boy is strangely transformed by its power.   He grooves down into a habit of labor.   It becomes a sort of necessity to him.   He finds that workmen in the business he is learning are receiving from twelve to twenty dollars a week.   It awakens his ambition: and this great defence against stealing—the ability to command a moderate salary by labor—is thrown around him.

Other things being equal, the country is the best place for these children, but the centripetal force drawing many of the city boys back into its streets is almost irresistible.   Farm-life is too slow for them.   Having developed in some measure their manual skill, if now a good trade, or a good place of labor, and a comfortable arrangement for board, can be secured in the city, the probabilities of a successful and virtuous life are greatly increased.   In many instances there are relatives requiring the assistance of the boy, and a touching appeal is made for his services.   The boy's own affections and sense of obligation have been awakened.   Having lived cleanly and comfortable for a year or more, he must continue to do so.   A room is found for the old mother or little group of sisters, and the boy goes bravely to work to support them.

A mature boy had a brother and two sisters in the Refuge. He gave but little promise when he came. The whole family was probably in the habit of stealing. His mother was nearly blind, and their quarters—one room, six by eight, with a slanting roof, near the Five Points—was as wretched as words can paint. He learned with us to labor, to be honest, and to pray. His bad eyes prevented his enlisting in the army. He objected to going into the country, because he clung to his old, blind mother, and to his brother and sisters. We arranged with a friend to secure a comfortable room for him, and a place of labor. He is now sustaining comfortably his mother and one sister. He has set his brother to work in a good position, while he boards him, and is arranging to have his other sister by the 4th of July.

As of faith, we may say, "all things are possible to him that" *worketh*. *Omnia vincet labor.* If you give these boys simply a higher form of education, you have only increased their ability to injure themselves and the community; but if you break up that terrible habit of indolence, of lazy lounging, start into life the sluggish blood in their veins, and turn the face and heart toward the heavenly Father in prayer, you have surrounded them with the best defences against temptation.

If there is any love of learning in a boy, he will find or make opportunities for its cultivation. "What more does a man need," said young Stone to the son of the Duke of Argyle, accounting for his power to read the *Mechanique Celeste*, "than a knowledge of the alphabet?" And if a boy has no inward appetite for it, you cannot crane him up above a moderate standard, with all your endeavor. How many boys, sons of lawyers, of ministers, of tender mothers, who had been living loafing and criminal lives, have borne testimony to the reforming power of this hard, constant work! It was their first introduction to honest labor, and, in entertaining the stranger, they have entertained an angel unawares.

There are certain ruinous habits that prey like wolves upon this class of children, and that yield to no treatment so soon as to regular and hard work, in connection with moral and religious instruction. Hard labor subdues the appetites, and makes sleep welcome in the instant that the weary body touches the bed, and sweet also, until the bell for refreshments and labor arouses the slumberer in the morning.

There would seem to be a serious objection suggested by this line of reasoning, to the proposition to pay families a consideration for assuming the custody of children requiring discipline, as proposed in the report of the Massachusetts Board of Charities. It is vital for the future well-being of the youth, that the habit of industry should be formed. Whatever pleasant tempers may be developed, the child's great implement for success and defence from temptation, outside of Divine influences, is a love of labor, and, if this is not secured, the experiment of reform has failed.

If the child works as a servant in the house, or a laborer out of doors, the services themselves form a large compensation for the outlay and care incident to its training, where the period of indentures extends through the minority. It is important that the family should kindly exact a proper amount of diligence; but if the board is paid or any considerable sum allotted, in addition to the services rendered, with well-meaning and kind-tempered parties this will be likely to prove a temptation to an indulgent indifference as to the amount of labor performed.   It will also be impossible to keep the child from learning the fact that, in addition to his work, the State will pay his employer a sum for his care.   There are always " disinterested " parties in every community that will feel called upon to inform the child of this fact, and it will be readily seen how his ambition will be quenched by such an intimation as this, and his sense of injustice be kindled by it.

A little fellow, under the direction of the writer, was placed in a most excellent farmer's family.   His health and habits required that he should be put to vigorous manual labor.   His own impression was, that he was earning his board by the sweat of his brow.   A wealthy relative of the family died, and he immediately rebelled against work.   There was too much money in the family, he said, for him to work upon a farm.

It is better for us all, young and old, to feel that the ability to eat and the provision for it depend upon faithful working.

By all means, we must preserve these children from even the *appearance* of pauperism.   Although with some considerable suffering, it is better for them early to feel that they are, under God, dependent upon their own resources; that they must fight down their evil tempers themselves; that they must stand up bravely under difficulties, endure patiently all ordinary hardships, and strike out hopefully for an honorable position, in a land where the boy of the alms-house struggles to the palace of the nation.

It will, from these suggestions, be seen, that a large institution, with all its liabilities, having its subjects for a year or more under perfect discipline, day and night, having regular hours of labor, having daily moral lessons, with prayers and the Word of God, having the Sabbath sanctified with appropriate services, and the most affecting and wholesome addresses from the wisest and best of Christian men and women, must make a salutary and lasting impression upon the minds of its inmates.

The institution is less like home, but more like the society into which the boy is to enter. He has learned the sanctity of law, the necessity and beauty of obedience, and the consequences of disobedience. He goes forth into a greater institution, where law constantly meets him, and will impress him as it never did before. Both habit and conscience will be his keepers, and there is great reason to hope that he will become "a law unto himself."

The discussions and correspondence of the conventions awakened much interest in European institutions of reform. The careful, personal examination of the more noted of these establishments, however, while rich in suggestions, develops no one model plan after which it is desirable to conform our own.

In the comparison of existing institutions for the redemption and reformation of exposed and criminal children, so far as comfort, convenience, sanitary appliances, adaptation for the ends sought after, and generousness of material provisions are concerned, we are incomparably in advance of European reformatories.* With a few exceptions in the old countries, old edifices,

---

* In the August number of the *Reformatory and Refuge Journal*, published in London, is an account of a "Social Meeting of Masters and Matrons" connected with reformatory and charitable institutions in that city. Among other speakers on this occasion was Mr. C. D. Fox, who is an active member of the Council of the English Reformatory and Refuge Union. He had just returned from a tour in this country, and "gave," says the Report, "a most

Character of Reformatory Edifices in Europe.

castles, hospitals, vacated and dilapidated schools, ancient and damp cottages, barns even, have been taken and made barely habitable for the occupancy of the children and their officers. In Liefde's entertaining sketches of some of the most successful establishments in Germany, Prussia, Holland, and France, only one or two are described as occupying buildings originally erected for the purpose to which they are now devoted, or without serious inconveniences arising from this cause. In the general cleanliness and wholesomeness of buildings, dress, and person, both American and English visitors render us in the United States the palm. In classification and variety of organization, missions for the virtuous poor, missions among the abandoned, truant homes, orphan homes, refuges for criminal children, and charities for all forms of want and suffering—in all these respects there seems to be little for us to learn from our brothers in Christian labor over the water; but we are able to

interesting account of his visit to the Reformatory institutions of the United States. Speaking first of their peculiarities, he referred to the almost total absence of corporal punishment. Emulation was their chief instrument of discipline. They carried on a great work among children, combining care for their spiritual welfare with active exertion for their bodily and mental wants. Their use of photographs, music, and flowers was quite unknown in England; while their thoughtfulness for the comfort of their little charges was most striking, and was seen in the arm-chair, separate desks, and covered play-grounds provided in most of the institutions. As a consequence of this treatment another peculiarity was, the great love between each child and the Superintendent; whenever he appeared among them they ran to him, and were to be seen clinging round him as if he were in truth their father. The system of adoption into families in the far West was also a peculiarity unlike any thing attempted in England; a most extensive correspondence was maintained with all who had been thus provided for. Mr. Fox then described the work being accomplished by the Five Points House of Industry, the Five Points Mission, the Howard Mission and Home for Little Wanderers, the Children's Aid Society, and the House of Refuge."

direct their grateful attention to many things which excite their commendation and imitation. In opportunities for the education of the poorest, for the elevation of the humblest, for securing every variety of form of labor with the highest compensation paid for it, and for obtaining at the smallest price the richest land, our new and democratic country affords unequalled facilities. There is no difficulty in finding a place for honest and remunerative labor for every active child in the land.

European institutions retain the children for a much longer period than the average of American reformatories, four years for boys and five for girls being considered the ordinary term, while two years is a high average with us. The capacity of an institution for relieving a given vicinity of its exposed children is thus greatly diminished.

There is no one form of organization and discipline in foreign institutions that is of itself so especially effective as to render it indispensable to the highest order of success. It is the magnetic power of the man that has secured the efficiency of the more noted reformatory establishments of Europe. There is not a finer institution for orphans in the world than Müller's, in Bristol, England, where he has congregated nearly two thousand children in half a dozen immense stone buildings. The well-known intelligent correspondent of the *Boston Journal* personally examined it, and says of Müller: "He is a man of great executive ability, and is the sole manager of this immense concern. I have been all over his establishment. It would do credit to any government on the face of the earth." It was not the family system, but Wichern and his beloved mother, that melted and, with the Divine blessing, recast the lives of the wretched little outcasts that kneeled under his thatched roof.

The institutions grew up around the men, and were informed to their utmost limits by the pervading spirit of their founders. They were men of extraordinary enthusiasm, piety, and perseverance. No obstacles were insurmountable to prayer and faith. In large uncouth buildings at Düsselthal, Christian Friedrich Georgi and his devoted wife made every member of their great communities feel that they were their loving parents, and inspired all their assistants with their own hallowed spirit. Boys and girls were brought under the same control; the girls separated by a wall, being gathered in five large families, living in a long two-story brick block. In the midst of a barren waste, recovered to tillage and beauty, near Hemmen, in Holland, Pastor O. G. Heldring has, in the exercise of marvellous faith and persistency, established three large congregated and eminently successful institutions, one for Magdalens, one for young exposed girls, and one for girls over sixteen, that would, without the sheltering arms of this Bethel, as it is significantly termed, be sent to prison and to inevitable ruin. It is the devoted Mr. Martin and his wife (of whom he touchingly said to a visitor, " Without my wife, sir, I should not have known many a time how to proceed; when a child is put into a cell for punishment, she goes there and talks with it, and God has blessed her words to the heart of many a one; really she can manage the boys better than any of us "), that have overcome the inconveniences of the badly-constructed congregate edifices of the Protestant Agricultural Colony at Sainte Foy, in the south of France, and made it to be a home of redemption for many young criminals. Indeed, every successful institution of reform in the world will be found to be an illustration of the truth that it is the man and not the system that has secured, with the Divine blessing, the encouraging results in the delicate work of human reformation. The presence or absence of Mr. Pillsbury from the Albany Penitentiary has been the criterion of success or failure at that institution.

But the fact should not be overlooked, that in these European establishments it is not the head of them alone by whom this great work is accomplished. In nearly every instance upon the Continent the first object of one proposing to inaugurate an asylum or school of reform has been to gather to his aid a body of devoted young persons of both sexes to become his assistants. They must all drink in his spirit, and coöperate in his movements. All the instructors in school, the foremen in the workshops, the assistants upon the farm, are devoted Christian disciples. These persons are drawn to these institutions in numbers much larger than the proportion of officers in our establishments. They receive no salary save their livelihood and the training they secure in conducting the discipline of the institution, and thus fitting themselves for the superintendency of similar establishments when hereafter called to them. Christian women, as in that wonderful collection of institutions which have grown up around the Deaconess House at Kaiserworth in Prussia, through the earnest ministry of Pastor Fliedner and his excellent wife, have devoted themselves without remuneration to years of faithful service, to learn the most efficient modes of exercising the womanly duties of nurse of the sick, and teacher and reformer of the abandoned of their own sex and of orphan and criminal children.

One cannot fail to see the influence of such a class of persons in the work of reform. If, instead of having officers filling their positions simply for hire, subject to constant changes, and being compelled, on account of the high rate of compensation with us, to employ in the workshops and upon the farm persons of inferior talent, and of a lower moral grade, the Superintendent could be supported in every position by a large force of trained and somewhat cultivated and always devoted persons, constantly seeking the one great end of the institution, what an overwhelming moral influence could thus be secured! This is one of the pressing demands in houses of reform at the present hour in this country.

In our city, in the conduct of several of the charities of the Protestant Episcopal Church, such as the "Sheltering Arms," and the "St. Barnabas Society," a number of devoted, intelligent Christian women, as we have seen in a previous page, have thus, for a limited period of years, offered their time and talents to Christ and to the necessities of those for whom He died, and are engaged in the offices incident to the rescue of the fallen, and the care of periled childhood, without pecuniary compensation.

In institutions supported by municipalities or by the State, it is not to be expected that persons will offer gratuitous service. Nearly every European institution of reform out of England is sustained by voluntary contributions, and grows out of the home-missionary operations of the churches. It is to small institutions thus originated in this country, that we may look for exhibitions of Christian sacrifice, and for models of Christian training and success. Certainly this is a legitimate field for the charity and piety of the churches, to gather up and save the youthful slaves of appetite and vicious habits. But while Christian people are slowly awakening to their duty and opportunity, the State, for its own defence, must step in, with a strong hand, and the broadest provisions, and gather into the readiest and most practicable institutions for moral and religious discipline, the tempted juvenile population of the streets.   These children have not a claim upon us simply because they are human, and are to be the companions of our own children, but because they are to be our rulers.   The poor and criminal streets of our cities govern, by their votes, the residents upon the parks and avenues.

The fact that these European institutions have, the most of them, been located at some distance from large cities, and have secured facilities for garden and farm labor, has not, of itself, been so striking an element of success, or induced such a taste for agricultural life as one might at first view suppose.

In the agricultural colony at Mettray, where the inmates are chiefly employed upon a farm, of eight hundred and fifty-six inmates, two hundred and twenty-three entered the army, and a large number went to mechanical trades, and followed the sea. At the beautiful Netherland Mettray, near Zutphen, in one of the charming districts of Guelderland, where every effort was used to train city boys to become farmers, nearly fifty per cent. of the inmates were found to have an unconquerable aversion to farm-labor, and the managers found it necessary to introduce various handicrafts to prepare the inmates for such positions as their natural tastes rendered most inviting, and gave the best promise of their following in subsequent life.   The difficulty is even more serious with us; other forms of labor than farm-work offer so much larger pecuniary compensation, and apparently afford so much more favorable opportunities of reaching a competence, in addition to the inherent longing of a city boy for the excitement of the town, that it is quite impossible to induce the more enterprising to remain for any time amid the quiet, monotonous, and slow pursuits of the country.   Our only

Religion the great Reforming Agent.

hope of securing in their behalf a life of honest industry is to
place them, with proper training, and under wholesome supervision, in some trade within the city limits, or to find for them a
good opportunity on shipboard.   If we attempt to force nature,
and place them even in the most distant West, under indentures
to farmers, they soon steal away, and hasten back to the city,
where, finding themselves without regular employment, they become a ready prey to the street prowlers, and fall again into
habits of crime.

There are two things that strike the mind forcibly in the
conduct of the work of reform in Europe.   The first is, the
prominence that is given to religious instruction, and the reliance
upon it for the accomplishment of the great end sought in all
reformatory efforts.   M. De Tocqueville, who was one of the
most hearty co-laborers with De Metz, says, with much empha-
sis, "No human power is comparable to religion for reforming
criminals; upon it especially the future result of penitentiary
reform depends."   Another thoughtful European writer has
admirably said, "Without religion prisons may be reformed—
prisoners never can."   The successful superintendents of the
most noted juvenile institutions are men of astonishing faith, like
John Falk, Müller, Wichern, Fliedner, Zeller, Fingado of the
orphan-house in Baden, the simple-hearted, sainted haberdasher,
whose motto was, "As for me and my house, we will serve the
Lord," the Dutch pastor Heldring, the French Martin and Bost,
and hundreds of others, "whose names are written in the book
of life," and also upon the grateful hearts of thousands of redeemed children.   They are men of like infirmities with others,
but also, like Elijah, powerful in prayer, and like St. John, of a
loving, gentle, and heavenly temper.   The whole discipline of

these institutions is pervaded with the spirit of the Gospel, and a large portion of the instruction given is devoted to the study of the Scriptures.

In England, as also with us, one of the most serious obstacles in the way of breaking up institutions into separate families, has been the difficulty of securing the right kind of men and women to place at the head of the several houses.   Rev. Sydney Turner, now inspector of reformatories in England, formerly superintendent and chaplain of Red Hill Philanthropic Farm School, in Surrey, says: "For these positions, you want a religious man; I mean a man who takes up his work as a mission; something given him to do by God; something in which he is responsible, not only for the means he uses, or the methods he pursues, but for the results he attains to.   Such a man views his work as one which he cannot, dare not, leave just to get more salary, more leisure, less worry, or less confinement.   Such a man conducts his work in the spirit and by the instruments of the missionary; not only teaching, but praying; not only admonishing and advising, but giving the daily example of patience, kindness, industry, endurance, and devotion in his personal life.   Before such men the stubborn tempers bend, the hard hearts soften, the idols of vice and crime are cast down. They need not be men of extraordinary talent, but they must be men of earnestness, love, and a sound mind."

The other noticeable fact is, the elevated social position of the persons interested in the discussion of questions of reform in Europe, and in the conduct of the institutions that have already been established.

The first legal minds of France have devoted their time without hesitation, and their best thoughts, to the consideration

of the question of adult and juvenile reformation.   The presiding manager of Mettray was a judge of the Court of Assize,
at Paris, and was first employed by the French Government to
visit and report upon the prisons of the United States.   De
Tocqueville had preceded him in this work, and heartily united
with him in his great experiment at Mettray.   The Empress
Eugenie has made herself a voluntary prison and reformatory inspector.   Her hand upon the shoulder of a boy would not cure
him of the king's evil, as was formerly believed, but it did something better for one—it melted his heart.   The large sums of
money bestowed upon the French queen by the city of Paris,
at the time of her marriage with the emperor, for the purchase
of a diamond necklace, and again, upon the birth of the prince
imperial, were devoted by the benevolent empress to the construction of a magnificent suite of buildings, with beautiful
grounds, for orphan institutions for boys and girls, in Paris.
Here, once a fortnight, she obtains a few hours of the purest
enjoyment of her life, in visiting these joyful little pensioners
upon her bounty.   Has any court upon earth a fairer or more
attractive set of crown jewels than these?   Long before Wichern
opened his thatched cottage at the Horn, Count von Der Recke
laid the foundation of the orphan and reformatory institutions at
Düsselthal, and presided over them until it pleased God to raise
up Mr. Georgi to catch his mantle as he ascended to the skies.
King William III. and the Queen-dowager of Holland were large
subscribers to, and personally interested in, the establishment of
the Netherland Mettray.   The lamented Prince Albert, of England, was greatly interested in the reformatory movements of
that country, and at the head of several organizations.   He laid
the corner-stone of the Agricultural Colony, at Red Hill, under

the auspices of the Philanthropic Society.   The first legal talent
of Great Britain, headed by the late Lord Brougham; the most
conspicuous among the nobility, like the Earl of Shaftesbury,
president of the Reformatory and Refuge Union; the highest
orders in the church, and a numerous body of the most intelligent and cultivated men and women in Great Britain, like Mary
Carpenter, one of the most voluminous and thoughtful writers
upon prison and juvenile discipline, now engaged upon a great
public mission of mercy to her sex in India, have given personal
attention even, to the management of local institutions, as well
as devoted their time and pens to the discussion of the fundamental principles involved in the work of reform.

This general interest, among educated and religious persons
of both sexes in England, has been secured by one feature in
the act of Parliament recognizing local reformatories, by which,
where any voluntary, municipal, or county institution is accepted
and held subject to the periodic inspection of officers appointed
by the government, a subsidy of some eight shillings sterling
per week for each inmate is allowed.   By this means, if a town
or county, or private individuals, secure the buildings, a large
part of the current expenses of the institution is paid by the
government.   The effect must be salutary.   It multiplies small
establishments, and secures the supervision and personal interest
of the best philanthropic and religious members of the community.   It awakens a deeper interest in the welfare of the im-
periled young, and becomes a double blessing, in the development of the zeal and charity of the persons engaged in this
Christlike work.   We must certainly have the missionary and
reformatory skill among us, although in a large degree it is now
latent.   It only awaits the occasion to call it forth.   The labor-

ers, male and female, in the Sanitary and Christian Commissions, bear witness to this.   If the State, under proper supervision, would allow a bare livelihood for the support of the children collected, and benevolent men and women were made to see at how small an additional outlay suitable buildings could be erected for the care and cure of juvenile criminals, small institutions would spring up in every direction.

The two great necessities in our country at this hour in the matter of juvenile reform are, first, some thorough, effectual measure for clearing the streets of our cities and large towns of vagrant, begging, and vicious children.   Mr. Oliver Dyer, in a report read at a public meeting in the city, from the results of a careful inspection made by several sanitary commissions, showing that about six hundred thousand persons are living in tenement-houses, most of them very inconveniently crowded, or in cellars and hovels, calculates that, of the one hundred and twenty thousand children included in this number, *forty thousand* of them are to be considered " destitute and outcasts," and that additional provisions of some kind must be made for them to save them from a life of pauperism or crime.*   We cannot but hope

---

* Of the moral character of these children, Mr. Dyer says in his report: " In the greater portion of this class, their surroundings and their training have produced their natural results.   Hundreds of them have already become confirmed drunkards, and thousands of them are accustomed to strong drink.   Children, from the age of fourteen years down to infants of four, are daily met in a state of intoxication.   They come drunk to the mission-schools. The little creatures have many a time lain stretched upon the benches of this institution (Howard Mission) sleeping off their debauch.

" Hundreds of these children have also become veteran thieves, and thousands more are in training for the same end.   Nine hundred and sixty girls, and three thousand six hundred and fifty-eight boys, between the ages of ten and fifteen years—making a total of four thousand six hundred and

that this is an exaggerated statement.   At least we are certain that, even from the squalidness, ignorance, and corruption of their present condition, many, as they grow older, will find employment which will awaken ambition, and aid them in struggling for a more hopeful fate in life.   But after making every rational deduction, what an army of exposed childhood will still remain !

We shall never come abreast of crime, and have a fair struggle with it, until the community is relieved of these immense gathering reservoirs of vice.   In certainly one city in Scotland, Aberdeen, the experiment has been successfully tried of cleaning out the streets of these children, gathering them into schools or refuges, or securing for them regular employment, and the result upon the criminal statistics of the city was truly wonderful.

If we understand the force of a late act of the English Parliament, all vagrant and unemployed children can be arrested, and, unless properly cared for by parents, can be disposed of in reformatories and by indentures, or by removal from the country, as is deemed advisable by the magistrate before whom the case is brought.   As the law, of course, would not execute itself, and no one sought the self-constituted and somewhat thankless task of complaining against the children in London, the Reform-

---

eighteen—were arrested during the year ending October 31, 1867, for drunkenness and petty crimes.

"No longer ago than Saturday, the 11th day of January last, a boy, thirteen years old, was sent to Blackwell's Island " (no boy of that age should have been sent to a penitentiary) " as a confirmed drunkard, and on the next morning (the Sabbath), his little brother, named Jacob Bullach, only ten years of age, who had also become accustomed to strong drink, in a fit of despondency, occasioned by his brother's fate, committed suicide at his mother's residence in this city."

atory and Refuge Union, two years ago, appointed an officer styled "the Boys' Beadle," and made it his duty to approach "all homeless children as a friend, to sift their cases thoroughly, and, as their various circumstances required, to take them to friends, to a school or refuge, to a magistrate, or to the police." A report of his efforts, which was read at the late meeting of the Social Science Association, held at Belfast, is both interesting and suggestive.*

The multiplication of street trades during the last ten or fifteen years has been of serious disadvantage to children. For the pittance earned in the sale of apples and nuts, of newspapers and matches, and in the vagrant labor of the bootblack, children are kept from school, and are also prevented from learning a trade which will hereafter enable them to support themselves and those that are dependent upon them. Almost all these street pedlars, both boys and girls, are vicious. A large proportion of our city children in the House of Refuge graduated here.

* The twelfth annual report of the Reformatory and Refuge Union, for 1868, referring to this agency, remarks: "The effects of the combined efforts of law and charity are plainly evident in the reduced number of Arabs to be met with in the streets of the metropolis. The boys' beadle, whose duty it is to look after the waifs and strays, has, since his appointment, dealt with upward of two hundred little wanderers, besides helping the teachers engaged in the Ragged Schools and Refuges in their self-denying efforts for those sometimes worse than homeless. . . . . The example of the Union has already been followed by one large town, Birmingham now having its 'Children's Visitor,' whose duties are similar to those of the boys' beadle. Before entering upon his labors, the agent who has been appointed paid a visit to London, and gathered all the information he could from the experience and advice of the agent of the Union, accompanying him upon his rounds, and thus seeing for himself the mode in which he works. The Council cannot but hope that, before long, each of our great provincial towns will have a visitor, whose special duty it shall be to relieve the streets of destitute children."

They are thievish, early becoming burglars, being accustomed to the streets at all hours of the night.   They attend the lowest drinking and dancing saloons, and theatres, and become, at a precocious age, the martyrs of the most loathsome forms of vice. The worst criminals upon our calendars are these young, hardened street venders, confirmed in evil by two or three terms of six months in the penitentiary.

Until the streets are cleared of these children without visible means of support, and some wholesome regulations established in reference to these young highway traders, so that at a proper age they shall go to some trade, and some restriction shall be placed upon their unattended visits to depraving places of amusement, and to the haunts of vice, the community will be obliged constantly to multiply its prisons, and watch thousands of its population going certainly, and to the injury and discomfort of the virtuous, down the broad road to ruin.

Who is the wise man to whom the heavenly Father has imparted the broad, effectual, humane plan by which the now predestined children of crime shall be saved to the community, to themselves, and to God?

The second want is some place of confinement between the House of Refuge and the penitentiary for confirmed young criminals.   The prisons and jails contain hundreds of young men between eighteen and twenty who are now revolving through their cells on short sentences, and at the same time are effectually trained to a life of crime, and hardened to the commission of the most fearful acts.   These young men ought to be taken in hand by the community, to be restrained and kindly watched over, and, solicited by religious culture, taught a trade; a portion of the proceeds of their labor secured to them upon condition of

good behavior; a position found for them when apparently reformed; and then they should be discharged at first upon a
ticket-of-leave, which, if forfeited by crime, secures their return
to the place of detention for the work to go on until they *are*
reformed.   If they have dependent friends, a portion of their
income from their labor might be paid, at their request, to them.
How much better for the community to burden itself with the
expense incident to such a course than to be obliged to submit
to the depredations of trained criminals, and to the loss of the
men besides !   It is simply shocking to enter some of our county
prisons and look upon the young men confined in the cells,
without work, without hope, with nothing before them for a
livelihood but a life of crime, without moral instruction, or instructive and religious reading, whiling away their time in mu-
tually recounting their vicious adventures and in playing cards.
We can see all this, and worse, everywhere in our municipal
and county jails.

A place of detention something of the character indicated
has been established in the Isle of Wight, England, and is called
the Parkhurst Prison.   From it boys are either transported to
Australia and indentured under the supervision of an officer, or
are discharged upon a ticket-of-leave permitting them to remain
at large during good behavior, and subjecting them to the surveillance of the police.

After the careful weighing of the various theories of juvenile
reform, the managers say in their Forty-second Annual Report :
" In the fulfilment of our duties, we are necessarily engaged
upon that vexed problem which has so long lain close to the
heart of the philanthropist, the solution of which involves not
only the welfare of its immediate subject, but largely also the

interests of society, as connected with the best practicable method of moral reformation to be applied to the large and growing class of neglected and vicious youth. . . We believe that the foundations of our system as a house of reform rest upon a solid basis, and we do not consider that the experience of others offers any very important improvement; that, within the limited means at our command, it would be difficult to devise a more judicious and effective method for the peculiar class with which we are called to deal, and that such has not been presented in any compact and single plan by the combined efforts of the various benevolent enterprises of the day, operating in the same field.

" We do not hesitate to say, whatever difficulties invest the general subject, and partial as the work of thorough reformation may be, that this Board accomplishes a great and beneficent work.   Not only is society saved from grave and immediate annoyance by our custody over so large a portion of its delinquent youth, but from more serious vices and crimes into which these neglected and unhappy lives would be sure to fall as their history matured.

" But while we are able to speak thus confidently of the general tendencies of what we do to improve the habits and elevate the moral standard of our charges, and while we can trace its happy effects in many instances, we are not able to convey fully by any arithmetical tables the value of our work.   Doubtless, under favorable circumstances, much of its fruit ripens beyond our jurisdiction into permanent reformation, and in others the good influences which have been brought to bear exercise a modifying power over lives which know no other restraint.   This Board do not believe in any panacea for a vicious and depraved nature. The methods employed must depend to a degree for their success on causes and conditions which cannot be fully estimated, and over which we can have only a partial control. The secret springs of thought and action lie beyond and out of our sight; but what virtue is found in well-adapted means we claim.

"The plan of our organization is such that while, in a community so large as ours, systematically to individualize our training and efforts would involve an amount of expenditure imposing a serious burden upon the State, compared with the present very moderate rate; still, obliged as we are to deal with the subjects of our discipline mainly in the mass, they are so broken up by divisions in each department and by separate classes in the schools, that the character of each child is studied and understood, and the training adapted to the nature of each. Comprehensively the design of the House of Refuge embraces the physical, moral, and intellectual care and culture of its inmates upon a basis which, while securing to our treasury the fruits of a well-arranged and limited system of labor, leaves a proper measure of time for instruction, recreation, and rest. . . . Our inmates may be said to form a large household where, under the guidance of a well-matured experience, benevolence and religion combine to hold the reins of authority. If these do not avail, if judicious restraints, industrious habits, wholesome advice, adequate instruction, and all under conditions favorable to health of body and of mind, fail, we are at loss to supply the necessary elements. We know of no better way."

The records of every succeeding year confirm the impression that, among these classified crowds, the searching and powerful moral influences of the House work out their benign results.

Boy of the Refuge becomes a Colporteur.

At fourteen years of age James C—— was sent to the House for stealing cotton upon the docks. His father was intemperate, and had left his mother in England, bringing James with him to this country. They had no home but hired lodgings, and took their meals wherever they happened to be at meal-time. It was said of him, when his record was taken upon entering the House, "He will require some training to cure him of his habits." He was indentured in a good family in this State, and favorable accounts were received of him from time to time. In 1860 he wrote himself as follows: ". . . You know I have served out my time as an apprentice, and I am at present travelling through the county of Greene, as a colporteur for the American Tract Society; and here I must inform you that this is the county where I was converted and joined the Church, and I feel anxious to spread that Gospel which has done so much for me. I must say I feel well, I like the business, it is the Lord's work. . . . I can now look back with pleasure on the day when I first entered the House of Refuge. *It was the starting-point in my life. I believe it has been the means of making me what I am.* I have gained very many kind friends, and, what is better, they are Christian friends. My associations and associates are Christian, and I am led to inquire how it would have been with me if I had been left to myself to run in the streets of New York, where so many youth and young men are ruined? I bless the day that I was ever taken from them, and I hope now, by the grace of God, to live a Christian life, and my desire is to serve Him continually. Oh, how I should like to see you all at the Refuge, and thank all of you for the kindness you showed to me while I was with you! I wish I could talk to the youth and young men under your care, and tell them

Visit of James to the House.

how I have been blessed by being in the same position they now are in. I would take them by the hand, and tell them what the Lord will do for them if they will receive Him. I hope the time will come when I shall be able to see you, and can assure you it will give me great pleasure to see you after so long an absence. But, my dear sir, should we never meet again on earth, we have the consolation that, if we are faithful in the service of our God, we shall meet in heaven."

A short time afterward he visited the House and passed the night, and we find this record of it upon the Daily Journal : " James C., No. 4,708, visited the House and stayed with us last night. He was indentured in August, 1851; his term of service expired in 1857, giving entire satisfaction. After this he attended school during the winter months, and worked on the farm in the summer ; by so doing he has obtained a good education. He is a worthy and exemplary member of the Dutch Reformed Church. He is now laboring in the employment of the American Tract Society in Greene County, N. Y., doing good and being well received. He closed the first division school with a very able prayer, which, on account of the peculiarity of his case, was quite affecting. His deportment and conversation were of a devoted character, and gave us strong evidences of his being a warm-hearted Christian."

CHAPTER IX.

THE CLOSE OF THE HALF CENTURY.

THE census of the institution began in 1865 to rise toward the full capacity of its immense halls.   During the early part of the war, for apparent reasons, the number of boys, especially of the maturer ones, if any thing, slightly decreased, but with its close the numbers rose rapidly from an average of six hundred to the good-sized village which it has now become, with a population of a thousand.

It is a matter of surprise to all intimately acquainted with the workings of the Refuge, and with the annual exposition of its benevolent designs and reformatory discipline, that many intelligent persons should still regard the House as a penal institution. This misapprehension greatly embarrasses the good work of the institution and brings unnecessary grief and chagrin to the hearts of friends.   The impression probably arises from the fact that the same officers of justice and the same tribunals commit to the prison and also to the House of Refuge; and from the additional fact that, while many of the courts clearly understand its beneficent design, some still have the same mistaken apprehension of its true character.

It is for this reason that we constantly meet with the remark, both from friends and presiding justices, that the child should

The Institution not penal.

be discharged " because he has been sufficiently punished," or
that he ought not to remain in the House, " as the crime charged
against him was so trivial." If the institution is to be considered as a place of punishment, it entirely fails of its object; for
the simple restraint within its walls for a short period, with its
full and wholesome diet, its hours of study and recreation, and
its opportunity for learning a trade, would be considered no
dreaded consequence of wrong-doing, and have no power to
awaken a fear of again committing a like offence. Six months
comfortable boarding and schooling would be no adequate punishment to a boy for larceny, but would rather create within
him a sense of impunity in wrong-doing. If it were a place of
punishment, there would be a cruelty in allotting, even for the
shortest period, confinement within its bounds for trifling larcenies, on the part of young children, thoughtlessly committed.
But if the early crime is in one sense forgiven by the community, on account of the youth and neglected condition of the
subject, and he is placed away from temptation under suitable
guardianship, where he may be trained for a useful life, and then
placed in a position to begin life for himself with a fair chance
of success, what might otherwise be accounted a wrong becomes
an invaluable charity. Simple punishment might require but a
short period of severe discipline, but training requires time.
Habits cannot be shed and renewed in a few months, and character grows very slowly. But this period, passed in physical,
mental, and moral culture, is of manifest advantage both to the
subject and to his friends. Indeed, as to the former, it is, in
most instances, the favorable decision of the question between a
life of indolence and crime, attended with their inevitable results of misery and ruin, and a life of activity and virtue crowned

with a good name.   Certainly no stain of the prison clouds the recollection of former inmates of the Refuge, who have purchased a good reputation by a worthy life.

If not a place of punishment, why should children be sent here whose parents have the pecuniary ability to care for them? The family tie should not be broken without adequate cause, and parents should not be too easily released from their obligation to support their children.   But there is even a paramount obligation that the community owes to the young; for, if parents neglect their charge, it is evidently the duty of the State, in some way, to assume the task, both for its own security and for the salvation of the youth.   Children have a natural and civil right to be kept from the temptations of the street, to be defended from the pernicious example of evil companions, to be secured from haunts of sin, to have instruction in the common branches of learning, to be taught habits of industry and the practices of virtue, and to be made acquainted with their duty to God and man, as revealed in the Holy Scriptures.   Whatever may be the pecuniary ability of the parents, this obligation to the children has not been met in reference to those committed to our care, except in the rarest instances.   Even in cases where it has been attempted, the child has been surrounded by such influences that the efforts of the parents have been overborne by them. Nearly all our children have been truants, if sent to school, and are almost utterly deficient as to the first steps in a common education.   They have also fallen into such indolent habits that they are only a burden upon their parents, and will ultimately be upon the community; and their moral nature has remained entirely unsolicited by religious culture.   The only chance for even a limited education, however respectable the parents seem

Its Moral Influence powerful.

to be, and for an established habit of industry and reverence for sacred things, is that offered by the House of Refuge.

There is another misapprehension existing in the community, sometimes even seeking expression in the public prints, destroying both the confidence of parents and the general public in the ability of the institution to accomplish its work. Its immense capacity and the large numbers gathered within its walls are supposed to peril its reformatory discipline, and to render it a school of vice rather than of morals. As a question of fact, the carefully accumulated statistics of nearly half a century give a most satisfactory answer to this erroneous judgment.

It is well to call to mind the weight of the moral influence we are enabled to exert over our inmates. In our city, from the same class of children, the Mission Sunday-schools are collected. The pupils of these schools are under wholesome tuition but a few hours upon the Sabbath, and are exposed, all the rest of the time, to the most baneful examples and severe temptations; yet, it is confidently affirmed and unquestioned, that a vast amount of good is accomplished by even these short periods of religious culture. But all this we have every Sabbath, with constant attendance, and, in addition to this, the impressive services of the chapel, adapted to their age and wants; the morning and evening prayer, the blessing at the meal, repeated religious addresses, the personal contact of Christian men and women; the regular hours of study; the absence of the temptations continually drawing them aside when in the streets—and all this continued for the period of a year or more. If any thing is accomplished in the Sunday-schools, how much more, with God's blessing, must result from this daily moral and religious discipline!

Intelligent men speak unadvisedly when they give utterance to distrust in reference to the influence of the Refuge, as some have frankly, and with much emotion, acknowledged when, on the Sabbath, they have united with us in the services of public worship, or have become familiar, by personal inspection, with our daily discipline.

With our large numbers we secure much of the character of a family institution by our many subdivisions. Walls divide us into four companies, and schools still further separate us into thirteen or fourteen classes, under different teachers; so that the powerful influence of personal character is brought to bear upon the individual child. The affectionate recollections which the children preserve for years, of their teachers and officers, manifested in a continued correspondence, show how powerful for good this influence is.

In March, 1863, Mr. Ketchum, who had held the position of Superintendent for fourteen years, closed at the same time his life and his charge of the House. He died in the peace of the Gospel, to which alone he had looked as the great reformatory agent in the work to which he had given the ripest years and best energies of his life. During nearly all this period he had enjoyed the support of Mr. I. C. Jones, as his assistant. With this long acquaintance with the responsibilities and details of the position—the fifth in this honored succession of first officers— Mr. Jones entered upon the administration of the House, and has fully confirmed the high expectations of the managers in his ability and executive energy.

In the same year Colonel Linus W. Stevens, who had been a manager for more than sixteen years, and devoted a large portion of his time to the service of the House, passed away from

Colonel Stevens.—Edmund M. Young.

earth. "In justice to his memory," say the Board, in the deserved tribute which they pay to his worth, "and in gratification of our feeling of regard, we desire to record our appreciation of his eminent services in the inception and successful completion of our present buildings. His sound judgment and unwearied perseverance were alike conspicuous in the many applications to the Legislature, and in the difficulties arising in the course of the erection of the House; his connection with the Building Committee from its original formation to the close of its labors brought his usefulness into constant requisition; his unswerving probity and stainless public life added weight at all times to his efforts in our behalf with the public authorities; and his admirable tact, his sagacious prudence, and simple suavity of manners seldom failed, as they were exerted to accomplish the worthy ends he had in view."

The succeeding year proved to be fatal to another one of the most respected and useful members of the Board, Mr. Edmund M. Young, an active, successful, and well-known merchant of the city. For about twelve years he had generously yielded his valuable services to the interests of the Refuge. From the hour of his election up to the time of his sudden and lamented death, he was faithfully and "efficiently engaged in the performance of his duties as a manager, serving, as he did, on several of the most important committees. Always prompt, of sound judgment, and rare executive ability, with clear views, and the strongest interest in the objects of the institution, his devoted services and usefulness were most highly appreciated by his associates, while his urbanity, his correct principles, and sincere Christian course as a man, endeared him to all."

The succeeding years placed the fatal star upon the record

against the honored names of Thomas B. Stillman, a highly-respected officer of the General Government, as well as a trusted citizen; Walter Underhill, for many years the faithful and efficient treasurer of the Society, a man of undoubted integrity, and enjoying the confidence of the community, whose interest in the institution and its unfortunate inmates rather increased than decreased with his advancing years; and James W. Underhill, the banker, prompt in business, the beloved and successful head of the Sunday-school of his church, and the abiding friend and wise counsellor of the House of Refuge.

All these, like the names of precious memory before them, rested from their earthly labors, and we and those that will follow us, are reaping, and will continue to reap, the harvest of their sowing.

The Board had long felt the importance of securing some personal supervision over its indentured children, an inspection of the homes of the inmates received from the cities of New York and Brooklyn, to aid the Indenturing Committee in deciding the important question of the expediency of a child's discharge to his parents, rather than upon indentures in the country, and an organ of communication with the magistrates from whose courts the majority of its subjects were received; they were also impressed with the importance of having a resident clergyman, now that the numbers of the House had become so large, and the moral condition of these children demanded that they should be touched at every possible point of contact by religious agencies; they therefore sought to combine these objects, by electing a permanent chaplain, and making the important duties above referred to his proper pastoral work.

The excellent gentleman, Rev. Richard Horton, who had held

Duties of the Chaplain.

the office of chaplain for the preceding eight years, being able only, through his business engagements, to yield his Sabbaths to the religious instruction of the children, tendered his resignation, and was succeeded by the present incumbent of the office.

In addition to the public Sabbath service, the chaplain now leads in evening prayer one of the divisions of the school, visits the sick in the hospitals, is visited by any inmate that desires an

RIVERSIDE PARSONAGE, RANDALL'S ISLAND.

interview, preaches to the officers on one evening in the week, and attends such funeral services and public occasions as are incident to the place and the times.

To render the exercises of the sanctuary a personal act of the children, rather than a performance to which they are simply to give their attention, a series of liturgical services, as has been intimated, were prepared under the direction of the Board, so varied as to meet the different exigencies of daily devotions and Sabbath worship, and interspersed with extemporaneous prayers, to give expression to the peculiar religious emotions and wants of the hour. This very elastic and simple form of worship has now been in use about five years, and it is only expressing the unanimous sentiment of all who have united with us in our services, representing almost every shade of Christian belief, that it rarely occurs, that what may be called the devotional parts of the service of the sanctuary, often in other congregations listened to with apparently little attention, are conducted with such universal interest and reverence.

It is an affecting illustration of the firm hold with which these devotional formularies seize upon the memories and hearts of the children, and of their "power of God unto salvation," that in the instance of a number of the older boys, who, at times, have manifested a deep and sincere interest in spiritual things, in their extemporaneous prayers in the voluntary services which they attended during a portion of their hours of recreation, in the school-room, these appropriate and peculiarly expressive sentences of Scriptural confession and supplication often occurred. This form of service, with the Bible, accompanies the child when leaving the institution for a new home. All the laws of association, and all the strength of memory and habit, will tend to keep the hours of devotion in the mind, while the familiar manual will offer the well-known channel for the utterance of religious emotions.

The visits of the chaplain, among the families into whose hands children had been placed by indentures, disclosed upon the whole a very satisfactory condition of things. Of one hundred and fifty-three to whom personal visits were made, or of whom information was obtained, during one summer and fall, thirty-nine only had been returned to the House, or had run away from their places. The remainder were doing well, and a large proportion of the families was all that could be desired.

To aid the Indenturing Committee in determining when they might safely yield to the importunity of parents, for the discharge of children back to their custody, instead of indenturing them in the country, the chaplain was made secretary of the committee, and such cases are committed to him for a personal examination of the homes and of the places of labor provided for the inmates when released. Written reports are made which are transcribed upon a permanent record for reference when required. The nature and importance of this service will be better understood by a few extracts from the journal of these visits.

"The chaplain had a very satisfactory conversation with Justice F—— T——, in reference to the case of J—— C——. By personal inquiry it was found that the boy had a bad reputation when at home; that the part of the city where his mother resided was the worst possible place for him; and two parties capable of forming a safe judgment earnestly protested against his return. When the justice learned with how much care every case brought before the committee was examined, and the principles upon which they acted, he expressed great surprise and pleasure, and intimated that he should hereafter rest quietly upon their decisions, after all the facts brought to his knowledge had been presented to them."

"In the case of B—— W——, the examination of the home developed much to awaken sympathy. A miserable drunken father was in the penitentiary on Blackwell's Island. The suffering wife felt assured that she was relieved from him forever.

A daughter, hardly recovered from a fever, unable to work, was living at home. The mother and daughter bear a good character, and need the aid of B——, for whom a position which she had previously occupied was open. There are good grounds to believe that the girl was innocent of the offence for which she was committed to the House a year since. Her case is commended to the favorable consideration of the committee."

"Justice C—— called the attention of the committee to the case of M—— S——, upon the recommendation of Rev. Father T——, of the Catholic Church of the Transfiguration. The chaplain had a pleasant call upon Father T——. He would on no account, he said, recommend the discharge of the girl to her parents unless they left the city. Should they go to R——, as they now propose to do, he thinks M—— may be safely returned to their care. The parents have been to him often before, and he has always refused their request to have her returned to them in the city."

"In the case of M—— H——, the chaplain reports that the home in Mulberry Street is as bad a place as possible for a girl, and that the mother assented to this proposition. The father has been an invalid for a long period, and appears to be near his end. It is recommended that M—— be taken to the city to see her father once more. The mother seems to be an honest and industrious woman. She needs any assistance that M—— could render her in the support of the family. She was advised to find a good place for her daughter and report it to the superintendent."

"Visited the home of P—— O'H——, and found as dreary and dirty a room as can well be imagined. Three or four nearly naked children were running about, exhibiting the utmost neglect. Seeing the impression made by the first appearance of things, a woman in the family remarked that they 'were about removing, as they had trouble with their landlord;' but to this statement Mrs. O'H—— objected, saying that they 'were not intending to move,' that there 'was no trouble,' and that 'she could speak for herself.' She said her husband had been receiving twenty shillings a day for his work, and was 'now upon a little strike for three dollars.' It might be stated that the clothing of Mrs. O'H—— was nearly as ragged and scanty as that of the children. She said they had no place provided for the boy to work, and simply wanted him at home, as his father was able to support him."

"Called at the home of J. J. B——, and found it to be a rear tenement-house, with terrible odors filling the passage-ways. The rooms, however, in the upper story, occupied by the family were comfortable, and the parents appeared very tidy and respectable. The scene upon entering the room was an affecting one in the extreme: the father, feeble, and evidently in the last stages of consumption, was sitting in an easy-chair, and the mother, an invalid, was lying upon the bed. All the earnings of the family have been exhausted by their sickness. There were three little children in the room, too young to do any thing for their own support. J—— has heretofore been able to earn six dollars a week, and is the only member of the family now able to do any thing for their support. He had fallen into bad company, but has been deeply affected since he has been at the Refuge, by a knowledge of the helpless condition of the family. He has in several instances given evidence of a manly character, and a desire to be a good boy.

When the chaplain intimated, during the visit, the possibility of his being discharged, the scene was truly a touching one. The mother rose up from the bed to shake hands with him, the tears running down her face; the father, unable to rise, stretched out his hand, and the children, one after another, followed the example of their parents. The mother insisted upon the chaplain's taking a sprig of the geranium which she was carefully cultivating in the window, as an expression of her gratitude. The circumstances of the case without the name were related to the boys of the second division at evening prayers. They all seemed much affected, J—— particularly so. To the question whether a boy in such a case might be trusted to go and take care of his helpless parents and family, there was a unanimous answer in the affirmative. With the consent of the Indenturing Committee, the chaplain accompanied J—— to his home. The scene at his return can be better imagined than described. Up to the present time the boy has fulfilled his promise, and faithfully provided for his parents. They have all removed from the city, and have secured employment and a good home in the West.

"Visited the mother of S—— J——, Baxter Street. His father has lately died. An uncle of the boy lives in Northfield, Vermont, and expresses much interest in the family, sending money to them. He says he can find work for S——, and offers to pay his fare, directing as to the route he should take. The mother intimated that she was about to remove there; but when it was proposed to place S—— on board the Troy boat whenever she was ready to start, she flamed up at once and said she would 'not leave New York for a kingdom,' and it was very evident that she did not intend that S—— should leave the city. The home is a rear-tenement, in about the worst neighborhood in the city. Northfield is the place for S——."

Boys in the Army and Navy.

"Called at the home of C—— C——. Found it with much difficulty. The mother was away from home. Her parents live in a crowded, rear tenement-house. The room was in the third story, and two little girls were looking out from it through broken panes of glass, being locked in. This it was found was the daily custom, as the mother goes out every day to wash. A neighbor said that Mrs. C—— *did* get drunk, but would do better if she were not so constantly abused by her husband. She said he also was intemperate, and that a short time since he had been placed in the penitentiary for cruelty and abuse toward his wife. All this confirms the sad story brought by the little girl to the House, our belief in which was somewhat shaken by the good appearance of the father. Her home would be a miserable place for C——."

These few, out of a large volume of records, already collected, will serve to indicate how important a knowledge of the actual condition of the home and the state of the family is, to enable the committee, considering the question of the final disposition of the child, to judge prudently and humanely between the legitimate home of the inmate and a new legal one in a strange family.

The last years in the history of the House have been made memorable by incidents connected with the great civil war through which we have passed. The boys entered fully into the spirit of the times, and among the older inmates there was an intense desire to enlist either in the army or navy. Between three and four hundred entered the service of the country, directly from the institution, during the struggle, and a much larger number of those that had been indentured or discharged found their way into the army or navy.

Many rose to positions of considerable distinction, both upon
the sea and land.   When bounties began to be paid, large sums
were placed by the boys in the Savings Banks, which became a
valuable capital for them upon their return from the army, or a
generous aid to their parents.

The constant perils of the war and the regular discipline of
the army seemed to have a favorable moral influence over the
young soldiers, keeping fresh in their minds the instructions of
the Refuge.   Very interesting and affecting illustrations of this
fact were constantly coming to our notice during the last years
of the war.

The following letter was received, in 1866, from the gentleman at the West to whom J. T. had been indentured: " He
remained with me," says the writer, " until August, 1861.
During the time he lived with me he felt very much at home,
was industrious and honest, and attended Sabbath-school and
church regularly.   During the last six months he was with us
he improved very much.   The religious instructions he had received were manifestly having a good effect.   In August, 1861,
he enlisted, with my consent, in the 42d Illinois Volunteers.   I
felt some fears that the temptations of camp-life would be too
much for him to withstand, but he conducted himself nobly on
the field, and won the confidence of his officers.   We kept up a
correspondence with him.   His letters grew more and more
interesting, and showed a radical change wrought in him.   He
expressed the strongest attachment to my family; called up
things that were done which were wrong, and begged our for-
giveness.   After the battle of Chickamauga, I received a letter
from a member of the Christian commission, informing me that
J. was severely wounded, and expressing a very favorable

opinion in regard to his Christian experience. He lay seven days upon the battle-field before he was brought in and cared for. I afterward had an interview with a Christian companion of his who was with him in the closing scene. In relating his conversation with him, he said he asked him this question: ' Did you not suffer terribly while you lay upon the battle-field?' ' Suffer,' he answered, ' how could I suffer when Jesus was with me?' We feel that he has left us a rich legacy in this simple expression, abundantly repaying us for all our anxiety, care, and trouble in his behalf. He died January 23, 1864."

The Daily Journal, during these memorable years, contains constant records like the following: "H. F. visited us to-day, after an absence of over two years, during which he has served his country in the Army of the Potomac, participating in nearly all the battles, but escaped without injury. During the seven days' battles he distinguished himself by his coolness and bravery, and was rewarded by being promoted to the rank of second lieutenant, and is now attached to the —— regiment of heavy artillery. He is an intelligent young man, and we predict for him a prosperous future."

" B. L. was sixteen years of age when he came to the House. He had become a pickpocket, and was deemed a hard case. After remaining at the Refuge about seventeen months, he was permitted to enlist as a private in the army. Three years from the date of his enlistment he visited the House, accompanied by his wife, a very well-appearing and intelligent young woman, who seemed quite proud of her husband, and in no measure disturbed to know that he was once an inmate of the institution. Without aid from friends, by his own good conduct and courage, he worked his way through all the intermediate positions until he had reached that of captain. He was still in the army, and wore his uniform with much grace."

" James C. visited the House this afternoon, accompanied by his wife. He was in the army, but was discharged on account of severe wounds received during the seven days' battles. He is now master of a vessel in the employment of the government, carrying supplies for the army. He is a fine-looking man, and has a neat, modest wife."

" James R. visited the House this morning. He was indentured seven years ago to Mr. S., of Connecticut, who represents him to have been a faithful apprentice. When the war broke out, he obtained his master's permission to enlist in one of the Connecticut regiments, and accompanied General Burnside on his expedition. He subsequently joined the Army of the Potomac, and took a part in the principal battles. His term of service having expired, he enlisted again, and received a bounty of seven hundred and two dollars, which he has securely invested. He is now in good health and spirits, having entirely recovered from a wound received in battle."

" George H. called to see us this morning. He is a soldier, having been in the Army of the Potomac nearly three years, and has been in many battles. He is now at home on a short furlough, and is suffering from the effects of a wound in the arm. He speaks favorably of a number of our boys who are in his regiment. All are in good spirits, and are determined to ' fight it out on this line.' "

" Philip J., a former inmate, visited the House this afternoon, having obtained a short furlough ashore while his ship is undergoing repairs at the Navy Yard. He has been for some time in the United States service, and has been promoted to the berth of master's mate, having passed through all the petty grades to his present position. He is a steady young man, and his future is promising."

" Charles S., who left the House in 1857, called to see us to-day. He entered the army when the war first broke out, was promoted through the several grades to captain, when his health failed, and he resigned his commission. He has lately come into the possession of quite a fortune, and is at the present time living in the city. He is a gentlemanly young man, and bears himself modestly."

" E. L. called to see us this morning and to attend the chapel service. He was discharged from the House two years ago, and shortly after enlisted in one of the New-York regiments for two years. He has served his time honorably, and has now re-enlisted, receiving a bounty of eight hundred and two dollars, which, added to his previous savings, makes him upwards of a thousand dollars on deposit in the Savings Bank. He is a fine-looking young man."

These quotations might be almost indefinitely multiplied, showing at the same time the good service rendered by the institution to the country in the hour of its greatest peril, and the effect of the previous discipline of these young men, to defend them against the peculiar temptations of the camp.

April 14, 1863, the Legislature of the State gave to the " Society for the Protection of Destitute Roman Catholic Children in the City of New York " an act of incorporation very similar to that of the Juvenile Asylum, and made it the duty of the Courts that, " whenever the parent, guardian, or next of kin of any Catholic child about to be finally committed, shall request the magistrate to commit the child to the Catholic institution, the magistrate shall grant the request."

This Society and institution owe their origin and successful establishment to the indefatigable and persevering endeavors of Dr. L. Silliman Ives. Large donations, in the beginning, were made by generous Catholics of the city; considerable sums of money have been raised by lectures and fairs; annual subscriptions are still taken up, a portion of the current expenses is raised by the labor of the children, and the remainder comes from annual donations from the State and the city.

The Society receives both sexes into its custody, but they are placed under separate administrations, the boys under the Christian Brothers and the girls under the Sisters of Charity. For several years the two branches of the institution were poorly accommodated in hired houses in the city; but in 1867 a brick building for the boys was completed on a large farm in Westchester County, about three miles from the Harlem Bridge, and the corner-stone of an edifice for girls was laid at a short distance from the boys' House. The boys' building is temporary, being intended for shops when the main edifice is completed; but it is very comfortably and economically arranged. The institution has been peculiarly successful in its choice of a Superintendent, Brother Telliow, a Prussian, a gentleman of warm and humane sentiments, of great practical wisdom, and of much quiet executive power. It has another advantage peculiar to the Catholic Church, at least in this country. Wichern, as we have seen, has secured the same object under Protestant auspices in Holland. It has twenty officers, all belonging to the order of the Christian Brothers. They give themselves to the church, when they take the vows of the order, to be teachers wherever they may be appointed to labor. They are looking to nothing besides. They will never be priests; they are expecting to pursue no form of business hereafter, but for life will remain in the office of instructors. Their salaries are simply the requisite provision for their living, sick or well. These men are constantly with the boys in school, work, recreation, and in the dormitory; and it can be readily seen what a moral power they are able to bring to the aid of the Superintendent in his work of reforming the young persons thus placed in their hands.

Brother Telliow appreciates the importance of securing habits of industry and the value of regular work in attaining good discipline in the House. Shop-work, for lack of securing as yet suitable contractors to employ the services of the boys, has not been as remunerative as it may be rendered, but the quality of the work is good, and the favorable effect of it upon the lads is beyond a question.

There is no exchange of labor between the boys and girls, excepting that the shoes for both departments are made by the former. Washing, tailoring, dressmaking, and mending, each sex attends to by itself.

The boys' institution is crowded, about seven hundred being gathered into it. One hundred and seventy girls form the female department. The average time of detention, on account of the crowded state of the institution, is short, being considerably within a year; and the Courts have been informed that their ability to accommodate other committals is exactly measured by the discharges they can make. Nearly all their inmates have been sent to them by the magistrates, although they have the power to receive children whose custody has been released to them by their parents or guardians.

The boys range young, the average age being much below the House of Refuge, and they seem to be from a much better class of street children.   Thus far most of the discharges have been to parents; but measures are being considered to effect the distribution of more of them in the country, especially at the West. The purchase of a large farm in some Western State has been recommended by friends of the Society, to which many of the children might be deported, and from whence they could be distributed throughout the farming districts of the country.   Very large and imposing buildings form the plan of the establishment, when its original purpose is carried out, and a decided impression will be made upon the juvenile crime of the city, when its full capacity is reached.

We can certainly bid our Catholic co-laborers in this work " God-speed;" and, after they have reached their utmost limits, we shall find the streets of the city crowded with children, who will more than fill our Asylums and Refuges, and who are perishing for lack of proper care and training.

The marked feature of the House of Refuge at the present time is the practical direction which has been given to its long-established system of grades, and the important office which it is made to accomplish in the discipline of the House.   So manifest has this latter effect become, that the "lock-ups," which were constructed in the House at its opening for separate and solitary punishment, have been, every one of them, removed, and a large open dormitory has been constructed in their place. Corporal punishment has been in this way reduced to an exceedingly small percentage, and a general appearance of cheerfulness and hopefulness has been secured throughout the institution.   In the Appendix to this volume the system is presented in detail. The boy is met when he enters the House (and the same is true of the girl) with the assurance that the hour of his discharge is in his own hands. The two simple rules of the Refuge are recited to him, and the effect of obedience to them upon his standing and comfort in the House, and upon the time of his discharge, is clearly and fully explained. If in the school, in the shop, in the yard, and everywhere, he always tells the truth, and does the best he knows how, he will receive and hold the grade (1). If he retains this grade for a year, and has advanced to the fourth class in school, he has purchased his discharge by good conduct, and the door that has detained him opens before him as soon as his friends or the institution can secure a suitable place for him.

As a barrier against the importunity of friends who have not always the best interests of the children at heart, especially in reference to their education, it is required that the inmate shall reach, at least, the third class in school before he is discharged. This acts as a wholesome spur to the ambition of an indolent or stupid boy. No one can be discharged that has not been in the grade (1) for at least six weeks. By carelessness, by idleness, or by wilfulness, shown when about his work or in school, a boy may sink by one degree a week to the lowest grade (or by some serious offence at once through all the grades), which is (4). In such a case four additional weeks to the six in the grade (1) are required before he can be discharged; and for every succeeding (4) two weeks are added to the previous accumulations. Every boy knows his position in reference to a discharge, and would respond at once if questioned, when, according to his badge, he can be released. As this change of badge is so serious a matter to an inmate, only the Superintendent, assistant superintendent, and matron (before whom the offence has not been committed, and who can consequently weigh calmly the charges brought against the children) administer this discipline. It is done in the presence of the inmate before the school, on Saturday evening, and is a very impressive occasion.

The labor of the boys and girls is let out to contractors, who supply their own overseers. But these overseers have nothing to do with determining the amount of work to be done by the inmates, and are not permitted in any manner to administer discipline. The daily stint of labor is settled by the officers of the House, and has been established after the most careful examination of a boy's ability at different ages, and at different stages of his advance in the knowledge of the trade, and is intended to be not more than two-thirds of what a boy in the same conditions of age and skill, outside of the Refuge, with the spur of a pecuniary reward, can easily accomplish. Every act of discipline in the shop is accorded by the assistant superin_ tendent upon the report of the House officer stationed in each shop.

The great object sought (and it has been gained) is, to have every inmate feel that perfect justice will be done him, and that he will have a fair chance to merit an honorable badge. A boy, who was just ready to be discharged, was irritated beyond his power of self-control by the unhappy manner of a workman, and, in a moment of excitement, used very improper language. There was but one course to be pursued. It was as severe a strain upon the sympathies of the Superintendent as upon the condition of the boy. He was degraded from his standing, and, although his friends had been requested to come for him, thirteen additional weeks were added to his detention. But justice

was equal in its balance; the workman was peremptorily discharged.   As might be expected, a powerful and wholesome impression was made by the affair upon the minds of the boys.

The absence of the assistant superintendent, a short time since,
brought the Superintendent into the shops in his place.   He
noticed a long string of boys assembled upon the line to be disciplined for failure in the work.   They were some of the best
boys in the institution.   The Superintendent talked with them,
heard their reasons for the failure, and also the testimony of the
overseer.   He sent the boys back again, after talking with them,
to their work.   He learned that this overseer had for some time
experienced this difficulty with his boys, and made this daily
complaint of a large portion of them.   The Superintendent was
fully convinced in his own mind that the trouble was not with
the boys, but with their overseer.   When he found the same
scene enacted on the succeeding day, he quietly remarked to
this man, that he would grant him a week longer to try the experiment with his "team;" if his trouble continued, he would
then be discharged.   The agent of the contractor, who defended
his man, was indignant, and confident that such a course would
break down the discipline of the House.   The Superintendent
was decided and even peremptory; and—the result was, that
not a boy was on the line the next day, and the work was
done.

As the consequence of this simple and easily-administered
system of grades, as we have remarked, the necessity of corporal
punishments has been almost entirely removed.   The boy's
strongest selfish interests coöperate with his highest purposes
to restrain him from wrong-doing, and to inspire him in the diligent discharge of his duty.   Although there were never before

this year (1868) so many inmates present in the institution, and particularly never more mature boys (indeed, they may be called young men, their ages ranging from seventeen to twenty), there never was a period in its history when the requisition for a rigid discipline was less urgent, or a better feeling prevalent throughout the whole establishment.

Up to the first of July, 1868, twelve thousand five hundred and sixty children had been received into the House.   During the greater portion of last year there have been a thousand inmates in the two departments—eight hundred boys and two hundred girls.   The largest number present at one time has been one thousand and twenty.

Last year there were eight hundred and four children received, and seven hundred and seventy-nine discharged.   There were nine hundred and seventy-one present on the first of January, 1867.   Between seventeen and eighteen hundred different children thus came under the training of the officers of the House during the year.

The current expenses for the year amounted to between one hundred and fifteen and one hundred and sixteen thousand dollars.   Of this amount the inmates earned, by their productive labor, over fifty-five thousand dollars—the girls earning about four thousand dollars of this sum, besides doing the usual housework of their own department, and the tailoring, dressmaking, mending, and washing for the whole establishment. This is quite an unprecedented result; no institution of reform for children in the world has thus far even approached it, excepting the sister institution at Rochester.   Every child, down to the youngest (six or seven years of age), is employed a given number of hours daily in labor suited to its age, health, and strength, and is better, physically, intellectually, and morally, for it. No child has been overworked.

Every day but the Sabbath, every child has enjoyed an average of four hours of schooling. In the period of a year, with these opportunities, besides the skill attained in labor, and the change in moral purposes, unless there is serious mental deficiency, the child, even if, as in a majority of cases, it has had no previous opportunity in school, will have acquired ability to read, write, and to understand the fundamental rules of arithmetic.

It is true that the promise founded upon the good order and submission which our inmates exhibit in their workshops, the progress they make in their studies, and their attentive interest in the religious services of the Refuge, is not always realized when they leave us. Some find their way back again through the devious paths of vice, and others become inmates of penitentiaries and State prisons, but these form only a small proportion of the number that are saved from a life of crime and vagabondism. The majority go forth to live honest and faithful lives. In exceptional cases they reach positions of distinction, and reflect much credit upon the institution, to which they freely render the tribute of gratitude for their redemption.

During the last year several have commenced their studies for the Christian ministry, who were indentured a few years since from the Refuge. One young man, in a peculiarly manly letter, recounts his pecuniary arrangements for prosecuting the study of the law.

There are two suggestions forced upon the convictions of the managers, by their experience with some of the maturer graduates of the House, which they have felt called to urge upon the Legislature. One is the establishment of a training-ship for boys

in the harbor of New York, under the charge of the Board-
" The benefits of such a step," says the president of the Society,
Oliver S. Strong, Esq. (who, for the period of nearly thirteen
years, has given daily attention to the various interests of the
House, and made himself familiar with the different experiments
in the work of juvenile reformation, both in this country and in
Europe, and who prepared the report for 1847), " would be very
great. Among the large number committed to the House, especially of the older boys, there are many possessing that bold and
adventurous spirit which would prompt them to choose the sea as
their vocation. After these have undergone the discipline of the
House for a year or more, and have learned habits of order
and self-control, it would be a great advantage to them and to
the country if they could have an opening afforded them in
the way proposed. It would be good for them, for they would
still be under the eye of the Society's officials, and be taught the
nautical profession ; it would be equally good for the country as
an important tributary to the navy and mercantile marine. . . .
The State of Massachusetts maintains two ships as a nautical
branch of the State Reform School at Westborough, but the
connection is merely nominal, the whole management of the
ships being under a separate Board of Trustees. The Westborough institution has power to transfer boys to the Nautical
Branch, but, to judge from the reports thus far made, the privilege is exercised only in the case of a few. By the Seventh
Annual Report of the Trustees of the Nautical Branch, it appears that, of two hundred and fifty-nine boys received, but six
were transferred from the State Reform School, while two hundred and forty-two were committed by the Courts fresh from the
streets, and without any previous training. The confinement

and restraint within the narrow limits of a ship, must necessarily be irksome to boys of this class, and render the task of reforming them much more difficult. Another objection to this course, both in a pecuniary and disciplinary point of view, arises from the impossibility of introducing labor on shipboard as one of the reformatory processes, and as a means of diminishing the cost of their support.

"The Massachusetts ships receive inmates without regard to the physical capabilities as well as the inclinations of the boys for a sea-life, and we find in consequence that nearly half of those discharged are returned to the land to learn trades. In this way the nautical training, continued on the average for nearly a year in each case, at a heavy cost to the State, is entirely thrown away upon those thus discharged. While, by the system of labor introduced into the House of Refuge, the net yearly cost of each child is reduced to a maximum of sixty dollars, the cost to the State of Massachusetts for the same period, for each boy in the Nautical School, is more than three times as great, with no reduction from the proceeds of labor.

"These statements are not made in any spirit of depreciation of the value of the Massachusetts school-ships as reformatories, but rather to show how we may profit by their experience, avoid the difficulties they have encountered, and, by making the training-ship an adjunct of the House of Refuge, accomplish a greater amount of good, at a less cost to the public. The managers, therefore, propose that a ship be placed under their management, properly equipped for the peculiar service required, to which they will transfer such boys as evince a natural aptitude for a seafaring life, after they shall have undergone the reformatory discipline of the House, learned the elements of education, and

earned this transfer as a promotion for good conduct and evidence of reformed dispositions.

"The time required for practice in seamanship and learning
navigation would probably not exceed three months; and, as
habits of order and subordination would already have been acquired, the necessity for a severe discipline would not be felt.
They could therefore be discharged, as opportunities might
occur, to enter upon their career as sailors, and so make room
for fresh accessions from the House. In this way a large number of boys could be prepared for sea on board one ship, at a
comparatively small cost *per capita*. The managers do not propose to restrict the benefits of the training-ship to the inmates
of the House of Refuge, but to extend them to candidates from
other reformatories in this State, possessing the same qualifications required in their own boys."

The second suggestion refers to "numbers of young men (to
whom reference has so often been made) beyond the age of sixteen, that may be still found in our prisons and penitentiaries,
serving their terms of sentence for a longer or shorter period,
who are thus shut out, both by the disgrace incurred and the
demoralizing influences of a penal institution, from all hopes of
reformation and of a better life. Their hearts are yet susceptible to influences of a reforming nature, and if only a hope be
held out to them of redeeming themselves by an encouragement
to do right, they can be elevated and reformed, under a proper
system of discipline, somewhat analogous to that pursued in the
House of Refuge."

Nothing can tend more certainly to secure the most hardened
and desperate criminals than the present system of short sentences. The young burglar, dismissed from the penitentiary,

has no opening of honest business before him, and theft seems to be the only means left to him to save himself from starvation. In the instance of such persons, where repeated offences have been committed, how wise would it be to pronounce upon them sentences limited only by their probable reformation, and have them placed where their daily labor will support themselves and perhaps gather a little capital upon which, with a certificate of good character, a place having been found for them, they can begin life afresh under honest auspices. Some of the soundest writers upon crime and its cure, men of wide legal erudition and of great experience, are giving utterance to such views both in Europe and in this country. They do not even shrink from saying, that if a young man is so helplessly weak, morally, that he cannot control his propensity to steal or to commit acts of violence, he must be always restrained of his liberty, for the peace of society, just as insane persons are confined, but in comfortable resorts, where his weak moral powers will be continually solicited and strengthened, and where he and his dependent friends can have some benefit from the work of his hands. His release is to be determined by his probable reformation, and his return to confinement will be the penalty for a new offence.

Mr. Mathew Davenport Hill, one of the ablest criminal judges of Great Britain, for nearly thirty years Recorder of Birmingham, said, as early as 1855, in a charge to the grand jury of that city: "Gentlemen, if you desire, as I most earnestly do, to see this principle" (that of allowing convicts to earn a diminution of sentence by good conduct) "universally adopted, you must be prepared to strengthen the hands of government, by advocating such a change in the law as will enable those who administer the criminal justice of the country to retain in custody all such as are convicted of crime, until they have, by reliable tests, demonstrated that they have the will and the power to gain an honest livelihood at large. You must be content that they shall be retained until habits of industry are formed, until moderate skill in some useful occupation is acquired, until the great lesson of self-control is mastered; in short, until the convict ceases to be a criminal, resolves to fulfil his duties both to God and to man, and has surmounted all obstacles against carrying such resolutions into successful action. But as no training, however enlightened and vigilant, will produce its intended effects on every individual subjected to its discipline, what are we to do with the incurable? Gentlemen, we must face this question; we must not flinch from answering, that we propose to detain them in prison until they are released by death. You keep the maniac in a prison (which you call an asylum) under similar conditions; you guard against his escape until he is taken from you, either because he is restored to sanity, or has departed to another world. If, gentlemen, innocent misfortune may and must be so treated, why not thus deal with incorrigible depravity? . . . It is my belief that if long terms of imprisonment, even to perpetuity, were placed before the public mind as indissolubly connected with the privilege to the convict of working out his own redemption from thraldom, by proving himself fit for liberty, it would require no great lapse of time to produce the change in opinion which I contemplate. Alarm on the score of expense ought not to be entertained, for two reasons: First, because no unreformed inmates of a prison, however extravagant its expenditures may be, cost the community so much as they would do if at large. This fact has been so often proved that I must be allowed to assume it as undeniable. But the second reason is, that prisons may be made either altogether, or to a very great extent, self-supporting."

It was natural that such an opinion, from a source commanding so much respect, should excite much discussion throughout the public press of Great Britain. The *London Times*, gathering up the sober judgment of thoughtful men as the debate developed the strength of the argument, remarked : " We believe it will be found the cheapest and most politic course, as well as the most humane, to leave no stone unturned to bring about the reformation of criminals, and not to discharge them upon society until they are reformed. In desperate cases we must even acquiesce in the conclusion of imprisonment for life." The *Spectator*, the ablest and most influential periodical in England, says, upon the same subject, that the detention of criminals until their reformation " would be justified upon the same grounds that justify the detention of the insane. As long as they are criminally disposed, thay are morally insane, and should be in safe custody. As soon as they have ceased to be criminally disposed, and become disposed, like ordinary people, to earn their livelihood in an honest way, they are cured of their insanity and may safely go at large." *

---

* Quoted from the Report upon Prisons and Reformatories, by Drs. Dwight and Wines, p. 275.

The Board of Managers are, at the present time, considering a plan which will inaugurate gradually a Division for the discipline of young men who have commenced a life of crime.

The following Report has just been submitted, at the request of the Board, for their consideration :

REPORT.

I. The establishment of such a Division is expedient for the following reasons :

These views indicate the direction that reform will take as the second half century opens upon this interesting work. A committee of the Board of State Charities, in conference with the managers of the Society for the Reformation of Juvenile Delinqents were pleased to express their interest in these suggestions, and desire to have them realized in successful experiments.

"Should the Legislature," the managers remark, " be pre-

1. To meet the necessities of a limited portion of the Second Division, who, after the usual average of detention, still remain incorrigible, and are not in a condition to be discharged, but require a more protracted and severer discipline.

2. For such mature boys, who, having been discharged, are returned by the police ; the discipline of the institution, as well as of the returned boys, requiring that they should be subjected to a more strenuous training.

3. As a practicable and economical trial of the experiment of attempting the reformation of criminal young men.

II. THE PROPOSED PLAN.—1. It is not deemed expedient at first to attempt a separation between the Second and Third Divisions as to shop, school, dining-room or dormitory, but to make the distinction rather a moral and penal one.

2. Boys of a long-continued low grade in the Second Division, and mature boys returned to the House for cause, shall be included in the Third Division.

3. No boy shall be discharged from the Third Division under two years, unless he reach his majority, or by a resolution of the Board upon the recommendation of the Indenturing Committee.

4. After six months of good behavior, the earnings of these boys over the cost of their maintenance shall be placed to their credit, to be paid to them upon their discharge from the House.

5. The details as to increased hours of labor, and as to pecuniary fines from their credited earnings for bad behavior, can be most wisely arranged by experiment under the supervision of the Indenturing Committee ; the compensation for the work of these boys can be best established by the Executive Committee, and the hours and character of the instruction in the schools by the School Committee.

6. A full statement of the plan may be made to the boys at an early day, and the Division go into operation on the 1st of January, 1869; those boys of the Second Division that continue to receive marks of dishonor from this time to be the first to enter the new Division.

pared to make an experiment with this object in view, they will most cheerfully undertake to carry out an act framed to meet the wants of this class of young criminals." To this offer they add the very appropriate words of a previous Report: " If these suggestions involve larger demands upon the public treasury than usual, we can only plead new conditions and the necessities of our situation. We would also add that the managers feel it to be their duty to state these questions fairly with reference to the public interests and to those of the institution they control."

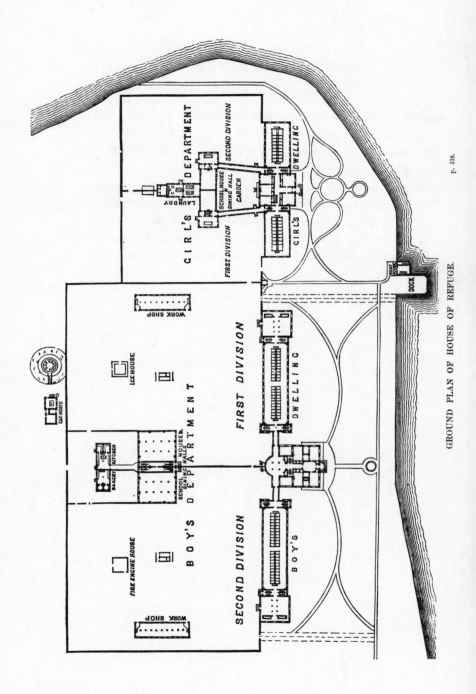

GROUND PLAN OF HOUSE OF REFUGE.

p. 318.

APPENDIX.

I.

DESCRIPTION OF THE BUILDINGS.

THE House of Refuge is located on the easterly bank of the Harlem River, on Randall's Island, and directly opposite that portion of the city of New York which is included between One Hundred and Fifteenth and One Hundred and Twentieth Streets. The buildings are of brick, erected in the Italian style. The two principal structures front the river, and form a façade nearly a thousand feet in length. The line of their fronts is exactly parallel with the city avenues. The larger of the two buildings is for the accommodation of the boys' department, the other for the girls'. Other buildings are located in the rear of these, and are enclosed by a stone wall twenty feet high. A division wall, of like height, separates the grounds of the boys' department from that of the girls', and in each department walls separate the inmates into two divisions.

The boys' house is nearly six hundred feet long. The dome-surmounted portions are devoted to the use of the officers; the central mass also contains the chapel; while the extreme portions contain the hospitals and lavatories. There are six hundred and thirty-six dormitories, five feet by seven, and seven feet high, in the portion between the centre and end buildings. In the rear is the school and dining-hall building, seventy by one hundred and thirty-eight feet. A central brick wall divides the building in each story into two equal parts, one for each division. The lower story is appropriated. to dining-rooms, and the upper story to school-rooms. In the rear of the school building are the kitchen and bakery, occupying a space twenty-five by ninety feet. The workshops are at the northerly and southerly extremities of the yard, and are each thirty by one hundred and fifty feet, and three stories high.

The girls' house is two hundred and fifty feet long—the central portion of which contains the apartments of the matron, assistants, and female teachers, while the wings contain two hundred and fifty dormitories for the inmates. In the rear, connected by two corridors or covered halls, is a building for school-rooms and dining-halls—the hospitals, sewing-rooms, and lavatories being at each end, with the laundry in the rear.

The whole establishment is supplied with Croton water, brought across the Harlem River in a three and one-quarter inch lead pipe. Tanks are in the attics of the principal buildings, and a reservoir, one hundred feet diameter, located beyond the enclosure, affords a reserve for extraordinary occasions, as well as a plentiful supply of ice in the winter.

II.

ACT OF INCORPORATION, AND IMPORTANT AMENDMENTS AND ADDITIONS.

An Act *to incorporate* the Society for the Reformation of Juvenile Delinquents, *in the city of New York.*

Passed March 29, 1824.

Whereas, by the petition of several inhabitants of the city of New York, it is represented, that they are desirous of establishing a Society and House of Refuge for the Reformation of Juvenile Delinquents, in the said city, and have prayed to be incorporated: Therefore,

I. *Be it enacted by the people of the State of New York, represented in Senate and Assembly,* That all such persons as now are or hereafter shall become subscribers to the said association pursuant to the by-laws thereof, shall be, and hereby are constituted a body corporate and politic, by the name of "The Managers of the Society for the Reformation of Juvenile Delinquents in the City of New York," and by that name they shall have perpetual succession, and be in law capable of suing and being sued, defending and being defended, in all courts and places, and in all manner of actions and causes whatsoever, and may have a common seal, and change the same at their pleasure, and shall be capable in law by that name and style of purchasing, holding and conveying any estate, real or personal, for the use of said corporation : *Provided*, That such real estate shall never exceed the yearly value of ten thousand dollars, nor be applied to any other purposes than those for which this incorporation is formed.

II. *And be it further enacted*, That the estate and concerns of the said corporation shall be conducted by a Board of thirty Managers, to be elected by a plurality of ballots of the members resident in the city of New York, being subscribers as aforesaid, and present at such election yearly, on the third Monday in November, at such place in the said city, and at such time of the day as the Board of Managers may from time to time appoint, and of which public notice shall be given, and if any vacancy shall occur by the resignation, removal, or otherwise, of any one of the said Board, the same shall be filled for the remainder of the year by such person or persons, being subscribers as aforesaid, as the Board for the time being, or a major part of them shall appoint; and until the election on the third Monday in November in the year one thousand eight hundred and twenty-five, the following persons shall compose the said Board of Managers, to wit: Cadwallader D. Colden, John Griscom, John Duer, Jonathan M. Wainwright, Isaac Collins, Thomas Eddy, Ansel W. Ives, John T. Irving, John E. Hyde, Cornelius Du Bois, James W. Gerard, Joseph Curtis, John Stearns, Ralph Olmstead, Robert F. Mott, Stephen Allen, Henry I. Wykoff, Samuel Cowdrey, John Targee, Arthur Burtis, Joseph Grinnell, Hugh Maxwell, Henry Mead, Peter A. Jay, Gilbert Coutant, Cornelius R. Duffie, and James Lovett, *And it is hereby further enacted*, that no Manager of the said Society shall receive any compensation for his services.

III. *And be it further enacted*, That if the annual election shall not take place on the stated day for that purpose, the said corporation shall not thereby be dissolved, but the members of said Board shall continue in office until a new election, which shall be had at such time and place and after such notice as the said Board shall prescribe, and in case of an equality of votes for any one or more persons as a member or members of the said Board of Managers, the said Board shall determine which of such persons shall be considered as elected, and such person or persons shall take his or their seats and act accordingly.

IV. *And be it further enacted*, That the said Managers shall have power in their discretion to receive and take into the House of Refuge to be established by them, all such children as shall be taken up or committed as vagrants, or convicted of criminal offences in the said city, as may in the judgment of the Court of General Sessions of the peace, or of the Court of Oyer and Terminer, in and for the said city, or of the Jury before whom any such offender shall be tried, or of the Police Magistrates, or of the Commissioners of the Alms House and Bridewell of the said city, be proper objects; and the said Managers shall have power to place the said children committed to their care, during the minority of such children, at such employments and to cause them to be instructed in such branches of useful knowledge as shall be suitable to their years and capacities; and they shall have power in their discretion to bind out the said children with their consent, as apprentices or servants during their minority, to such persons and at such places, to learn such proper trades and employments as in their judgment will be most for the reformation and amendment, and the future benefit and advantage of such children: *Provided*, That the charge and power of the said Managers upon and over the said children, shall not extend in the case of females beyond the age of eighteen years.

[See addition to this section by Act of April 10, 1860.]

V. *And be it further enacted*, That all and singular the clauses and provisions in the act, entitled " An Act concerning apprentices and servants," relating to the covenants to be inserted in the indentures of apprentices and servants, made by the Overseers of the Poor, and the provisions of the sixth, ninth, tenth, eleventh, twelfth and thirteenth sections of the last-mentioned act, shall apply to the apprentices and servants, and the persons to whom they may be bound, under and by virtue of this act.

VI. *And be it further enacted*, That the said managers under this act, may from time to time make by-laws, ordinances and regulations relative to the management and disposition of the estate and concerns of the said Corporation, and management, government, instruction, discipline, employment and disposition of the said chil-

dren while in the said House of Refuge, or under their care, not contrary to law, as they may deem proper, and may appoint such officers,
agents and servants as they may deem necessary to transact the business of the said Corporation, and may designate their duties; *and
further*, That the said Managers shall make an annual report to the
Legislature, and to the Corporation of the city of New York, of the
number of children received by them into the said House of Refuge,
the disposition which shall be made of the said children by instruct-
ing or employing them in the said House of Refuge, or by binding
them out as apprentices or servants; the receipts and expenditures
of said Managers, and generally all such facts and particulars as may
tend to exhibit the effects, whether advantageous or otherwise, of
the said Association.

VII. *And be it further enacted*, That this act shall be and is
hereby declared a public act, and that the same shall be construed in
all courts and places benignly and favorably for every humane and
laudable purpose therein contained.

VIII. *And be it further enacted*, That the Legislature may at
any time hereafter, alter, modify, or repeal this act.

An Act *to amend an Act entitled " An Act to incorporate the Society
for the Reformation of Juvenile Delinquents in the city of New
York," passed March* 29, 1824, *and for other purposes.*

Passed January 28, 1826.

§ 1. *Be it enacted by the people of the State of New York, represented in Senate and Assembly*, That the Managers of the Society
mentioned in the act hereby amended, shall receive and take in the
House of Refuge, established by them in the city of New York, all
such children as shall be convicted of criminal offences in any city or
county of this State, and as may in the judgment of the Court before
whom any such offender shall be tried, be deemed proper objects;
and the powers and duties of the said Managers in relation to the
children which they shall receive in virtue of this act, shall be the
same in all things as are prescribed and provided by the act entitled
" An Act to incorporate the Society for the Reformation of Juvenile
Delinquents in the city of New York," passed March 29, 1824, in
respect to children which the said Managers have received or may

receive in virtue of that act. [The remaining sections relate to funds for the support of the institution.]

II. Rev. Stat. 701.

Chapter 1st, Title 7, Section 17.

§ 17. Whenever any person under the age of sixteen years shall be convicted of any felony, the court, instead of sentencing such person to imprisonment in a State prison, may order that he be removed to and confined in the House of Refuge, established by the Society for the Reformation of Juvenile Delinquents in the city of New York; unless notice shall have been received from such Society, that there is not room in such House for the reception of further delinquents.

[As amended: Laws of 1840, chap. 100.]

AN ACT *to amend the Act to incorporate the Society for the Reformation of Juvenile Delinquents in the city of New York.*

Passed April 12, 1833.

The People of the State of New York, represented in Senate and Assembly, do enact as follows:

§ 1. Nine members of the Board of Managers of the said Society shall constitute a quorum for the transaction of business, and for the performance of all the powers and duties of the board, except the appointment and removal of any officer of the institution, for which business, twelve members of the said board shall constitute a quorum.

AN ACT *to amend an Act entitled " An Act to create a fund in aid of the Society for the Reformation of Juvenile Delinquents in the city of New York, and for other purposes.*

Passed February 1, 1839.

The People of the State of New York, represented in Senate and Assembly, do enact as follows:

§ 1. No theatre, circus or building, garden or grounds for exhibiting theatrical or equestrian performances in the city of New York, shall be opened for such exhibitions, unless the manager or proprietor thereof shall first, and annually, obtain from the mayor of the said city a license therefor, which license the said mayor is authorized to grant, to continue in force until the first day of May next ensuing the grant thereof; and every manager or proprietor, neglecting to take out such license, or consenting or allowing such performances without first taking out the same, and every owner or lessee of any building in said city, who shall lease or let out the same for the purpose of being occupied as such theatre or circus, or building for exhibiting theatrical or equestrian performances, or shall assent that the same be used for the purposes aforesaid; and the same shall have been so used by any manager or proprietor thereof who shall not have previously obtained such license, shall be subjected to a penalty of five hundred dollars for every such neglect or omission, which penalty the Society for the Reformation of Juvenile Delinquents in the said city, are hereby authorized, in the name of the people of this State, to prosecute, sue for and recover, for the use of said society.

§ 2. The said mayor is hereby authorized to grant licenses for said theatrical and equestrian performances for any term less than one year, and in any case where such license is for a term of three months or less, the said mayor is hereby authorized to commute for a sum less than said five hundred dollars, but in no case less than two hundred and fifty dollars for a theatre, or one hundred and fifty dollars for a circus.

§ 3. Upon granting every such license authorized by this act, or the act hereby amended, the said mayor shall receive from the person to whom the same shall be granted, the amount of said license, which amounts, as respectively received by him, shall be paid over to the Treasurer of the Society for the Reformation of Juvenile Delinquents in the city of New York, for the use of said Society.

§ 4. In case any manager or proprietor of any theatre, circus or building, garden or grounds, for exhibiting theatrical or equestrian performances, shall open or advertise to open, any theatre, circus or building, garden or grounds, for any such exhibition or exhibitions in said city, without first having obtained license therefor as is provided for by this act or the act hereby amended, it shall, and may be lawful for the said Society for the Reformation of Juvenile Delinquents in the said city to apply to the Chancellor of this State, or the Vice-Chancellor of the first circuit, for an injunction to restrain the opening thereof, until they shall have complied with the requisitions of this act, and the act hereby amended, in obtaining such license, and also complying with such order as to costs as the Chancellor or Vice-Chancellor may deem just and proper to make, which injunction may be allowed upon a bill or petition, to be exhibited in the name of said Society, in the same manner as injunctions are now usually allowed by the practice of the Court of Chancery.

§ 5. Any injunction allowed under this act may be served by posting the same upon the outer door of the theatre or circus, or building wherein such exhibitions may be proposed to be held, or if the same shall be in a garden or grounds, then by posting the same at or on or near the entrance-way to any such place of exhibition, and in case of any proceeding against the manager or proprietor of any such theatre, circus or building, or garden or grounds, as aforesaid, it shall not be necessary to prove the personal service of the injunction, but the service hereinbefore provided shall be deemed and held sufficient.

§ 6. The fourth and fifth sections of the act hereby amended are repealed.

§ 7. This act shall take effect immediately.

AN ACT *to amend an Act entitled " An Act more effectually to provide for common-school education in the city of New York, passed May* 7, 1844. "

Passed May 11, 1847.

The People of the State of New York, represented in Senate and Assembly, do enact as follows :

§ 1. The act entitled " An Act more effectually to provide for common-school education in the city and county of New York," passed May 7, 1844, is hereby amended in the following manner :

The eleventh section of said act shall be amended by inserting after the words " The School of the Mechanics' Society," the words " The School of the Society for the Reformation of Juvenile Delinquents in the city of New York, and the School of the Mechanics' Institute."

§ 2. To determine the shares of school money to which the School of the Society for the Reformation of Juvenile Delinquents in the city of New York, and the School for the Mechanics' Institute shall be entitled, in accordance with the general provisions of the twelfth section of the act hereby amended; the average number of children who shall have actually attended such school, without charge, during the preceding year, shall be ascertained by adding together the number of such children present at each morning and evening session of said schools, and dividing the sum by four hundred and eighty, and all the provisions of said twelfth section inconsistent with this section are hereby repealed, so far as they affect the school of the said Society for the Reformation of Juvenile Delinquents.

The eleventh section above amended and the substitute for the above second section now stand as sections twenty-two and fifteen of "An Act to amend, consolidate and reduce to one Act the various acts relative to the common schools of the city of New York," passed July 3, 1851.

§ 15. The said Board of Supervisors shall annually raise and collect, by tax upon the inhabitants of the said city and county, a sum of money equal to the sum specified in such notice, at the time and in the same manner as the contingent charges of the said city and county are levied and collected; also a sum of money equal to one-twentieth of one per cent. of the value of the real and personal property in the said city, liable to be assessed thereon, and pay the same into the city treasury, to be applied to the purposes of common schools in the said city; and the Board of Education shall apportion the money so raised to each of the schools hereafter provided for by this act, except the Free Academy and the evening schools, according to the number of children over four and under twenty-one years of age, who were actual residents of the city and county of New York, at the time of their attendance on such schools, without charge, the preceding year; and the average shall be ascertained by adding together the number of such children present at each morning and afternoon session of not less than three hours, and dividing the sum by four hundred and sixty; and if any school shall have been organized since the last annual apportionment, the average shall be ascertained by dividing by a number corresponding to the actual number of morning and evening sessions, of not less than three hours each, held since the organization of such school; and the sum apportioned to any schools, other than the Ward Schools, shall be paid to the Trustees, Managers or Directors of such schools, respectively, by drafts on the City Chamberlain, to be signed by the president and clerk of said board, and made payable to the order of the Treasurers of said Trustees, Managers or Directors.

OF THE SCHOOLS ENTITLED TO PARTICIPATE IN THE APPORTIONMENT.

§ 22. The New York Orphan Asylum school, the Roman Catholic Orphan Asylum school, the schools of the two half-orphan asylums, the school of the Mechanics' Society, the school of the Society for the Reformation of Juvenile Delinquents in the city of New York, the Hamilton Free school, the school for the Leake and Watts' Orphan House, the school connected with the almshouse of the said city, the school of the Association for the Benefit of Colored Orphans, the schools of the American Female Guardian Society, the schools of the Society for the Promotion of Education among Colored Children, the schools organized under the act entitled "An Act to extend to the city and county of New York, the provisions of the general act, in relation to Common Schools passed April 11, 1842," or an act to amend the same passed April 18, 1843, or an act entitled "An Act more effectually to provide for Common School Education in the city and county of New York," passed May 7, 1844, or any of the acts amending the same, and including such Normal Schools for the education of teachers as the Board of Education may organize, and the Normal School of the Public School Society for the education of teachers, and such schools as may be organized under the provisions of this act, shall be subject to the general supervision of the Board of Education, and shall be entitled to participate in the apportionment of the school moneys as provided for by this act, but they shall be under the immediate direction of their respective Trustees, Managers and Directors, as herein provided.

AN ACT *in relation to the confinement of juvenile offenders under sentences of the Courts of the United States.*

Passed July 21, 1853.

The People of the State of New York, represented in Senate and Assembly, do enact as follows :

§ 1. It shall be the duty of the respective keepers of the House of Refuge in the city of New York, and the Western House of Refuge, to receive and safely keep in their respective houses, subject to the regulations and discipline thereof, any criminal under the age of sixteen years, convicted of any offence against the United States, sentenced to imprisonment therein by any court of the United States sitting within this State, until such sentence be executed, or until such convict shall be discharged by due course of law; the United States supporting such convict and paying the expenses attendant upon the execution of such sentence.

§ 2. This act shall take effect immediately.

AN ACT *in relation to the theatres in the city of New York.*

Passed March 18, 1859.

The People of the State of New York, represented in Senate and Assembly, do enact as follows:

§ 1. It shall not be lawful for any owner, lessee, manager, agent or officer of any theatre in the city of New York, to admit to any theatrical exhibition, held in the evening, any minor under the age of fourteen years, unless such minor is accompanied by and is in the care of some adult person.

§ 2. Any person violating the above provision shall be guilty of a misdemeanor, and shall be liable to a fine, not less than twenty-five dollars nor more than one hundred dollars, or imprisonment for a term not less than ten nor more than ninety days, for each offence.

§ 3. All moneys recovered under the provisions of this act for fines, shall be paid over to the Treasurer of the Society for the Reformation of Juvenile Delinquents in the city of New York, for the benefit of such Society.

AN ACT *to amend an act entitled " An Act to incorporate the Society for the Reformation of Juvenile Delinquents in the city of New York, passed March* 29, 1824.

Passed April 10, 1860—three-fifths being present.

The People of the State of New York, represented in Senate and Assembly, do enact as follows:

§ 1. The act entitled " An Act to incorporate the Society for the Reformation of Juvenile Delinquents in the city of New York," passed March 29, 1824, is hereby amended, by adding to the fourth section thereof the following words:

The Managers of the said Society shall receive into the house of refuge established by them in the city of New York, whenever they may have room for that purpose, all such children as shall be taken up or committed as vagrants, in any city or county of this State, and might now, if convicted of criminal offences in such city or county, be sent as directed by law to said house of refuge, if in the judgment of the court or magistrate by whom they shall be committed as vagrants, the aforesaid children shall be deemed proper persons to be sent to said institution. The powers and duties of the said Managers in relation to the children whom they shall receive in virtue of this act, shall be the same in all things as now provided by law in case of children convicted of criminal offences and committed to the charge of said Managers.

AN ACT *to preserve the public peace and order on the first day of the week, commonly called Sunday.*

Passed April 17, 1860—three-fifths being present.

The People of the State of New York, represented in Senate and Assembly, do enact as follows :

§ 1. It shall not be lawful to exhibit, on the first day of the week, commonly called Sunday, to the public, in any building, garden, grounds, concert-room or other room or place within the city and county of New York, any interlude, tragedy, comedy, opera, ballet, play, farce, negro minstrelsy, negro or other dancing, or any other entertainment of the stage, or any part or parts therein, or any equestrian, circus or dramatic performance, or any performance of jugglers, acrobats or rope dancing.

§ 2. Any person offending against the provisions of this law, and every person aiding in such exhibition, by advertisement or otherwise, and every owner or lessee of any building, part of a building, ground, garden or concert-room, or other room or place, who shall lease or let out the same for the purpose of any such exhibition or performance, or assent that the same be used for any such purpose, if the same shall be used for such purpose, shall be guilty of a misdemeanor, and, in addition to the punishment therefor provided by law, shall be subjected to a penalty of five hundred dollars, which penalty the Society for the Reformation of Juvenile Delinquents in said city are hereby authorized, in the name of the people of this State, to prosecute, sue for and recover for the use of said Society; in addition to which every such exhibition or performance shall of itself forfeit, vacate and annul and render void and of no effect, any license which shall have been previously obtained by any manager, proprietor, owner or lessee, consenting to, causing or allowing, or letting any part of a building for the purpose of such exhibition and performance.

§ 3. This act shall take effect immediately.

Chapter 281.

An Act *to regulate places of public amusement in the cities and incorporated villages of this State.*

Passed April 17, 1862—three-fifths being present.

The People of the State of New York, represented in Senate and Assembly, do enact as follows :

§ 1. It shall not be lawful to exhibit to the public in any building, garden, or grounds, concert-room, or other place or room, within the city of New York any interlude, tragedy, comedy, opera, ballet, play, farce, negro minstrelsy, negro or other dancing, or any other entertainment of the stage, or any part or parts therèin, or any equestrian, circus, or dramatic performance, or any performance of jugglers or rope dancing, acrobats, until a license for such exhibition shall have been first had and obtained pursuant to and at the same rate provided for theatrical performance in an act entitled " An Act to amend an act entitled an act to create a fund in aid of the Society for the Reformation of Juvenile Delinquents in the city of New York, and for other purposes, passed February first, eighteen hundred and thirty-nine," and every manager or proprietor of any such exhibition or performance, who shall neglect to take out such license, or consent to, cause or allow any such exhibition or performance, or any single one of them, without such license, and every person aiding in such exhibition and every owner or lessee of any building, part of a building, garden, grounds, concert-room, or other room or place, who shall lease or let the same for the purpose of any such exhibition or performance, or assent that the same be used for any such purpose except as permitted by such license and without such license having been previously obtained and then in force, if the same shall be used for such purpose, shall incur the penalties and be subjected to the proceedings for an injunction provided for by the other provisions contained in the said act, which penalty the Society for the Reformation of Juvenile Delinquents, in said city, are hereby authorized to prosecute, sue for, and recover for the use of the said Society, in the name of the people of the State of New York.

§ 2. It shall not be lawful to sell or furnish any wine, beer, or strong or spirituous liquors to any person in the auditorium or lobbies of such place of exhibition or performance mentioned in the first section of this act, or in any apartment connected therewith, by any door, window, or other aperture; nor shall it be lawful to employ or furnish or permit or assent to the employment or attendance of any female, to wait on or attend in any manner, or furnish refreshments to the audience or spectators, or any of them, at any of the exhibitions or performances mentioned in the first section of this act, or at any other place of public amusement in the city of New York.

§ 3. No license shall be granted for any exhibition or performance given in violation of the second section of this act, and any and every exhibition or performance at which any of the provisions of the second section of this act shall be violated, shall of itself vacate and annul and render void and of no effect any license which shall have been previously obtained by any manager, proprietor, owner or lessee consenting to, causing or allowing or letting any part of a building for the purpose of such exhibition and performance; and any license provided for by the first section of this act, may be revoked and annulled by the officer or officers granting the same, upon proof of a violation of any of the provisions of this act. Such proof shall be taken before such officer upon notice of not less than two days, to show cause why such license should not be revoked; said officer shall hear the proofs and allegations in the case, and determine the same summarily; and no appeal shall be taken or review be had from such determination. And any person whose license shall have been revoked or annulled, shall not thereafter be entitled to a license under the provisions of this act. On any examination before an officer pursuant to a notice to show cause as aforesaid, the accused party may be a witness in his own behalf.

§ 4. Any person violating any of the provisions of this act, or employing or assenting to the employment or attendance of any person contrary to the provisions of this act, shall be deemed guilty of a misdemeanor, and upon conviction, shall be punished by imprisonment in the penitentiary for a term not less than three months nor more than one year, or by a fine not less than one hundred dollars nor more than five hundred dollars, or by both such fine and imprisonment.

Managers divided into Classes.

§ 5. It shall be the duty of every Chief of Police, Sheriff, Deputy Sheriff, Constable, Captain of Police, Policeman, and every other police officer, to enter at any time said places of amusement, and to arrest and convey any person or persons violating any provision of this act, forthwith, before any Police Justice, or Recorder, or Magistrate, having jurisdiction in said city, there to be dealt with according to law.

§ 6. The provisions of this act shall apply to all the cities and incorporated villages of this State, but the license to be obtained in every city or incorporated village, other than the city of New York, shall be issued under such terms, and under such regulations, as the municipal authorities of the said cities or villages may respectively prescribe ; and the fines and penalties for any violation of any of the provisions of this act, in such other cities or incorporated villages, respectively, other than as mentioned in section four of this act, shall be sued for and recovered in the name of the Overseer of the Poor of such city or incorporated village, or the town in which such incorporated village is situate, or such other officer as the municipal or village authorities thereof may direct, for the benefit of the poor thereof.

§ 7. This act shall take effect immediately.

An Act *to amend an act entitled " An Act to incorporate the Society for the Reformation of Juvenile Delinquents in the city of New York," passed March* 29, 1824.

Passed March 22, 1865—three-fifths being present.

The People of the State of New York, represented in Senate and Assembly, do enact as follows:

§ 1. The Managers of the Society for the Reformation of Juvenile Delinquents shall, as soon as conveniently may be after the next annual election of the Society, arrange themselves into three classes of ten each, to be determined by lot, to serve respectively one, two, and three years; and at every subsequent election, at the expiration of the terms thus designated, ten persons shall be chosen as Managers to serve for the term of three years; any vacancy that may occur in any class during the term of service of said class may be filled by the Board of Managers for the unexpired portion of said term.

§ 2. The fourth section of the act entitled "An Act to incorporate the Society for the Reformation of Juvenile Delinquents in the city of New York," passed March 29, 1824, is amended, by striking out the following words: "Provided that the charge and power of the said Managers upon and over the said children shall not extend in the case of females beyond the age of eighteen years."

§ 3. It shall be the duty of all courts and magistrates, by whom any juvenile delinquent shall be committed or sent to the House of Refuge in the city of New York, to ascertain the age of such delinquent by such proof as may be in their power, and to insert such age in the order of commitment, and the age thus ascertained shall be deemed and taken to be the true age of such delinquent.

§ 4. In cases where the age of the delinquent so committed is not so ascertained and inserted in the order of commitment, the said Managers shall, as soon as may be after such delinquent shall be received by them, ascertain the age of such delinquent by such proof as may be in their power, and cause the same to be entered in a book to be designated by them for that purpose, and the age thus ascertained shall be deemed and taken to be the true age of such delinquent.

§ 5. All children under the age of sixteen in the several counties, which are now or hereafter shall be designated by law as the counties from which juvenile delinquents shall be sent to the House of Refuge in the city of New York, deserting their homes without good and sufficient cause, or keeping company with dissolute or vicious persons against the lawful commands of their fathers, mothers, guardians, or other persons standing in the place of a parent, shall be deemed disorderly children.

§ 6. Upon complaint made on oath to any Police Magistrate or Justice of the Peace against any child within his county, under the age of sixteen, by his or her parent or guardian, or other person standing to him or her in place of a parent, as being disorderly, such Magistrate or Justice shall issue his warrant for the apprehension of the offender, and cause him or her to be brought before himself or any other Police Magistrate or Justice of the said county for examination.

§ 7. If such Magistrate or Justice be satisfied, by competent testimony, that such person is a disorderly child within the description aforesaid, he shall make up and sign a record of conviction thereof, and shall, by warrant under his hand, commit such person to the

House of Refuge established by the Managers of the Society for the Reformation of Juvenile Delinquents in the city of New York; and the powers and duties of the said Managers in relation to the said children shall be the same in all things as are prescribed as to other juvenile delinquents received by them: *Provided*, however, that any person committed under this act shall have the same right of appeal now secured by law to persons convicted of criminal offenses; but on any such appeal mere informality in the issuing of any warrant shall not be held to be sufficient cause for granting a discharge.

§ 8. This act shall take effect immediately.

III.

JUDICIAL OPINIONS.

SUPREME COURT.

The People, &c., on the Petition on behalf of Thomas Tobans *against* The Governors of the House of Refuge.	Opinion, December, 1859.

A. B. James, *J.*:

A writ of *habeas corpus*, issued on the petition of the father of Thomas Tobans, directed to the Governors, &c., of the House of Refuge, commanding them to produce the body of said Thomas, &c., was served upon the officers of that institution, to which they returned, that at the time of the allowance of said writ, the said Thomas was not, nor had he at any time since been, nor was he now, in the possessson or custody, or under their control, power or restraint, or by them restrained of his liberty; that the said Thomas, in August, 1857, was convicted as a vagrant, and committed to the House of Refuge; that he was received under such commitment, being a minor, and remained until April, 1858, when he was placed by the managers of said institution at employment with Wesley McDowell, of Lexington, Illinois; but that no indentures of apprenticeship had been executed; and hence the respondents were unable to produce the body of said Thomas, as commanded by said writ.

S. H. Stewart, for Petitioner.
H. A. Cram, <i>for Respondents.</i></div>

The only question presented for consideration is, the sufficiency of the excuse offered by the return for the non-production of the body of Thomas Tobans.

The truth of the return not being controverted, it appears that the respondents had not, at the time of granting the writ, nor at any time since, the custody or possession of the person named; and although they had such custody at a time long prior to the granting of such writ, it does not appear that such custody was parted with in bad faith, or for the purpose of unlawfully restraining the said Thomas of his liberty, or of evading the command of said writ.

It is, however, insisted by counsel that the excuse is wholly insufficient; that the transfer of said Thomas to McDowell was wholly without authority, illegal and void; that the Managers of the House of Refuge, by the terms of their charter, could only put the said Thomas to employment within the provisions of that institution, or bind him out to some farmer residing within the State; and that having sent him beyond the State, they should be compelled to produce him, in answer to the command of the writ.

The statute of 1824 authorized the Managers of the House of Refuge to receive children convicted of vagrancy, and gives power to place them, during their minority, at employment suitable to their years and capacities, and in the discretion of said Managers, with the consent of said children, to bind them out as apprentices, servants, &c.

The legal rights of the respondents, therefore, to place the said Thomas at employment, is clear, and the question of binding him was a matter wholly in their discretion.

There is nothing in the act limiting the employment of such children to the provisions of said institution, or their binding out to persons residing within the State.

Such a construction would greatly circumscribe the institution in its efforts to care for the well-being of those committed to its charge, without benefiting any one.

The statute wisely gives to the Board of Managers a broad discretion in the matter, leaving to their determination the kind of employment and instruction, the persons with whom, and the place where, it shall be given; and I can see no security of its being limited to this city or this State, so long as the future well-being of the child is considered, if suitable persons can be found out of the State who will take charge of them. I see no legal objection to their selection.

In this case, the respondents made a lawful disposition of Thomas. For aught that appears or is pretended, he is in the care and custody of a proper and suitable person. He is not now, nor was not at the time of granting the said writ, in the possession of the respondents; and this being so, the excuse for the non-production of the body is sufficient, and the writ should be discharged.

SUPREME COURT—KINGS COUNTY.

The People, *ex rel.* Thomas Hoey *against* The Superintendent of the House of Refuge.	*April,* 1860.

W. H. Scrugham, *Justice:*

The return to this writ of *habeas corpus* is made by the Superintendent of the House of Refuge, on Randall's Island, and states that Joseph Hoey is held and detained there by the Managers, on the authority of a warrant of commitment which is annexed to said return, and which recites the conviction of the said Joseph Hoey, on the day of its date, of petit larceny, before James H. Cornell, Esq., Police Justice of the city of Brooklyn, sitting as a Court of Special Sessions.

The return is objected to on the ground that it is not verified, and that the Superintendent of the House of Refuge is not a sworn public officer.

I will allow the return to be amended in that respect.

The prisoner had the right on the return of the writ to deny on oath any of the material facts set forth in the return, or allege, on oath, any fact to show either that his imprisonment or detention is unlawful, or that he is entitled to his discharge, and thereupon evi-

dence could have been offered in support of and against his detention: but failing to make such sworn denial or allegation, I must
regard the facts stated in the return as true.

They are certainly sufficient to justify the detention of Hoey, and
the statute makes it my duty to remand him to the House of Refuge.

Upon the argument, the conviction of Hoey, as set forth in the
return, was not denied, and in the petition for the writ and upon the
argument it was stated on behalf of the prisoner, and admitted by
the respondent, that no certificate of this conviction was ever filed in
the office of the Clerk of King's county, pursuant to sec. 67, title 3,
chap. 2, part 4, R. S., 5th ed., and it was claimed on behalf of the
prisoner that he was therefore entitled to his discharge.

It cannot be contended that the filing of this certificate is necessary to the perfection of the judgment. The judgment of the court
follows in its sentence immediately after the conviction, and is immediately put in execution by the commitment; while by the statute
the certificate need not be filed until twenty days after the conviction, and if it were intended that this should be necessary to perfect
the judgment, it would undoubtedly have been provided that no
commitment should issue until such certificate should be filed; for it
would be manifestly improper to allow a judgment to be put in execution before it was perfected.

The Court of Special Sessions is not a Court of Record, and in
the absence of this statute its judgment would require the same
proof as is required of the judgment of other Courts not of Record.
It was, among other things, to avoid the trouble and inconvenience
of this method of proof that this provision was made requiring a certificate to be filed and allowing it to be evidence of the facts stated
therein.

It is not declared that it shall be the only evidence of those facts,
nor can it be regarded as any thing more than a convenient substitute
for the primary or best evidence of them, and such evidence would
be received to prove them as well as the certificate.

The omission to file the certificate was a neglect of duty on the
part of the magistrate, which, if wilful, would subject him to punishment as for a misdemeanor, but it cannot invalidate the judgment
of the Court of Special Sessions held by him.

To hold otherwise would be to determine that a judgment in a
criminal case, duly and properly rendered, is to be annulled, and a

prisoner undergoing sentence thereon to be discharged, merely because the magistrate who held the court in which such judgment was rendered afterward neglected a duty, the performance or omission of which could in nowise affect the regularity or justice of the conviction.

OPINIONS OF GOVERNORS OF THE STATE UPON THEIR RIGHT TO PARDON INMATES OF THE HOUSE OF REFUGE.

EXTRACTS OF LETTERS.

October 7, 1839.

. . . . . As the Board of Commissioners (Managers) exercise the power of discharging persons from the House of Refuge, convicted of offences less than felony, I shall very cheerfully refer applications to them unless there be extraordinary circumstances, which shall seem to justify a different course.

(Signed) WM. H. SEWARD.

May, 1843.

In reply to a letter from Hon. Stephen Allen, then President of the Board of Managers, stating that " the removal by pardon, of the delinquent children placed in the care of the Managers, will not only be attended with great injury to the children, but will destroy the corrective influence of the institution upon those who remain," &c., &c. Gov. Bouck says : . . . . . In the mean time I wish to assure you of my willingness to coöperate in rendering the institution, over which you preside, effective and useful. I have granted a few pardons to those confined in the Refuge, under impressions that the law authorized it. I will, however, examine the subject and apprise you of the course I shall feel it my duty to pursue.

(Signed) WM. C. BOUCK.

All applications subsequently made to Gov. Bouck were referred by him to the Managers.

June 26, 1845.

. . . . . I have been studying the law too in relation to these subjects of that prison, and I cannot determine from my present researches, what they are in a legal sense, how to consider them or how they are to be got out, when once put there. I have ascertained from the office of the Secretary of State, that they are not considered subjects for the exercise of the pardoning power, for there has never been a pardon issued for one of them. They cannot therefore have been considered convicts in a legal sense. I conclude they must be considered as apprentices to the Corporation and subject solely to the disposition of the Managers within the terms of their act of incorporation and the laws modifying it. . . . . .

(Signed)   SILAS WRIGHT.

October 4, 1845.

. . . . . If not in positive conflict with your rules and what you consider your legal powers, I hope you will find in the circumstances of this case, an inducement to comply with the suggestions made by the Recorder of Buffalo, and which it seems had the approbation of the other judges and of the jury, which pronounced the verdict against these very juvenile offenders. . . . . If my feelings are urging me to ask of you what it is improper that you should do or what is against your positive rules or your settled conviction of your legal powers, I trust you will pardon me upon the assurance that I am not conscious that such is the character of my request. If, on the contrary, there shall be no such objections, then I hope you will permit me again to urge your patient examination of the case as presented by the recorder, before you reject our joint applications. . . . . .

(Signed)   SILAS WRIGHT.

December 30, 1846.

. . . . . All these papers satisfy me that you are better able to dispose of this young lad safely and justly than I am or can be, and as I have issued no pardon in any case to the House of Refuge, I cannot bring myself to begin at this late period of my official life. . . . . .

(Signed)   SILAS WRIGHT.

October 10, 1849.

The Managers of the House of Refuge have the power to discharge those committed to them. I have referred the case of your two boys to them, with a special request, &c., &c. . . . . .

(Signed)   HAMILTON FISH.

Supreme Court of Pennsylvania.

January 17, 1853.

. . . . . I have ascertained that I was mistaken in supposing that I had the power of discharging convicts from the House of Refuge. I am satisfied Governor Wright's decision is correct. . .

(Signed) HORATIO SEYMOUR.

June 23, 1857.

. . . . . I have come to the conclusion that the authority of the Managers of the House of Refuge over children under their care, should not be interfered with or embarrassed, by any act of the Executive of the character referred to (pardon), but should be left free to carry out the clear and laudable purposes, for which these institutions were founded. I erred therefore in granting pardon to N., &c., &c.

(Signed) JOHN A. KING.

DECISION OF THE SUPREME COURT OF PENNSYLVANIA.
DECEMBER TERM, 1838.

[Ex parte Crouse.—Habeas Corpus.]

PHILADELPHIA, *January* 3, 1839.

PER CURIAM.—The House of Refuge is not a prison, but a school; where reformation, and not punishment, is the end. It may, indeed, be used as a prison for juvenile convicts who would else be committed to a common jail; and in respect to these, the constitutionality of the act which incorporated it, stands clear of controversy. It is only in respect of the application of its discipline to subjects admitted on the order of a court, a magistrate, or the managers of the Almshouse, that a doubt is entertained. The object of the charity is reformation, by training its inmates to industry; by imbuing their minds with principles of morality and religion; by furnishing them with means to earn a living; and, above all, by separating them from the corrupting influence of improper associates. To this end, may not the natural parents, when unequal to the task of education, or unworthy of it, be superseded by the *parens patriæ*, or common guardian of the community? It is to be remembered, that the public has a paramount interest in the virtue and knowledge of its members, and that, of strict right, the business of education belongs to it. That parents are ordinarily intrusted with it, is because it can seldom be put into better hands; but where they are incompetent or corrupt, what is there to prevent the public from withdrawing their faculties, held, as they obviously are, at its sufferance? The right of parental control is a natural, but not an unalienable one. It is not excepted by the declaration of rights out of the subjects of ordinary legislation; and it consequently remains subject to the ordinary legislative power, which, if wantonly or inconveniently used, would soon be constitutionally restricted, but the competency of which, as the government is constituted, cannot be doubted. As to abridgment of indefeasible rights by confinement of the person, it is no more than what is borne, to a greater or less extent, in every school; and we know of no natural right to exemption from restraints which conduce to an infant's welfare. Nor is there a doubt of the propriety of their application in the particular instance. The infant has been snatched from a course which must have ended in confirmed depravity; and, not only is the restraint of her person lawful, but it would be an act of extreme cruelty to release her from it.

Remanded.

OPINION.

In all civil societies the individual members are held to a strict obedience to the laws. They are presumed to be acquainted with whatever is enjoined upon them as a social duty, and they are punished for a disregard or violation of it. This principle of accountability is essential to the prosperity and even the existence of society, and as a general rule, it exacts compliance and conformity from every individual. In its practical application, however, the rule is not universal. Many persons are partially exempt from its operation, and not a few are entirely beyond its reach. A rigid enforcement of the principle alluded to, implies the existence both of capacity and free agency on the part of those who are its objects. If either the ability to judge or the means to exercise a sound judgment be wanting, accountability is no longer imputed to the individual, or obedience exacted from him under the sanctions which generally apply. Persons who are thus exempt from the ordinary operations of the laws are subject necessarily to provisions which are peculiar to themselves. As they are not liable to the consequences of their own conduct, it is indispensable for the good of others as well as themselves that their conduct should be regulated and restrained. These regulations and restraints have been at all times applied with peculiar interest and care to persons of immature age. Contracts made by them are either considered of no binding force whatever, or are governed by rules which give them only a beneficial operation. Even as to crimes they are regarded with great indulgence; an indulgence which amounts to entire impunity if the capacity for deception be unformed. When very young they are also placed under restrictions that are unqualified and absolute; and during the whole period of non age they are the subjects of provisions which, if applied to other persons would be tyrannical or unjust. Parents, guardians and masters exercise an authority of this description. No one can doubt the propriety of it in its particular application, founded as it is, in an obvious necessity, and dictated by a kind and tender consideration for incompetency to self-control, and consequent proneness to error. The greater or less degree of restraint which is imposed by these Superintendents of youth must depend upon circumstances, and cannot be made the subject of any precise estimate. As long as it is governed by a regard to the best interests of the young, it has, perhaps, no other limits, and must be in its character discretionary with those by whom it is exercised.

It may frequently happen that none of the relations which have been mentioned exist. It does not, however, therefore follow, that the children who are without them must be either unprotected or unrestrained. Their condition as respects both capacity and proneness to error is the same, whether they have the good fortune to be connected with natural or legal guardians, or are unhappily destitute of both. Society is not to be exposed to the consequences of their present feebleness and freedom from restraint; they themselves are not to be exposed to the enduring evils of ignorance and idleness merely because of an accidental and unfortunate deficiency. On the contrary, the various evils to which they are exposed are the rather to be guarded against, because the deficiency exists, and the deficiency itself is to be anxiously supplied. Children in the condition supposed are thrown upon society at large for their guardians; and no system can be at all adequate to the exigencies of society, unless special provision is made for them by the laws. Such laws as are enacted for the mutual protection of themselves and others are wise and salutary in their design; and if they are imperfect or injurious

in application, it is only because their execution and details do not
conform to the theory and intention which it is their object to effec-
tuate.

The establishment of a House of Refuge ought to be entirely
agreeable to the principles which have been adverted to. It professes to exercise simply the salutary influence, which the condition
and incapacity of those who are its objects would seem to require:
to provide a substitute for parental authority and superintendence,
which have been either lost by misfortune or forfeited by misconduct: to apply a system of prevention and care to those who, from
their peculiar situation, are without the advantages in these respects
which others enjoy. The laws which have been enacted by the
Legislature of Pennsylvania have purely these ends in view. They
are similar in design, and only an improvement in their results to
those which almost every community has found itself under the
necessity of providing for in the shape of poor laws: which are, in
truth, liable to all the objections substantially, which are made to
those on which a House of Refuge is founded.

It is mainly objected, as I understand, to the law in question, that
punishment is inflicted without the ordinary preliminaries of trial and
conviction. Into this the principal difficulties resolve themselves,
which have forced their way into the minds of persons of high intelligence. The error on which the objection is founded is twofold.
First, in supposing that the mere commission of crimes is the reason
for admission into the house; and secondly, in imputing to the consequences of that admission the character and name of punishment.
An individual who is certified to be a proper subject for the discipline
of the house, is only brought into view on the particular occasion,
because he has done something wrong. His condition was such in-
dependently of his fault, as to require the discipline and care of the
establishment. The crime he has committed is satisfactory proof of
his condition and requirements. It manifests his unfitness for self-
government, and the absence or abuse of domestic authority and influence. Where this state of things is apparent, there is a corresponding necessity no less obvious for the interposition and exercise of that
paternal superintendence which, in the abstract, resides at all times
in the source of all authority, although the practical use of it is reserved for extraordinary occasions. In some countries this sovereign
authority is vested in the king. With us it belongs to the people.

An exercise of it cannot be safer or more salutary than when it is confided to the agents of the representatives of the people, under such limitations as the law, in its wisdom, may provide. It is not in place here to dwell on the superior kindness and humanity which would dictate an omission to convict, and consequently to degrade and render infamous, or the cruelty of an unnecessary exposure of young persons to so fatal a result. On principles of mere municipal and constitutional law, there is a clear right to provide for the education and improvement of the young: and in the attainment of these great objects all the assistance that can be derived from discipline and restraint in the due and wholesome exercise of them is within the limits of that authority conferred by the Constitution on the Legislature.

What real difference is there between the power thus necessarily exercised through the medium of the law, and that which parents and their ordinary substitutes are in the constant habit of resorting to? Every child that is sent to school is obliged to submit to a discipline which is more or less rigid, according to the rules of the establishment or the temper of the scholar. Sometimes it is vastly more severe than that of a house of refuge. Probably all the boys who are placed on board of ships are subjected to regulations more strict, to a confinement more unrelenting, to a course of discipline in every way more stern. Does it render the act of the parent or guardian illegal, that the particular kind of instruction and restraint has been appealed to, because of particular evil propensities or positive misconduct on the part of the child?

It is a fundamental principle of these institutions for the welfare of the young, that no punishment whatever is inflicted for any thing that may have happened before their admission into the house. Instead of being subjected to, they are saved from punishment. Past crimes are forgotten, and future ones are prevented. The mode in which these important objects are accomplished by the laws of Pennsylvania, is, in my opinion, perfectly consistent with the true principles of civil government, with a strict regard to the liberty of the citizen, with an entire deference to parental authority, and with the constitution of Pennsylvania and its general system of jurisprudence. J. R. INGERSOLL.

WASHINGTON, *January* 27, 1835.

I concur in the above opinion. My only regret is, that my engagements, since the application was made to me, have not allowed me time to put my views upon paper, but I have not the less confidence in the opinion on that account. The subject has long been familiar to my thoughts, and I have never doubted the constitutional competency of the Legislature to make the law, nor the constitutional validity of the law that has been made. Extreme cases may, indeed, be suggested, when the exercise of such a power would become odious and inadmissible. I have heard arguments against the power of the Legislature founded upon the possibility of abuse. But it must be assumed, in general, and it may be safely assumed in the present case, that the object is truly and *bona fide* what it professes to be. Namely, a pure purpose of policy and benevolence, embracing not less the welfare and happiness of the individuals over whom the control is exercised, than the general interests of society, and just as essential to the one as to the other. Thus understood, I cannot persuade myself that there is any doubt of the constitutional power of the Legislature to establish the interesting institution which has proved itself to be so valuable a charity.

JOHN SERGEANT.

WASHINGTON, *January* 27, 1835.

THE HOUSE OF REFUGE

vs.

THE STATE OF MARYLAND,

ON THE RELATION OF MARTIN ROTH.

} *In the Supreme Bench of Baltimore City.*

Upon the motion of the HOUSE OF REFUGE *to have heard and determined in this Court a matter of law decided in the Baltimore City Court.*

The motion in this case standing ready for hearing, was argued by counsel for the parties, and the proceedings have since been considered. And it appearing to this Court, for reasons set out in the opinion herewith filed, that there is error in matter of law in the judgment of the Baltimore City Court, rendered in this case on the thirty-first day of December, eighteen hundred and sixty-seven. It is thereupon, on this fifth day of February, in the year eighteen hundred and sixty-eight, by the Supreme Bench of Baltimore City, adjudged and ordered that the said judgment be, and the same is hereby reversed.   GEORGE W. DOBBIN,

                                                    HENRY F. GAREY,

                                                    ROBT. GILMOR, JR.

THE HOUSE OF REFUGE *vs.* THE STATE OF MARYLAND, ON THE RELATION OF MARTIN ROTH.	*In the Supreme Bench of Baltimore City.*

Upon the motion of the HOUSE OF REFUGE *to have heard and determined in this Court a matter of law decided in the Baltimore City Court.*

The matter of law which the House of Refuge asks to have reheard and determined in this Court, arose and was decided in an application for the release, by *habeas corpus*, of Frank Roth, the son of the relator, who was held as an inmate of the House of Refuge, upon a commitment by a Justice of the Peace, under the 18th section of the 78th article of the Public General Code. The boy was committed on the complaint of his father, "that he had rendered his control beyond the power of his father by reason of his own incorrigible conduct; and had made it manifestly requisite that, from regard for the morals and future welfare of said minor, and the peace and order of society, he should be placed under the guardianship of the Managers of the House of Refuge." The commitment is in the very words of the Code prescribing the manner of receiving inmates into the House of Refuge, and gratifies in all particulars the first of the modes therein prescribed; the justice also, in attempted but very meagre compliance with the requirements of the 20th section, annexed to the commitment, the statement that the testimony of Henry Yeager, proved the boy to be one of the same depredators and thieves prowling around and stealing. Upon the hearing, the boy was discharged by the Court, upon the ground that the commitment by the justice was a trial and conviction of the boy for crime, without indictment, and without a jury, in violation of the 21st and 23d articles of the Declaration of Rights; and that so much of the

provisions of the 78th article of the Code as professes to give such
authority to a Justice of the Peace, is in violation of the Constitution of the State, and is utterly null and void. It was stated in the
argument of the present motion, that it is with no special wish to
retain this particular boy as an inmate of the House of Refuge, that
its managers now ask to have this case reconsidered, and that except
for the desirableness of this reconsideration, they would willingly
acquiesce in the remanding of this boy to the custody of his father ;
but the decision of the Baltimore City Court so deeply affects the
usefulness of the institution as a reformatory asylum (whose place is
not supplied by any other institution in the State), that they feel it
to be their duty, in the discharge of the important philanthropic trust
committed to them, to ask that that decision, made by a single judge,
should be reviewed, and passed upon by the whole Supreme Bench.
We also are impressed with the importance of the case considered, with
reference to the interests of other benevolent institutions of like character, by the declaration of the counsel for the relator, that since the
pendency of this case, he has had an application to take, by *habeas
corpus*, from the care of the Children's Aid Society, a little girl of
eight years of age, now under the charge of that institution. Impressed with the importance of these considerations, this Court could
not hesitate to give to this motion a prompt and patient hearing, and,
after the assistance derived from elaborate and learned arguments,
they have brought to the determination of the case their most con-
siderate judgment. The motion gives rise to two inquiries : the first
having reference to the jurisdiction of this court to review the decision of a matter of law decided in a *habeas corpus* case in any of
the courts of original jurisdiction in the City of Baltimore; and the
second, involving the consideration of the constitutionality of the
provisions of the code under which this boy was committed to the
House of Refuge. The constitution of this court being new to our
judicial system, it is to be expected that, until it shall have a body
of precedent to guide its action, questions of jurisdiction will be of
frequent occurrence. The solution of these questions must be sought
for alone in the 33d section of the 4th article of the Constitution;
for, though in the argument we were referred to our own rules as a
measure of our powers, it is too obvious to need discussion, that we
have no authority whatever either to enlarge or abridge the limits
prescribed to us in the Constitution. In construing any new statutory

or constitutional provision, it is a wise rule to have respect to the
state of things existing under the antecedent law, in order to see
what change was desirable, and how the new enactment may affect it.

In this retrospect we find that, under our late judicial system, as
applicable to the City of Baltimore, there existed five independent
courts, of separate, and in most respects, dissimilar jurisdiction, each
presided over by one judge, and, however eminent and able each of
such judges might be individually, no provision was made by which
the suitor and the public could have the benefit of their united de-
liberation and judgment. The consequence was, that the law pronounced in one court was repudiated in another; and the suitor, in
choosing his forum, could also, in some sense, determine his law.
This evil was so apparent, that in one instance, involving the proper
construction of a clause in the Constitution, affecting a large class of
cases, and great public considerations, in which the Superior Court
had determined the question in one way, and the Court of Common
Pleas in another, the Court of Appeals felt it due to the public interests to express its opinion on the point in a case where it was not
necessary to be determined, and placed its departure from the usual
rule of decision upon the ground of the public inconvenience and
injury arising from this diversity of judgment. (State *vs.* Mace, 5 Md.)

For the adjudication of the important interests of this populous
commercial city, a system which admitted, and indeed, looking at the
frowardness of human judgment, almost encouraged, this diversity
of judgment, was deemed unsuitable and inadequate, and accordingly
the present scheme was devised, by which, whilst the number of
courts is continued, and their separate efficiency in the dispatch of
business is promoted, by apt provisions for mutual assistance and
interchange of labor, and for the division of the mass of business
among them, its chief merit was supposed to lie in the fact, that the
five judges, in their united capacity of the Supreme Bench, were
charged with the duty of making rules for them, so as to secure uni-
formity of practice, and with the hearing and determining controverted points of law, so as to insure harmony of decision.

The language of the Constitution, by which this latter duty is
imposed, is as follows: "It shall also have jurisdiction to hear and
determine all motions for a new trial in cases tried in any of said
courts, when such motions arise either on questions of fact, or for

misdirection upon any matters of law, and all motions in arrest of judgment, or upon any matter of law determined by the said judge or judges while holding said several courts." It will thus be perceived, that the jurisdiction of the court is of a twofold character: it is original, so to speak, in motions for a new trial when such motions arise on questions of fact, and on motions in arrest of judgment; and it is appellate upon motions for a new trial, when such motions are based upon misdirection upon matters of law, and upon motions upon any matter of law determined by the judge or judges, while holding said several courts.

These several subjects of jurisdiction have a distinctly recognized legal meaning, and we have no difficulty in determining that the present motion, which asks for a new trial upon the ground of mistake of law, and misdirection of law, in the order of the Baltimore City Court, cannot be entertained by us as a motion for a *new trial*, that form of motion being only applicable to the rehearing of a case which has been tried before a jury. But the motion also asks us to revise and determine the matter of law decided in the Baltimore City Court, and this brings us to the consideration, whether this, being a case of *habeas corpus*, in which, heretofore, in this State, no appeal has been allowed, is now, under the terms used in the Constitution, and under the construction we must give to these terms, in view of the evils they were supposed to remedy, and the benefits they were intended to confer, brought within the reviewing and appellate jurisdiction of this court.

It was argued before us, with great earnestness, that the allowance of an appeal in a *habeas corpus* case is an encroachment upon the liberty of the citizen. This, we think, is taking a narrow and restricted view of the value of that aim of remedial justice, which is intended to secure a deliberate trial, and a well-considered judgment. The petitioner for the benefit of the writ of *habeas corpus* may, indeed, rejoice in the finality of the judgment which liberates him; but what would be the opinion of the same petitioner, if the judgment chanced to be against him, and especially if it turned upon some controverted or doubtful point of law. No reference need be made, beyond a mere suggestive allusion, to the value, in *favorem libertatis*, of an appeal in times of high political excitement, when partisan judges may refuse the benefits of the writ, under the influence of corrupt motives, and in utter disregard of the principles of law and liberty. The liberty of the citizen is but protected by giving to him, as matter of right, a refuge from the fallibility of any single tribunal; and in every enlightened system of laws, such a resort is furnished in all cases, except where the trivial nature of the thing in controversy, or the preponderating convenience of the public, renders an appeal undesirable. It furnishes no reply to the argument which maintains the desirableness of an appeal, to say that its place is supplied by the fact, that the judgment of one judge is not conclusive upon another, and a petitioner may apply to any number of judges in succession, since it is now well recognized to be the law and practice applicable to the writ: that after a case has been once acted upon, the subsequent application ceases to be one of right, and becomes a mere matter of discretion—so that, at the very time when the necessity for the demand of an appeal, *ex debito justiciæ,* may be most apparent, weak and timid judges, fearful of responsibility and mindful only of their own or their party's interests, may, without incurring the censure of violating the law, take refuge under the former judgment, and refuse the application as *res adjudicata.* (*Ex parte* Lawson, 5 Bin., 304; *Ex parte* Campbell, 20 Ala., 89.) Our own Court of Appeals has said: "Very strong reasons should be required to induce the Court to refuse a party the benefit of an appeal; and any interference with the right, wherever it exists, must be upon strong grounds, and a clear manifestation on the part of the Legislature, that they designed to withdraw it." (Williams *vs.* Williams, 7 Gill, 304.)

The same reasoning will apply with equal cogency and force to the giving an appeal in every instance in which the case, from its nature, will admit of an appeal, without detriment to the cause of justice, and the convenience of the public, and when the Legislature have used such terms as will admit the appeal. The inquiry naturally arises, then, does the writ of *habeas corpus* present such a case that an appeal may be given without injury to the cause of justice, and the convenience of the public? If we consider the writ as we have been long accustomed to do, as the inestimable privilege of a free people, and the best safeguard of personal liberty, surely, then, any provision of law which tends to secure the just and well-considered application of its benefits, increases, rather than diminishes, its nature. If it be the refuge of the oppressed, to be cherished in the proportion that it affords him speedy and impartial justice, its true value must be measured by the certainty that he will be able to obtain justice when he makes the appeal. Now, it reverses the whole theory of the administration of justice to say that, in the proportion that you give the suitor an opportunity to have his case reviewed, you diminish his chances of obtaining justice; nor is there any thing, in the mode of administering justice by the usual practice under the writ, which makes an appeal impracticable or greatly inconvenient, especially when the appeal is based upon the determination of a matter of law, as in this case.

It is no novelty in the law, that an appeal in *habeas corpus* should be allowed, as it is granted with the same freedom as in other cases in some of the States, as in New York, Virginia, Florida, South Carolina, Mississippi, Texas, and Ohio, and is especially provided for in the recent statutes of the United States, giving the benefits of the writ, and prescribing the practice under it. It is there enacted, that " from the final decision of every judge, justice, or court, inferior to the Circuit Court, an appeal may be taken to the Circuit Court of the United States for the district in which the said cause is heard ; and from the judgment of the said Circuit Court to the Supreme Court of the United States, upon such terms, and under such regulations and orders, as well for the custody and appearance of the party alleged to be restrained of his or her liberty, as for sending up to the appellate tribunal a transcript of the petition, writ of *habeas corpus*, return thereto, and other proceedings, as may be prescribed by the Supreme Court, or in default, as the judge hearing the said cause may prescribe," etc.

Nowhere are two successive appeals given in cases of *habeas corpus*, and a mode provided by which the whole case, both in law and in fact, may be presented to the appellate tribunals.

If this be a practical and expedient method as applied to the successive appeals by which the cause finally reaches the Supreme Court of the United States, and presents to the review of each Court, in succession, both the facts and the law, why may not a similar practice be adopted by us, especially in the limited appeal claimed by this motion, of having only the matter of law determined in the Baltimore City Court reviewed and determined ?

It does not seem to have been considered by the Congress of the United States, that the inconvenience and delay incident to the practice in *habeas corpus*, which they have prescribed, abridges the liberty of the citizen in any degree commensurate with the advantage it gives him in having his cause thoroughly tried, and the judgment therein well considered; though the Supreme Court sits but once a year, and at a place which may be remote from that in which the cause arose. How little, then, in comparison with the benefits of an appeal, should the consideration of inconvenience weigh with the judges of this Court, who are engaged nearly every day in the year in judicial labor under the same roof, and may be brought into the same room at any time, upon an hour's notice!

It is indeed true, that heretofore, in this State, no appeal would lie to the Court of Appeals, in a case of *habeas corpus*, but the reason of that is, in the fact that, in the acts defining the right of appeal to the Court of Appeals, the words used do not include in their meaning the writ of *habeas corpus*, and, although the Court, in so determining, in Bell *vs.* the State, in 4th Gill, state certain characteristics of the writ which, in their judgment, do not bring it within the class of cases which, by the law of Maryland, has been considered as proper subjects for an appeal, it is not asserted in that case, that if the acts of 1785 and 1804 had used terms sufficiently comprehensive to have included the writ of *habeas corpus*, any other consideration connected with the writ would have forbidden the extension of an appeal to it. Is this court, then, subject to the same restrictions, or are the words of the Constitution, by which we are required to hear and determine appeals in certain cases, sufficiently broad and comprehensive to include within their meaning the proceedings on the writ of *habeas corpus?* The obligation imposed upon us by the Constitution is, " to hear and determine all motions upon any matter of law determined by the said judge or judges, while holding said several courts." By what process of reasoning can we come to the conclusion that a judgment pronounced in a *habeas corpus* case, by which an act of Assembly is declared to be unconstitutional, and null and void, is not the determination of a matter of law, whilst the same judgment pronounced in our action of trespass for the detention of this boy would be a matter of law, and reviewable by us? yet this would be the result of our rejection of this jurisdiction.

It was argued at the bar, that the jurisdiction to grant the writ of *habeas corpus* of the courts in Maryland, and of the judges out of of court, having been given by statute, presents a case of special and limited jurisdiction, and must follow the rule applicable to such superadded jurisdiction, and no appeal will lie unless expressly given, by words descriptive of the writ, in the same statute. This conclusion, we think, is drawn from unsound premises. The writ of *habeas corpus* is coeval with the earliest times of the common law, and its origin dates so far back that it cannot now be traced. It was in use as a common-law writ of right, *ex debito justiciæ*, before Magna Charta; and the practice under it was reduced to regularity as far back as the Statute of 31st Charles II., commonly known as the *Habeas Corpus Act*. It was imported into the colony of Maryland with the earliest settlers, and the *Habeas Corpus Act* of the reign of Charles II. is one of those reported by Chancellor Kilty to have been in force here. Our own statutory enactments on the subject are but little more than an adaptation of the statute of Charles to the altered condition of our institutions and times, and no more create a special and limited jurisdiction in our courts than an act of Assembly, which regulated the proceedings in trespass or covenant, could be said to confer a special jurisdiction. It is not necessary, therefore, upon this ground, at least, that an appeal shall be given, *totidem verbis*, in *habeas corpus*, but it may be included in any general terms sufficiently comprehensive certainly to embrace it. In New York, by the force of such general terms, it was held that a writ of error would lie in such a case (Yates *vs.* The People, 6 Johns, 337), and in the Supreme Court of the United States the same point had the authoritative support of such names as Taney, Story, McLean, Wayne, and Catron, though the case came to no decision, from a divided court. (Holmes *vs.* Jennison, 14 Peters, 540.) This point has not been again considered in the Supreme Court of the United States, except in the case of Barry *vs.* Mercein, 5 Howard, 120, which arose under a different clause of the judiciary act, and in which the right to a writ of error was limited to cases where the amount in controversy exceeds two thousand dollars. Chief-Justice Taney delivered the opinion of the Court, in which it was ruled, that, as no pecuniary value could be assigned to a controversy involving only the consideration of the custody of a child, no writ of error would lie under that section. But he expressly refers to the 25th section, in which no such limitation is prescribed, and distinguishes the case then under consideration from cases arising under the 25th section. In coming to the conclusion, that this court has had conferred upon it and is bound to exercise the duty of reviewing the determination of the Baltimore City Court in this case, we cannot disguise that we are acting under a deep sense of the magnitude of the public interest involved in this decision; whilst the humble citizen is entitled to demand at our hands the fullest protection to his liberty and happiness, the great body of the people may, on the other hand, equally claim that a great philanthropic enterprise, which has for its object the rescuing of the young from the dangerous contamination of immorality and crime, shall not be stricken from its usefulness by a view of the constitutional protection to personal liberty now for the first time acted upon.

The magnitude of the interests involved in the judgments often pronounced in *habeas corpus* cases is not overstated by an American law-writer, treating of this subject of appeal, when he says: " Questions of the most serious moment are often raised in this proceeding; questions relating to the unconstitutionality of an act of the State Legislature, or of Congress, and to the jurisdiction of courts, the highest, it may be, in the land, and to the validity of the process emanating from them. These questions, when they arise, it is supposed to be the duty of the judges hearing the *habeas corpus* to determine. Such questions claim the most deliberate consideration of the wisest who are charged with the administration of justice, and it is neither safe nor consistent with the general spirit of American law to intrust their final decision, in a summary proceeding, to a single judge, sitting apart, at chambers, without a record, shorn of the majesty of a court." (Hurd on *Habeas Corpus*, 569.)

Assuming, then, that this court has had conferred upon it jurisdiction to entertain this motion, the remaining question to be considered is: is the law constitutional and valid which empowers a justice of the peace to commit Frank Roth to the House of Refuge, on the complaint, and upon due proof made to him by his father, that, by reason of incorrigible or vicious conduct, the said Frank Roth had rendered his control beyond the power of his said father, and made it manifestly requisite that, from regard for the moral and future welfare of said Frank Roth, and the peace and order of society, he should be placed under the guardianship of the House of Refuge. These are the precise terms of the conditions in which a minor, in Frank Roth's position, can be committed, and are the very conditions stated in the warrant upon which he was committed. Let us now see whether the justice had lawful authority to act in the premises; for, if he had, and has acted within the scope of his authority, it is conceded that there is no power in the Baltimore City Court to reverse that judgment in this proceeding, it being well settled that a *habeas corpus* cannot be made to perform the office of a writ of error. It is commonly said of the State, in view of its absolute authority over all within its limits, that it is *parens patriæ*, by which it is understood that it possesses, and is bound to exercise for the common good, dominion and control over the persons of all its people. This dominion and control the State never exercises except where the good of society demands that it shall be called into use, and then its right is indisputable. Thus, it confines the insane, it finds a home for the pauper, it imprisons the criminal, it binds the apprentice, it drafts the soldier. These are some of the cases in which the State gives practical evidence of its right to control personal liberty, growing out of the special exigency of the case; but there is another large class, who are, in contemplation of law, always in the special care and custody of the State, and this class is composed of all persons within her borders who are in their minority. In contemplation of law, the state of minority is a state of custody, and when questions affecting the condition of minors arise upon *habeas corpus*, the inquiry is not, shall the minor be set at liberty, but to whose custody shall he be committed? This is a condition necessarily consequent upon the disability under which the law places him. He can make no valid contract; he can bring no suit except through the agency of a next friend; and hence the law, in disabling him from protecting himself, must assume him to be in the guardianship of some protecting custody. The mode in which this care and custody is exercised varies with the varying needs of the subjects of it.

Those whose natural progenitors were able to care for all their wants it intrusts to the helping of parents, relying upon the natural instincts of paternity to discharge this duty faithfully and well; those who have estates, and are orphans, are placed by the agency of proper courts in the care of suitable, chosen guardians; those who need only education, which their own means will not supply, are supplied with public schools, which, in many instances, they are compelled to attend; but there is still left a large class of minors, some of whom are without means—often without parents or friends, and as often with such as are careless and dissolute—for whom the State, as their nursing-mother, is bound to find the means of support. Now, as the State is but a corporate entity, and can only use the instrumentality of public eleemosynary institutions for performing this duty, and as these institutions must be adapted to the wants of the classes of minors specially confided to them, we find necessity for Manual-Labor Schools, Children's Aid Societies, Orphan Asylums, Poor Boys' Homes, and Houses of Refuge for juvenile delinquents. As the case we are considering concerns alone an institution of the kind last named, it is only needful to notice its character and objects. The House of Refuge is an incorporated society, originally started upon private subscriptions, but now become an institution of such value to the public, that annual appropriations from the public treasury are made for its support. It is under the management of a board of twenty-four directors, chosen annually, ten of whom are elected by the members of the association, ten are appointed by the Mayor and City Council of Baltimore, and four by the Governor of the State, thus insuring that the conduct of it shall be under the charge of our most responsible citizens. Its distinctive character is declared, in the law, to be a place of reform, and not of punishment, and the means used to carry out its object consist in the supply of abundant clothing, wholesome food, educational and moral training, the cultivation of music, and the teaching of such proper trades and employments as, in the judgment of the managers, will be most conducive to the reformation and the future benefit and advantage of its children. The institution is intended for the benefit of that class of minors commonly called juvenile delinquents, and to those only should its benefit be extended. But, as it is established for this class only, and is not to be used by those who, being of good character, need only the public aid in their support and education, and for whom other institutions, as the Manual-Labor School, Children's Aid Society, and Poor Boys' Home, are founded, it is obvious that some mode of admission should be prescribed by which the reformatory benefits of the institution shall be conferred upon those only who are the proper subjects for them. These may be briefly stated to be: *First*, by the action of a justice of the peace, on the complaint of the father, that the minor is of incorrigible or vicious conduct; *Secondly*, by the same authority, upon proof that the minor is a vagrant or incorrigibly vicious, and that the parent of such minor cannot, or will not, exercise proper discipline over him; *Thirdly*, by contract with the parent

of an incorrigible and vicious child, for his support and maintenance
during temporary restraint and discipline; and, *lastly*, children convicted of felony, and committed by sentence of court. The case we
are now considering arises under the first of the above-mentioned
modes of admission, it being by a commitment of a justice of the
peace, upon the complaint of the father. To find the facts upon
which the justice has acted, we must look to the commitment itself,
because, in order to try the question of jurisdiction in the justice, we
must assume the facts which he declares to have been the basis of
his action to be true. The jurisdiction is plainly given by the act of
Assembly, if the Legislature had the power to confer it, and it is the
denial of that power by the judgment of the Baltimore City Court, in
this case, as being in violation of the 21st and 23d sections of the Bill of
Rights, which constitutes the matter of law this court is called upon to
review. It seems to us that the mere statement that this commitment
was upon the complaint and request of the father is an answer to the objection, unless we mean to assume that the framers of the Bill of Rights
designed by those sections to take from a father of a minor twelve
years old the right to subject him to a reformatory restraint, without
indicting him by a grand jury and procuring his conviction of crime.
This is certainly not the view of the law under which society has
reached its present point of civilization and culture. In all time
heretofore, the rights and duty of the parent, under the allowance of
the State, to control his child by any discipline, not barbarous and in-
human, which the incorrigible and vicious conduct of such child may
render necessary, have been always admitted and acted upon. Could
our constitutional lawgivers have intended to destroy this right by
the sections in the Bill of Rights protecting personal liberty? If they
did, we have been a long time in ignorance of it, for these provisions
were in our first Bill of Rights, and have never before been applied to
the limitation of parental discipline, either exercised directly by the
parent himself, or, in default of his ability to afford it, through the
instrumentality of a public institution. The jurisdiction of the
justice thus exercised by the authority of the State to commit an incorrigible and vicious minor, upon the complaint and due proof made
by the father that he was such, seems to be too plain for argument.
Let us look, then, at the character of his action, to see how far it is
conformable to the authority conferred upon him. The authority to
commit in this case is conferred by the 18th section of the 78th Ar-

ticle of the Public General Code, which prescribes the four classes of cases which should be received, and the manner of receiving them into the House of Refuge. This commitment was made under the first mode set forth in the section, and is in the very words of the law, stating neither more nor less than the law requires. But a subsequent section—the 20th—makes it the duty of the justice, when committing a vagrant, or incorrigible, or vicious minor, in addition to the commitment, to annex the names and residences of the different witnesses examined before him, and the substance of the testimony given by them respectively, on which the adjudication was founded, and the same duty shall be performed by the clerk of any court the judge whereof shall make such commitment. It may very well be questioned whether the proper construction of this requirement will extend it to the case of a commitment upon the application of the father, or whether it ought not to be confined to the second class of cases named in the 18th section, where the commitment is made upon the testimony of strangers, who proved not only the vicious character of the minor, but also the moral depravity of the parents. In the first case, the authority and right to control and confine the incorrigible child already exist, by force of law, in the father; and he is entitled to exercise them, for disciplinary purposes, according to his own judgment of their necessity. His application to the justice is not to obtain the authority to confine, but for the purpose of obtaining the benefit of the institution in the mode which has been prescribed to prevent its abuse. His own commitment of the minor, if the institution would receive him, would be as valid as the justice's. Moreover, he is, by law, the sole and final judge of the conduct of his child and his necessity for discipline, and his testimony, that, by reason of the vicious conduct of such child, it is manifestly requisite that he or she should be placed under the guardianship of the House of Refuge, ought to be sufficient, without the necessity of his spreading out at length the particular delinquencies of the child, to remain a record long after the reformatory influences of the Refuge may have made him a useful and honest member of society. In the case of the commitment upon the testimony of strangers, where the proof must be not only the delinquency of the minor, but the moral depravity of the parent, the authority to commit is in its nature judicial and it results from the judgment of the justice applied to the facts proved before him. Hence arises the propriety of requiring the justice to state the substance of the testimony upon which his judgment is founded. But, conceding that the requirements of the 20th section are applicable to this case, is compliance with such requirements a necessary part of the commitment to the extent of making the commitment void if not complied with? We do not think it is. The commitment itself states, with exact particularity, the facts necessary to be proven, and states, with equal distinctness, that they were so proved. The requirement of the 20th section is not, that the justice shall state the whole evidence upon which the adjudication is founded, so that another court, subsequently investigating the case, can see whether his judgment was right, but he is to state the substance of the testimony, that is, just so much, by his own abridgment of the facts, as will show the general character of the matter proved. Surely it could not have been intended that the validity of the commitment should be made to depend upon the literary and technical legal accuracy of the justice, in compressing into a few words that which, in its delivery, occupies many. This is made apparent, also, by the provisions in the same section, which requires that, when the judge of a court shall make the commitment, the clerk of the court, who is not required by his duty to listen to the evidence, who is not called upon, and is incompetent, to judge of its admissibility, its weight, or its technical significance, is to make the same statement of the substance of the evidence; and yet, according to the construction contended for, the commitment of the judge is to stand or fall by the technical accuracy of the clerk's discharge of this duty. In this case the justice did not omit altogether the performance of this duty, but, to justify his adjudication, that the boy was incorrigibly vicious, stated that he was proved to be one of a gang of depredators and thieves prowling around and stealing. This, although not a very full and satisfactory compliance with the act of Assembly, is not sufficient to render the commitment bad. We do not think there is any thing in the objection that the statement of the justice convicts the boy of a crime. The thing to be proven to the satisfaction of the justice was, that the boy was of incorrigibly vicious conduct, and he was so proven. If, in the statement of the substance of the testimony, the justice states that one of the items of proof which led to that conclusion was, that he belonged to a gang of depredators and thieves, it does not follow that he was specifically charged with being a thief, or that his being adjudged to be incorrigibly vicious convicted him of larceny or felony. Proof within the terms used by the justice might have been exhibited to him, as that the boy frequented the society of depredators and thieves, against the remonstrance of his father, and that he was perversely forsaking the path of rectitude for that of vice, would fall far short of a conviction of crime, in a legal sense, and yet be quite sufficient to sustain the judgment that he was incorrigibly vicious. A large part of the argument before us, in behalf of the relator, was expended in the attempt to show that the inquiry before the justice was a "criminal prosecution," in the sense of the 21st section of the Bill of Rights, and that, therefore, the party charged was entitled to a trial by jury, and to the other privileges set out in that section, and that the proceeding also violates the 21st section, by depriving the minor of his liberty, without the judgment of his peers, or, not according to the law of the land. It is sufficient for us to say that, in our view, the complaint and proof by Martin Roth, that his son, twelve years old, was incorrigibly vicious, and the consequent judgment therein, that he should be placed under the guardianship of the House of Refuge, is not a "criminal prosecution" which demands the intervention of a jury; and if we are right in the proposition heretofore laid down in this opinion, as to the legal status of minors with reference to custody, the proceeding in question is not one by which the minor is deprived of his liberty, but only one in which is determined, on grounds of public expediency, the transfer of his custody. The case we have now considered and decided is not now for the first time brought to the notice of a court of justice. In the State of Pennsylvania there exists a House of Refuge, after which our own was copied, and from whose charter we have taken the precise modes of admission to the benefits of the institution which they had previously adopted. Upon a case exactly resembling the one we have been reviewing, except that the conviction was made on the complaint of the mother, and the *habeas corpus* applied for on the relation of the father, the Supreme Court of Pennsylvania heard and decided the case upon precisely the objections taken in this; that is, that the authority conferred on a justice to commit was in contravention of the Declaration of Rights, which contains the same provisions as our own. We give the unanimous opinion of the Court, in full, the judges being Chief-Justice Gibson, and Rogers, Huston, Kennedy, and Sergeant, associates. The case is *Ex parte* Crouse, 4 Wharton, 9 :

Per Curiam.—" The House of Refuge is not a prison, but a school, where reformation, but not punishment, is the end. It may, indeed, be used as a prison for juvenile convicts, who would else be committed to a common jail, and in respect to these, the constitutionality of the Act which incorporated it stands clear of controversy. It is only in respect of the application of its discipline to subjects admitted on the order of a court, a magistrate, or the managers of the Alms House, that a doubt is entertained. The object of the charity is reformation, by training its inmates to industry, by imbuing their minds with principles of morality and religion, by furnishing them with means to earn a living, and, above all, by separating them from the corrupting influence of improper associates.

" To this end, may not the natural parents, when unequal to the task of education, or unworthy of it, be superseded by the *parens patriæ*, or common guardian of the community ?

" It is to be remembered, that the public has a paramount interest in the virtue and knowledge of its members, and that, of strict right, the business of education belongs to it. That parents are ordinarily intrusted with it, is because it can seldom be put into better hands; but when they are incompetent or corrupt, what is there to prevent the public from withdrawing the faculties held, as they obviously are, at its sufferance? The right of parental control is a natural, but not an inalienable one. It is not excepted by the Declaration of Rights out of the subjects of ordinary legislation, and it consequently remains subject to the ordinary legislative power, which, if wantonly or inconveniently used, would soon be constitutionally restricted, but the competency of which, as the Government is constituted, cannot be doubted.

" As to abridgment of indefeasible rights by confinement of the person, it is no more than what is borne, to a greater or less extent, in every school, and we know of no natural right to exemption from restraints which conduce to an infant's welfare. Nor is there a doubt of the propriety of their application in this particular instance. The infant has been snatched from a course which must have ended in confirmed depravity; and not only is the restraint of her person lawful, but it would be an act of extreme cruelty to release her from it. Remanded."

In conformity with the opinion we have now expressed, we reverse the judgment of the Baltimore City Court.

In testimony that the aforegoing is a true copy, taken from the opinions of the majority of the Supreme Bench of Baltimore City, and filed in this office for [SEAL.] record, February 5, 1868, I hereunto subscribe my name, and affix the seal of the Supreme Bench of Baltimore City, 6th day of February, A. D. 1868.

GEO. ROBINSON, *Clerk.*

THE HOUSE OF REFUGE	
vs.	*In the Supreme Bench of*
THE STATE OF MARYLAND, ON THE RELATION OF CHARLES BOYLE.	*Baltimore City.*

Upon the motion of the HOUSE OF REFUGE *to have heard and determined in this Court a matter of law decided in the Baltimore City Court.*

The paper-book shows that this case differs from Roth's case, just decided, only in the fact that the commitment in this case was made under the second provision of the 18th section of the 78th article of the Code, which provides for the commitment to the House of Refuge of incorrigibly vicious minors, whose parents, by reason of their own moral depravity, or otherwise, are incapable or unwilling to exercise the proper care and discipline over them. The reasons which we have given, in the opinion filed in Roth's case, for entertaining jurisdiction to hear and determine matters of law in a *habeas corpus* case, and for sustaining the jurisdiction of a Justice of the Peace, as conferred by the article of the Code above referred to, apply equally to this. The proceedings of the justice more fully conform to the law in this case than Roth's, the statement of the substance of the testimony annexed to the commitment is, in all particulars, a compliance with the law. The objection taken, that it convicts the minor of a crime, we think, can hardly be sustained by the fact that, in giving the testimony upon which is founded his adjudication, that the minor was, in consequence of vicious conduct, a proper subject for the guardianship of the House of Refuge, the justice stated that the minor, a child between ten and eleven years old, had been caught in the act of stealing two dollars and thirty-eight cents. To have taken any other notice of such an offence, committed by a mere child, except to subject him to parental discipline, or, in default of that, to the reformatory care of the House of Refuge, and especially to have committed one of his tender years to the contamination of a Penitentiary, would have aroused the moral sense of the community in a far higher degree than it is likely to be disturbed by any apprehended invasion of the right to personal liberty. For the reasons given in the opinion in Roth's case, and in this, we reverse the judgment of the Baltimore City Court in this case.

THE HOUSE OF REFUGE *vs.* THE STATE OF MARYLAND, ON THE RELATION OF CHARLES BOYLE.	*In the Supreme Bench of* *Baltimore City.*

Upon the motion of the HOUSE OF REFUGE *to have heard and determined in this Court a matter of law decided in the Baltimore City Court.*

The motion in the case standing ready for hearing, was argued by counsel for the parties, and the proceedings have since been considered. And it appearing to this Court, for the reasons set out in the opinion herewith filed, that there is error, in matter of law, in the judgment of the Baltimore City Court, rendered in this case, on the eleventh day of January, in the year eighteen hundred and sixty-eight,

It is, therefore, on this fifth day of February, in the year eighteen hundred and sixty-eight, by the Supreme Bench of Baltimore City, adjudged and ordered, that the said judgment be, and the same is hereby reversed.

GEORGE W. DOBBIN,
HENRY F. GAREY,
ROBT. GILMOR, Jr.

I hereby certify that the foregoing is a true copy, taken from the records of the Supreme Bench of Baltimore City, on file in this office. In testimony whereof, I [SEAL.] have hereunto subscribed my name, and affixed the seal of the said Supreme Bench, this sixth day of February, in the year of out Lord one thousand eight hundred and sixty-eight.

GEORGE ROBINSON, *Clerk.*

IV.

RULES FOR THE ENFORCEMENT OF DISCIPLINE IN THE NEW YORK HOUSE OF REFUGE.

I.—TELL NO LIES.

II.—ALWAYS DO THE BEST YOU CAN.

III.—The boys and girls are divided into four grades, according to conduct.

Grade 1—Includes the best behaved and most orderly boys and girls; those who do not lie, nor use profane language; who are neat and tidy in their persons, and cleanly in their habits; who do not wilfully or carelessly waste, injure, or destroy property belonging to the House, and who are always respectful to the officers.

Grade 2—Embraces those who are fair in conduct, but not entirely free from faults mentioned above.

Grade 3—Consists of those whose conduct is not so good as those in Grade 2. The first Grade of a boy or girl is always 3.

Grade 4—Is the lowest, and one of disgrace, it is only given in cases of continued or gross misconduct; a former inmate returned for fault is placed in Grade 4.

IV.—For violation of rules, boys and girls are degraded from 1 to 2, from 2 to 3, and from 3 to 4; for improvement in conduct they are raised in Grade from 4 to 3, from 3 to 2, and from 2 to 1. Any boy or girl continuing for thirteen weeks in succession in Grade 1, is advanced to the Class of Honor, and wears an appropriate badge.

V.—The Grades are determined every Saturday evening, in the presence of the whole division, according to the marks made during the week.

VI.—Five marks lower the Grade one step ; four leave it the same as the previous week ; less than four are forgiven.

VII.—In the Second Division, punishment with the strap degrades to 4; except when the subject is in the Class of Honor, in which case it degrades to 2.

VIII.—Boys and girls gain their release from the Refuge by retaining Grade 1 for fifty-two weeks in succession, and by attaining to the highest class in school—and they are discharged from the House when a proper place is provided for them.

IX.—No applications from parents or friends of children will be entertained by the Indenturing Committee, until the inmate applied for shall have been in Grade 1 at least six weeks next preceding the time of application, and shall have reached at least the third class in school.

X.—When an inmate has been degraded to 4, an addition of four weeks' continuance in Grade 1, required by the foregoing rule, will be made, before an application for discharge can be heard ; and two weeks more are added for every other Grade of 4 received.

XI.—Grades can be changed only by the Assistant-Superintendent, in case of boys, and by the Matron, in case of girls, for offences committed out of school; and by the Principal for offences occurring in school.

XII.—Any officer in charge of boys or girls may give, for disorderly conduct, not to exceed two marks during any one week, provided the marks given, added to those already imposed by others during the same week, do not exceed four.

XIII.—Before any marks are given, the boy or girl must be required to tell the number of marks already received, and the statement must be taken and noted.

XIV.—In case an inmate makes a false statement, which will be discovered at "Badge call," the offender shall be degraded at least two Grades, or may be punished according to the discretion of the officer in charge. In the latter case the Grade will be 4.

XV.—When the aggregate marks for the week amount to four, and other offences are counted, the boys out of school must be reported to the Assistant-Superintendent, and the girls to the Matron; and all cases in school, either boys or girls, must be reported to the Principals. After a report is made to the Assistant-Superintendent, Matron, or Principal, no marks can be altered or cancelled except by their approval; nor can these officers cancel any marks legitimately given by the subordinate officers previous to the report.

XVI.—When the Grade is determined at the calling of the badges at the close of the week, it cannot be changed except by the consent of the Superintendent.

V.

A DISCOURSE

ON OPENING THE NEW BUILDING IN THE HOUSE OF REFUGE, NEW YORK; ESTABLISHED FOR THE REFORMATION OF JUVENILE DELINQUENTS. DELIVERED DECEMBER 25TH, 1825, IN PRESENCE OF THE MANAGERS OF THE INSTITUTION, THE HONORABLE THE MAYOR AND COMMON COUNCIL OF THE CITY, SOME OF THE MEMBERS OF THE LEGISLATURE, AND MANY OF ITS PATRONS AND FRIENDS. BY JOHN STANFORD, A. M.

> Once rude and ignorant we were,
> With natures prone to stray!
> Blest now by Pity's kindest care,
> We hear of Wisdom's way.
>
> The soul untaught is dark as night,
> Where every evil dwells;
> All hail Instruction's sacred light,
> Which all this night dispels!—SS.

" *Take this child away and nurse it for me, and I will give thee thy wages.*"—Exodus ii. 9.

It has frequently been asserted, that when a child is destined for some eminent station and usefulness in life, its birth is usually accompanied with some strong marks of distinction. This certainly was the case with Moses, who was designated by the Almighty to be the deliverer of the Israelites from their bondage in Egypt; and afterward to become their Lawgiver, Prophet, and General, as they passed through the wilderness to inherit the land of Canaan. About the 320th year of the Hebrew captivity, it is said, *There arose up a new king over Egypt, which knew not Joseph.* Which, I presume, is not to be understood, that he was ignorant such a person lived in Egypt, was raised from obscurity to dignity, and preserved multitudes alive amidst the ravages of famine: but, that he had no esteem for him, because he was an Hebrew; and therefore cultivated an implacable enmity to Joseph's brethren, who had so exceedingly increased that it alarmed his fears for the safety of his kingdom. This excited his cruelty to lay unjustifiable burdens upon this people; but *the more he afflicted them the more they multiplied and grew.* Disappointed in this measure, he commanded, that when the Hebrew women should bring forth their male children, the midwives should destroy them in their birth. In this also the king was disappointed; for, to the humanity and honor of those females it is said, *the midwives feared God, and did not as the king of Egypt commanded them, but saved the men children alive;* and then made an excuse for their conduct. This so exasperated the king, that *he charged all his people, saying, Every son that is born ye shall cast into the river, and every daughter ye shall save alive.* Cruel wretch, in the character of a king! his edicts are here recorded as perpetual brands of his infamy.

At this time lived Amram and Jochebed, two pious Israelites of the tribe of Levi. God had already blessed them with a son whose name was Aaron, and a daughter called Miriam. Now, a third child is added to the number; it was a son of a beautiful countenance, and excited the most ardent affections of his parents. But, the edict! the cruel mandate of Pharaoh, which sentenced the lovely child to death in the waters of the Nile, overwhelmed them with sorrow. The fond parents determined to conceal the infant as long as possible, and retained it within their arms for three months, but could do so no longer. God, who foresees all events, to accomplish His own purposes, no doubt dictated to the mother the expedient of making an *ark,* or close basket of bulrushes; and it is said, *she daubed it with slime and with pitch,* to keep out the water. Into this ark she laid her tender infant, closed the lid, and, in faith on the God of Israel, laid it in the flags by the river's brink, whether for life, or death.* Say, ye tender mothers! what were your feelings, when, on the loss of an infant by death, it was laid in the coffin, and, before the lid was closed, you gave with your lips the last token of affection! Ye best can tell the feeling of the mother of Moses, when in tears she closed the lid of the ark, and left him in the waters of danger.

On this very day, the providence of God directed the feet of Pharaoh's daughter, in company with her maidens, to go down to the river and wash. Whether this was for the purpose of pleasure, for health, or as an act of idolatrous worship, is not so material for us to determine. As she walked by the river, she saw a something among the flags; curiosity prompted an order to her maidens to fetch it; the lid was opened; she saw the child; and behold! *the babe wept.* Had we been present, we should have perceived her surprise; the tears of Moses in distress awakened her sympathy; her generous bosom glowed; she had compassion on him, and instantly exclaimed, *This is one of the Hebrews' children!* A nurse was immediately provided, and the princess honored her own feelings by thus addressing her: *Take this child away, and nurse it for me, and I will give thee thy wages.* This was accepted, *and the woman took the child and nursed it.* Those who have read the sequel of this history need not be told that, from this most striking occurrence, Pharaoh's daughter adopted this rescued child as her own son; she caused him to be instructed in all the learning of Egypt; and, that he afterward became one of the most distinguished and honored characters that adorn the pages of the Old Testament.

As we are this morning assembled in this new building, to offer our prayers to the Almighty for His gracious benediction upon this benevolent Institution, perhaps I may not better perform the duty assigned me, than by drawing a few lines of comparison between the forlorn exposure, and the relief of little Moses, and those young unfortunates whom this Society rescues from misery, granting them protection in this House of Refuge.

I. Let us recollect the danger to which the infant Moses was exposed. He was laid among the flags which grew on the brink of the Nile, and in danger of being carried away by the stream, and

* Hebrews xi. 23.

seen no more. And who does not know, that iniquity has too long
run down our streets like water; and that the floods of the ungodly,
like the rising of the waters of the Nile, have frequently overflowed
the safety and peace of our city? The rising generation, for successive years, have been exposed to this polluting current, and many of
them have been carried away and destroyed. Often have we seen
the children of the lower orders of society, for the want of education
and restraint, plunging into this iniquitous stream; and such are the
force of example and the fascinations of vice, that we are not without some instances of other young persons, of respectable connec-
tions, being unhappily carried away from the paths of virtue, lodged
in houses of criminal confinement, lost to all expectation by their
parents of retrieving their characters and becoming useful members
of society. But now, the pitying eye, like that of Pharaoh's daughter, is directed to such young offenders; and, the hand of kindness
is extended, at once to rescue them from destruction, and safely conduct them to this House of Refuge.

Let us not forget that little Moses was also in danger of being
devoured by the crocodile. This amphibious animal is a native
inhabitant of the Nile, living both on land and water; it frequently
grows to an enormous size, is of great strength, and extremely vora-
cious. It has the largest mouth of all monsters, opens both his jaws
at once, which, being furnished with a great number of sharp teeth,
can snap a man asunder in a moment, and gorge the body. To this
dreadful monster the infant Moses was exposed; and we cannot but
shudder at the apprehension of his exposure. Perhaps you may
inquire, Have we any such dangerous animals in our city, or in its
rivers? We have only seen them exhibited in show, and so confined
as to admit of no danger to the visitors. Where then can be the correctness of this comparison between little Moses and the miserable
young beings who wander in our streets? I venture to affirm that,
among us, we have crocodiles in human shape; persons whose conduct is as dangerous to the interest of civil society as are the ravages
of the monsters in the Nile. They may well be denominated amphibious, for they are capable of committing their ravages upon the
land, or on the water. Indeed, it is well known that, by various
methods, such unhappy characters form their criminal practices into
a system. They first learn the rudiments of their art in secret; perhaps in some obscure cellar, and there form combinations. Occasion-

ally, a party sally forth to try their skill in less crimes; till, eventually, some of them are detected, and sentenced to the penitentiary. There, for the want of room to make the necessary classification, they horde too much in mass, and soon find those who are more proficient in criminal practices than themselves; from whom they receive greater aid to carry on the course of bad instruction. So true is it, that *evil communications*, not only *corrupt good manners*, but certainly make bad manners much worse. Here, too, they formerly met with the juvenile offender; perhaps sentenced for his first offence. As with the false tears of the crocodile, they pretended to commiserate his misfortunes, ingratiate themselves into his tender feelings, and by such insinuations he gradually listens to the story of their own vicious conduct; and finally imbibes those depraved principles which soon make him to resemble their own likeness. Thus advanced in their vicious education, no wonder they should resolve to form a new gang on their liberation; so that, on the expiration, it may be said of some of them, they are competent to take their first degree of BACHELOR in the ART of crime.

Now, a new scene appears. Instead of cultivating repentance for past offences, such is the strength of sinful habits, they improve their criminal system, and form stronger combinations to execute their purposes. Their rapacity, like that of the crocodile, increases; and, with extended jaws, they lay in wait to catch the young offender that he may aid in their dark designs. This becomes indispensably necessary, in order to perform those operations of which a grown person is incompetent. The little boy must watch the opening door; climb the fence; or, urge his way through the cellar bars. Having gained admission, the urchin conceals himself, perhaps beneath the bed; within the vacant closet; or, in the garret's corner, until all is hushed in silent sleep; when, behold! he descends the stairs, unlocks the door, and admits the gang to accomplish their plunder. This is no false representation; facts like these have too frequently occurred; and I personally know a youth, of about fifteen years of age, now in one of our prisons, who, by such early instruction and practices, has been pronounced competent to take the lead of a gang. What generous soul but shudders on beholding scenes like these, and ardently wishes to rescue such young delinquents from the jaws of total destruction? Such public depredations, however, seldom go long without detection; and, the perpetrators are deservedly conveyed to the

State Prison. Here, likewise, for the want of adequate means to classify the criminals, their intercourse with each other, especially in the shades of night, is favorable for that conversation which can only produce a stronger growth of vicious principles, and which outbraves the watch of their keepers, and the moral lessons which they constantly receive. And here, too, the old offenders seldom fail to ensnare the young, and instill stronger principles of mischief into their minds, and thus stimulate them to the perpetration of more flagrant offences. From such a mass of criminals, so long in the cultivation of vice, no wonder that some of them should become so proficient as, at the expiration of their sentence, they may be said to take their second degree, of MASTER in the ART of criminality.

Let us look again at the infant Moses, and we shall perceive him exposed to danger from the officers of Pharaoh's court. Had they passed along by the river side, and perceived something in the shape of a basket, they would have been excited to ascertain its contents. Opening the lid, they would have found the Hebrew child; and although they might have been affected by perceiving its tears, the inexorable edict of their king would have compelled them to take away its life by drowning him in the river. This is similar to the case of our delinquent children; for, the civil law of our country knows no distinction in the detection of crime, whether committed by old or young. When, therefore, our officers of justice perceive the unwary youth, wading in the stream of iniquity, notwithstanding they may have compassion for his tender years, they are bound to arrest. And, although the natural life of the offender be not in danger, like that of Moses, still, the condemnation and criminal confinement of a young person generally produce the moral death of his character, and destroy the hope of society in his favor. How generous, then, is that hand which can rescue a fallen youth from such extreme danger!

What adds a final grade to the distressing exposure of poor little Moses is, that he was unconscious of his danger. Is not this the case with our unwary youth? Ignorant of the criminality of their conduct, their offences against God, and their accountability to the laws of society, they go astray, regardless of its fatal consequences. Like as Moses knew not his danger of being carried away by the stream, or devoured by the monster of the Nile, so our unfortunate children are insensible of the current of vice, or of those older, abandoned characters, whether male or female, who lay in wait to destroy them! Nor is it uncommon for such old offenders, having succeeded in decoying the young under a promise of gain, on their detection, to turn evidence against them, and thus seal their condemnation.

Let this general statement of our dissipated youth, and the dangers to which they are exposed, produce the necessary impression upon our mind, and we shall instantly perceive the importance of the laudable efforts of this Society in rescuing them from the paths of the destroyer, and giving them a place in this House of Refuge. As the means which the Almighty employed to extricate the infant Moses from his danger are so remarkably interesting, and, as the circumstances attending it are so admirably calculated to afford us a few lessons of instruction on the design of the present assembly, we will make them the subject of the second part of this discourse.

II. By the intervening providence of God, the feet of Pharaoh's daughter were directed to the waters of the Nile. How minutely does the Almighty perform His operations! Had the princess, with her maidens, come down on the morning before, Moses had not been there: had she been confined to her chamber, and visited the river on the following day, the child might have been drowned, or devoured by the monster. This, therefore, was the very *set time* for God to favor Moses; and all circumstances combine to produce the event. Permit me to say, that many years ago, I cultivated a commiseration for the vagrant children in our streets; and especially for those miserable little creatures who were confined in our prisons. In the year 1813, I presented to the Honorable the Common Council the outlines of a plan for the establishment of an asylum for their relief; but, it was like the morning, too soon! The set time for such an operation had not arrived; now, the providence of God appears in their favor, and the public mind is generously excited to rescue them from the polluted waters of destruction, and employ every possible means for their restoration to usefulness and happiness.

The address of the princess of Egypt to the nurse is as expressive as it is kind and benevolent; and affords us a charming impression of the strong interest which she took in the future welfare of the infant. *Take this child away*, said she, from its present danger, though it be an Hebrew. Carry it to your home, *and nurse it for me*, as though it were my own. I require not this care at your own expense; for I am able, and promise to *give thee thy wages.* Excel-

lent princess! what more could she have said? How justly may all
these items be applied to the good intention of the Society now assembled! Let us examine them: *Take this child away;* remove the
miserable little objects from the paths of idleness, beggary, vanity,
and inducement to crime, by the crafty and the wicked who lie in
wait to allure and destroy them. But whither shall these juvenile
delinquents be conveyed? Where is the hospitable door that will
open to receive them? Here it is! The House of Refuge is now
open: its door unfolds to receive and protect them, as the arms of
the nurse were extended to embrace the rescued Moses.—What attention are they here to receive? They are to be nursed. What this
means is easy to be understood. They come to you in rags, and you
must clothe them; they are hungry, and you will feed them; destitute of virtuous friends, you clasp them to your bosom; mentally
diseased by idleness and sin, you afford them the religious means for
restoration. Nursing is, indeed, anxious labor; and those who have
the government of this Institution will frequently find a sufficiency
of care to fill both their hands and their hearts. Still, who is to
supply? From whence are the necessaries to be obtained to feed
and to clothe so large a family? Remember, Pharaoh's daughter
said unto the nurse, I will give thee thy wages; and if the nurse
could trust the princess of Egypt, surely we may confide in the
providence of the Almighty, for the silver and the gold are His to
bestow. Besides, the public mind has already been so benevolently
interested in its favor, that methinks I hear their voice to you this
morning, "We will give thee thy wages." For, indeed, you nurse
these poor miserable creatures for the public peace and safety; and
therefore they will not fail to give you the most ample supply.

The reflections I have already made lead me to institute an
inquiry: What may be the public expectation of benefits arising
from this new establishment? The first I will name is, the extraction of THE CORE OF PAUPERISM. It is well known, that we seldom
see men and women, with baskets on their arms, going from house to
house, soliciting charity; for the trade of mendicity has been carried
on principally by the children of the indolent and worthless. While
this practice was pursued, Societies for the cure or prevention of
pauperism may hold their meetings, and publish their annual reports,
without any other benefit than what would accrue to the paper-mill,
and the printing-press. Remove such children from the streets, and

nurse them well; then, though the strings of the core of pauperism
may draw hard in its extraction, it is the best, if not the only method
of cure. The public will likewise expect these children will be
instructed in the rudiments of plain education; the importance of
cultivating habits of industry; and some of the more useful mechanic
arts; by which, hereafter, they may obtain an honest livelihood,
whether on the land, or on the seas. To which must be added, their
reformation, and improvement in morals; without which, very little
good will be obtained. No man will expect that you can change
their vicious little hearts; for this is alone the prerogative of God,
by the operation of the Holy Spirit of His grace. But, as this is
frequently produced by the use of means, you can teach these ignorant children to read their once neglected Bible; show them the
nature and danger of sin and transgression in the sight of God and
man; you can point them to a compassionate Saviour, who not only
died for our sins, but, in the days of His flesh, took children in His
arms and blessed them. And it will be easy for you to contrast
their former state of ignorance and degradation with the privileges
of instruction and good examples which they now receive, in the
cheering hope of their interest and happiness in the world. These
are some of those duties which you owe to them, and to the public;
and, if faithfully performed, I hope God will succeed your endeavors,
and the expectation of our citizens will be happily realized.

ADDRESSES.

THE ladies who have so generously engaged their services to visit
and to watch over the female department of this House of Refuge
will accept my congratulation upon this occasion. You have no
need for me to intimate the duties you have to perform. You pos-
sess a parental feeling; and nothing but motives of tenderness and
kindness could have prompted your exertions to aid in this noble
design of restoring the fallen children of your own sex to the paths
of virtue and happiness. Permit me to remind you of Pharaoh's
daughter, as your noble example. True, she was an Egyptian; an
idolatress; no matter for the color of her complexion; she came to
the brink of the river; she saw the helpless infant; she had compassion, and she saved him! Had that distinguished woman lived in
a Christian land, and had her heart been enriched with the Gospel

To the Mayor and Common Council.

of Christ, I would exhibit her in the attitude of relieving the distressed, and then say to you, BEHOLD THE LOVELIEST PICTURE OF CHRISTIAN CHARITY! Go, worthy ladies, and do likewise.

THE HONORABLE THE MAYOR, AND THE MEMBERS OF THE COMMON COUNCIL OF THE CITY; AND THE GENTLEMEN OF THE NEW YORK DELEGATION TO THE STATE LEGISLATURE, who have honored this Society with their presence, cannot but feel a lively interest in beholding this rising institution. You must be convinced, gentlemen, that this is not an object of simple charity. It is strongly combined with the safety, honor, and happiness of the whole community. If such little offenders were permitted to range at large, their criminal habits would grow with their years; their number by example would increase; and, by these means, town and country would be overrun, and our public prisons be crowded, not failing to produce an enormous expense to the State! To prevent these calamitous consequences, the House of Refuge is erected, and makes a strong appeal for public support. But, my humane friends, the prevention of the growth of crime is not all that is intended by this Society; it is their moral design, by every method possible, to reclaim these juvenile delinquents, that they may become useful and honorable members of society. This enhances the value of the institution so highly, that I have no language sufficiently to express its importance! While, therefore, we cherish the hope that our own CORPORATION will look with a benign aspect on the House of Refuge, our CITY DELEGATION also will make such a favorable representation of it, that our STATE LEGISLATURE will form a sort of echo, "We also will aid, and pay thee thy wages."

THE MANAGERS OF THIS ESTABLISHMENT: I cannot but congratulate you, gentlemen, on the completion of this new building. The smiles of Heaven have thus far succeeded your efforts, in favor of the young unfortunates committed to your care. The duties requisite in every new institution must generally be known as the result of observation and experience; of course you will have much to learn, as well as much to perform. Begin your services in the fear of your God; duly reflect on the magnitude of the object for which you are engaged; while you combine tenderness and faithfulness in all your operations; it is my sincere wish that the whole may be crowned with the most abundant success.

THE CHILDREN.

CHILDREN: I must not omit claiming your attention, and soliciting you to indulge the most serious reflections on the privileges you now enjoy. The erection of this building, together with your support, must give you strong conviction, how much a benevolent public are interested in your present and future welfare. Had you been left alone to yourselves, in poverty, idleness, and sin, instead of insuring you peace and pleasure, iniquity would have proved your final ruin. You are to look at the walls which surround this building, not so much as those of a prison, as an hospitable dwelling, in which you enjoy comfort, and safety from those who once led you astray. And, I may venture to say, that in all probability, this is the best home many of you ever enjoyed! You have no need for me to tell you, that the consideration of all these favors should stimulate you to submission, industry, and gratitude. You are not placed here so much for punishment, as to produce your moral improvement. By these indulgent means, we hope that, instead of your spending your days in idleness, disgrace, and misery, you may become useful to yourselves, honorable in society, and share in the true happiness of your fellow-creatures. Although you are now young in years, you must have some consciousness that the errors of life, and the evils of your heart, expose you to the displeasure of the Almighty; that you need the tender mercy of the Saviour to pardon your iniquities; to renew your depraved minds by the virtue of His grace, and thus save you from the desert. of your transgressions. We hope, therefore, that, while you are within these walls, the Lord may command His merciful kindness upon you, and enable you to devote yourselves to His adored Name, and His most delightful service! Moses could never forget the humanity and kindness of Pharaoh's daughter, in delivering him from the danger to which he was exposed; and I would indulge the charming impression, that there is no youth in this House of Refuge, but what will bear in devout remembrance the deliverance and the favors which you have here received, and evince the sincerity of your gratitude by the amiableness of your temper, and the virtue of your future conduct.

CONCLUSION.

The time on which we have now assembled is usually called "Christmas Day." Whether this recognizes the very day on which

An appropriate Christmas Service.

Jesus was born in Bethlehem, is not now my business to examine. If any man prefers keeping this, or any other day to the Lord, I am not disposed to interrupt him in the enjoyment of his privilege. The text on which I have this morning addressed you, combined with the narrative of Moses laid among the flags on the brink of the river, remind me of the angel's address to the shepherds in the field while watching their flock by night : *Fear not : for, behold, I bring you good tidings of great joy, which shall be to all people. For unto you is born this day in the city of David a Saviour, which is Christ the Lord. And this shall be a sign unto you ; ye shall find the babe wrapped in swaddling-clothes, lying in a manger.* Immediately the shepherds left their flocks; *and they came with haste, and found Mary, and Joseph, and the babe lying in the manger.** This is that true Moses, the prophet, which the Lord our God promised to *raise up, like unto him in all things, whom his people should hear.*† How singularly striking were the circumstances which attended their infancy! Yes, the babe of Bethlehem, found in a manger, was Christ the Lord; and, *his name was called Jesus, for he was to save his people from their sins.* If Moses that was found in the ark of bulrushes was born to deliver the Israelites from their bondage in Egypt, and conduct them through the wilderness on their way to Canaan : we are certain, that our blessed Saviour was born to deliver from the more dreadful bondage of sin and misery, and safely conduct His redeemed to the rest of immortality and glory. Yes, Jesus was born to live, to suffer, and to die upon the cross for our sins; and after He was laid in the grave, He burst the bands of death, ascended up to heaven, and sat down on the right hand of the Majesty on high, from thence to shower down the multiplicity of his mercies upon mankind. And who, on this occasion, but will most devoutly pray—LORD, RESERVE A BLESSING FOR THIS HOUSE OF REFUGE! Amen.

---

* Luke ii.   † Deut. xviii. 15; Acts vii. 37.

VI.

LIST OF MANAGERS OF THE SOCIETY FOR THE REFORMATION OF JUVENILE DELINQUENTS IN THE CITY OF NEW YORK, FROM 1824 TO 1868.

*The names in Italics are connected with the Board at the present time. Those marked (*) thus are deceased.*

Elected.		Retired.	Elected.		Retired.
1824	* Cadwallader D. Colden,	1832	1826	* Samuel Wood,	1831
"	* Stephen Allen,	1852	1827	* Isaac S. Hone,	1830
"	* Peter A. Jay,	1827	"	* Heman Averill,	1834
"	* John T. Irving,	1829	"	* Joseph Curtis,	1829
"	* John Griscom,	1833	"	* William W. Fox,	1853
"	* Henry J. Wyckoff,	1839	"	* James Kent, LL. D.,	1828
"	* Cornelius Du Bois,	1846	"	* Benjamin L. Swan,	1830
"	* Ralph Olmsted,	1835	"	* David Stebbins,	1829
"	* Robert F. Mott,	1826	"	* M. Van Schaick,	1834
"	* Arthur Burtis,	1829	1828	* John Hunter,	1835
"	* Isaac Collins,	1829	1829	* Jacob Harvey,	1842
"	* Samuel Cowdrey,	1829	"	Rufus L. Lord,	1852
"	* Gilbert Coutant,	1826	"	* Dennis McCarthy,	1835
"	* John Duer,	1826	"	* Nathaniel Richards,	1834
"	* Cornelius R. Duffie,	1826	"	* Najah Taylor,	1830
"	* Thomas Eddy,	1829	"	* John W. Wyman,	1836
"	James W. Gerard,	1829	1830	* Russell H. Nevins,	1836
"	* Joseph Grinnell,	1830	"	James J. Roosevelt, Jr.,	1831
"	* John E. Hyde,	1831	"	* Frederick A. Tracy,	1837
"	* Ansel W. Ives, M. D.,	1831	"	* Robert D. Weeks,	1853
"	* James Lovett,	1850	"	* William L. Stone,	1844
"	Hugh Maxwell,	1848	1831	* Jacob Drake,	1845
"	* Henry Mead,	1826	"	* William Kent,	1834
"	* John Stearns, M. D.,	1835	"	* Peter R. Starr,	1837
"	* John Targee,	1826	"	* Charles Town,	1832
"	* J. M. Wainright, D. D.,	1827	1832	* Silas Brown,	1847
1825	* Robert C. Cornell,	1845	"	* B. L. Woolley,	1849
1826	William A. Davis,	1827	1833	* Samuel Stevens,	1844
"	* Thomas Gibbons,	1827	1834	* Benjamin S. Collins,	1844
"	* William F. Mott,	1839	"	* Eli Goodwin,	1837
"	* Richard Riker,	1827	"	* John R. Townsend,	1846
"	* Frederick Sheldon,	1834	"	* John R. Willis,	1844
"	* Peter Sharpe,	1842	1835	* Augustin Averill,	1853
"	* Arthur Tappan,	1827	"	* Ira B. Underhill,	1840
"	* Gabriel Wisner,	1827	1836	* Cornelius W. Lawrence,	1842

List of Managers.

Elected.		Retired.	Elected.		Retired.
1836	* Anthony Lamb,	1850	1850	Thomas W. Gale,	1851
"	* William Mandeville,	1843	"	*Edgar S. Van Winkle.*	
"	* Oliver M. Lownds,	1839	"	* George F. Hussey,	1858
1837	* Robert I. Murray,	1841	"	* M. L. Seymour,	1852
"	* Chandler Starr,	1840	1851	Ogden Haggerty,	1852
1838	* David C. Colden,	1850	"	*Frederick W. Downer.*	
"	* Oliver T. Hewlett,	1839	1852	Samuel L. Mitchill,	1854
"	* Revo C. Hance,	1839	"	Wm. H. Maxwell, M. D.,	1857
1839	* Mahlon Day,	1840	"	* Edmund M. Young,	1865
"	* Robert Kelly,	1856	1853	*John J. Townsend.*	
"	*Shepherd Knapp.*		"	*Andrew Warner.*	
1840	* Leonard Corning,	1841	"	* David Sands,	1859
"	* Thomas Eddy,	1842	"	John Bigelow,	1855
"	Harvey P. Peet,	1850	1854	R. L. Kennedy,	1857
"	* Marinus Willett,	1841	"	*Richard M. Hoe.*	
1841	* G. P. Disosway,	1844	"	Charles C. Leigh,	1865
"	* Samuel Downer, Jr.,	1846	1855	* Thomas B. Stillman,	1865
"	* Israel Russell,	1858	"	William C. Russel,	1864
1842	John H. Gourlie,	1854	"	*Oliver S. Strong.*	
"	* Charles M. Leupp,	1859	1856	*William M. Prichard.*	
"	* James Marsh,	1846	"	* James P. Cronkhite,	1860
1843	William Moore,	1844	"	*James M. Halsted.*	
"	* John T. Adams,	1847	"	*Edgar Ketchum.*	
1844	*John A. Weeks.*		1857	*Peter McMartin.*	
"	* Joshua S. Underhill,	1857	"	* Mark Spencer,	1859
"	Cornelius Du Bois, Jr.,	1845	"	*Henry A. Cram.*	
1845	* Mahlon Day,	1854	1858	*D. Jackson Steward.*	
"	*James N. Cobb.*		"	Francis P. Schoals,	1862
"	* P. A. Schermerhorn,	1845	"	* William Gale,	1862
"	* Walter Underhill,	1866	1859	* Henry H. Barrow,	1862
"	JamesVan Nostrand,	1847	"	*Henry M. Alexander.*	
"	Elias G. Drake,	1856	"	*William Cromwell.*	
"	* George J. Cornell,	1857	"	* Joel Rathbone, Albany,	1864
1846	John W. Edmonds,	1854	1860	*Cyrus P. Smith,* Brooklyn.	
1847	* T. T. Luquere,	1849	1862	*Henry K. Bogert.*	
"	R. L. Schieffelin,	1849	1863	*Morris Franklin.*	
"	* James W. Underhill,	1866	1864	Howard Potter,	1866
"	C. E. Pierson, M. D.,	1855	1864	*Henry Q. Hawley,* Albany.	
"	* Linus W. Stevens,	1864	1865	*D. Thomas Vail,* Troy.	
"	* Smith W. Anderson,	1849	1865	*Samuel W. Torrey.*	
1848	* Daniel Seymour,	1850	1866	*Geo. W. Clinton,* Buffalo.	
1849	James W. Beekman,	1855	1866	*Benj. D. Silliman,* Brooklyn.	
"	* Richard H. Ogden,	1853	1866	*Nicholas D. Herder.*	
"	*J. W. C. Leveridge.*		1866	*John A. Stewart.*	
1850	*B. B. Atterbury.*				

List of Officers of the Society.

List of Officers and Managers filling the various Committees of the Society for the Reformation of Juvenile Delinquents in the City of New York, from 1824 to 1868.

PRESIDENTS.

Elected.		Retired.	Elected.		Retired.
1824	Cadwallader D. Colden,	1832	1852	Robert Kelly,	1856
1832	Stephen Allen,	1852	1856	OLIVER S. STRONG.	

VICE-PRESIDETNS.

Elected		Retired	Elected		Retired
1824	Stephen Allen,	1832	1848	David C. Colden,	1850
"	Peter A. Jay,	1827	1850	Rufus L. Lord,	1852
"	John T. Irving,	1829	"	SHEPHERD KNAPP.	
"	John Griscom,	1833	1851	Robert Kelly,	1852
"	Henry J. Wyckoff,	1839	1852	Israel Russell,	1858
"	Cornelius Du Bois,	1834	1853	Charles M. Leupp,	1859
1827	James Lovett,	1850	"	John H. Gourlie,	1854
1829	Peter Sharpe,	1842	"	Joshua S. Underhill,	1857
1832	Hugh Maxwell,	1848	1854	Mahlon Day,	1854
1833	William W. Fox,	1853	"	John A. Weeks,	1856
1834	Robert C. Cornell,	1845	1855	JAMES N. COBB.	
1840	Samuel Stevens,	1844	1856	Linus W. Stevens,	1864
1843	Jacob Drake,	1845	1857	Walter Underhill,	1866
1845	Anthony Lamb,	1850	1858	James W. Underhill,	1866
1846	Cornelius Du Bois,	1846	1860	JNO. W. C. LEVERIDGE.	
"	Augustin Averill,	1853	1863	B. B. ATTERBURY.	
"	Robert D. Weeks,	1853			

TREASURERS.

Elected		Retired	Elected		Retired
1824	Ralph Olmsted,	1828	1848	Joshua S. Underhill,	1857
1828	Cornelius Du Bois,	1846	1857	Walter Underhill,	1866
1846	Israel Russell,	1848	1866	JOHN A. STEWART.	

SECRETARIES.

Elected		Retired	Elected		Retired
1824	Robert F. Mott,	1826	1835	John R. Townsend,	1843
1826	Samuel Cowdrey,	1827	1843	John H. Gourlie,	1853
1827	Isaac S. Hone,	1828	1853	James W. Underhill,	1854
1828	Frederick Sheldon,	1833	1854	ANDREW WARNER.	
1833	Ralph Olmsted,	1835			

CHAIRMEN OF THE ACTING COMMITTEE FROM 1824 TO 1854.

Elected		Retired	Elected		Retired
1824	Stephen Allen,	1825	1829	William W. Fox,	1841
1825	Cornelius Du Bois,	1827	1841	Augustin Averill,	1851
1827	Robert C. Cornell,	1829	1851	Robert Kelly,	1854

List of Officers.

SECRETARIES OF ACTING COMMITTEE FROM 1824 TO 1854.

Elected.		Retired.	Elected.		Retired.
1824	Joseph Curtis,	1825	1829	F. A. Tracy,	1831
1825	R. C. Cornell,	1827	1831	R. D. Weeks,	1842
1827	Isaac Collins,	1827	1842	John H. Gourlie,	1847
"	M. Van Schaick,	1828	1847	James W. Underhill,	1853
1828	Nathaniel Richards,	1829	1853	Fred. W. Downer,	1854

Managers who have acted on the Indenturing Committee, and the term of years each has served, from 1827 to 1868.

James Lovett,	3		Daniel Seymour,	2
Frederick Sheldon,	1		Walter Underhill,	1
Wm. F. Mott,	6		George F. Hussey,	1
Heman Averill,	5		James N. Cobb,	7
Benjamin L. Swan,	1		Elias G. Drake,	2
R. C. Cornell,	4		David Sands,	3
Nathaniel Richards,	2		Richard M. Hoe,	6
M. Van Schaick,	1		James P. Cronkhite,	3
Benjamin S. Collins,	8		O. S. Strong,	1
Silas Brown,	4		William Gale,	2
Jacob Drake,	5		FRED. W. DOWNER,	10
Robert I. Murray,	3		EDGAR KETCHUM,	5
Augustin Averill,	2		Charles C. Leigh,	4
John R. Willis,	5		William C. Russel,	2
Robert Kelly,	2		Thomas B. Stillman,	1
James Marsh,	2		H. K. BOGERT,	6
J. S. Underhill,	4		WILLIAM CROMWELL,	6
Israel Russell,	15		MORRIS FRANKLIN,	4
Mahlon Day,	9			

Organization of the Finance Committee in January, 1841 to 1868.

1841	Robert C. Cornell,	1845	1848	Robert Kelly,	1856
"	James Lovett,	1845	1856	Edmund M. Young.	
1845	Charles M. Leupp,	1859	1859	Shepherd Knapp.	
"	Joshua S. Underhill,	1848			

Organization of the School Committee, January 7, 1847. The following Managers have acted on this Committee up to 1868.

CHAIRMEN.

1847 to 1849—Charles E. Pierson, M. D.; Charles M. Leupp; John A. Weeks.
1850 to 1852—C. E. Pierson, M. D.; C. M. Leupp; B. B. Atterbury.
    1853—C. E. Pierson, M. D.; B. B. Atterbury; F. W. Downer.
    1854—C. E. Pierson, M. D.; B. B. Atterbury; F. W. Downer; J. W. Underhill.

List of Officers.

1855—B. B. Atterbury; F. W. Downer; J. W. Underhill; T. B. Stillman.

1856—O. S. Strong; F. W. Downer; Wm. C. Russel.

1857—O. S. Strong; F. W. Downer; James M. Halsted.

1858 to 1861—O. S. Strong; James M. Halsted; P. McMartin.

1861 to 1868—O. S. Strong; James M. Halsted; P. McMartin; Henry M. Alexander.

Building Committee for New House on Randall's Island. Organized October 1, 1851, up to 1868.

Elected.		Retired.	Elected.		Retired.
1851	Charles M. Leupp,	1859	1851	Elias G. Drake,	1856
"	Robert Kelly,	1852	"	Jno. W. C. Leveridge.	
"	George J. Cornell,	1852	1856	Richard M. Hoe.	
	Linus W. Stevens,	1864	1857	Walter Underhill,	1866
"	J. S. Underhill,	1857	1859	Thomas B. Stillman.	
"	John H. Gourlie,	1853			

Members of the Executive Committee since the removal of the Refuge to Randall's Island. Organized November 3, 1854, to 1868.

Linus W. Stevens,	6 years.		John J. Townsend,	2 years.	
Robert Kelly,	1 "		H. H. Barrow,	2 "	
Edmund M. Young,	1 "		James N. Cobb,	7 "	
Wm. M. Pritchard,	1 "		Cyrus P. Smith,	7 "	
O. S. Strong,	1 "		D. Jackson Stewart,	3 "	
B. B. Atterbury,	12 "		Nicholas Herder,	2 "	
C. C. Leigh,	1 "				

Organization of the Law Committee, November 3, 1854.

1854	George J. Cornell,	1857	1857	Wm. M. Pritchard.
"	John A. Weeks,	1856	1857	Henry A. Cram.
1856	John J. Townsend,	1857		

PHYSICIANS.

1825	John Stearns, M. D.,	1834	1836	Jno. C. Cheesman, D.D.,	1838
"	Ansel W. Ives, M. D.,	1832	"	James B. Nelson, M. D.,	1838
1832	H. A. Field, M. D.,	1835	1855	H. N. Whittlesey, M. D.	
"	Galen Carter, M. D.,	1854			

CHAPLAINS.

1825	Rev. John Stanford, D. D.		1855	Rev. Richard Horton,	1863
1835	Thos. S. Barrett, M. D.,	1853	1863	Rev. B. K. Peirce, D. D.	
1854	Rev. Franklin S. Howe,	1855			

List of Officers.

SUPERINTENDENTS.

Elected.		Retired.	Elected.		Retired.
1824	Joseph Curtis,	1826	1844	Samuel S. Wood,	1849
1826	Nathaniel C. Hart,	1838	1849	John W. Ketchum,	1863
1838	David Terry, Jr.,	1844	1863	ISRAEL C. JONES,	

MATRONS.

Elected.		Retired.	Elected.		Retired.
1824	Phœbe Curtis,	1826	1843	Phœbe Wood,	1846
1826	C. E. Andrews,	1828	1846	Ann Carter,	1850
1828	Catharine Gowey,	1830	1850	Phœbe Ann Daly,	1853
1830	Rebecca Oram,	1833	1853	Ann Carter,	1854
1833	Rebecca Goldsmith,	1834	1855	Maria Osgood,	1861
1834	Susan C. Taylor,	1838	1861	Julia O'Brien,	1865
1838	M. T. Myrich,	1839	1865	Kate Logan,	1867
1839	Susan C. Taylor,	1841	1867	JULIA O'BRIEN.	
1841	M. A. Elmendorf,	1843			

THE END.

PATTERSON SMITH REPRINT SERIES IN
CRIMINOLOGY, LAW ENFORCEMENT, AND SOCIAL PROBLEMS